The
Ku
Klux
Klan

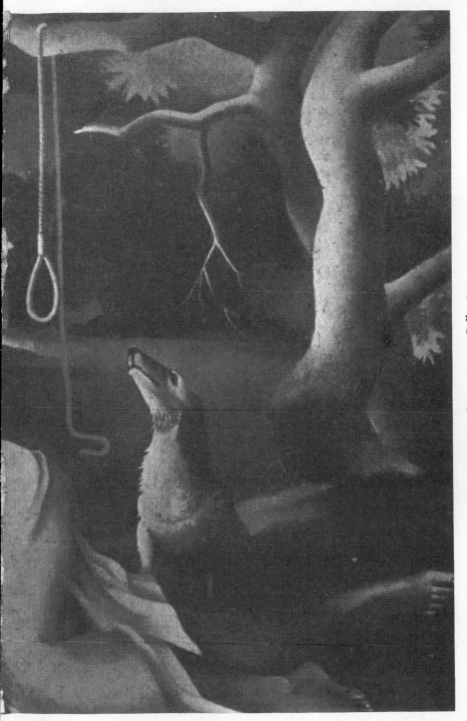

American Justice by Joe Jones.   New York Public Library Picture Collection

THE
KU
KLUX
KLAN

A

Century

of

Infamy

BY

William Peirce Randel

CHILTON BOOKS
A Division of Chilton Company
Publishers
Philadelphia   New York

Library of Congress Catalog Card Number 65-13920

Manufactured in the United States of America by
Quinn & Boden Company, Inc., Rahway, N.J.

To all victims of racism

PREFACE

What are we really like, we Americans? We pride ourselves on being tolerant, civilized, law-abiding; yet there is considerable evidence that we are a violent people. Not all of us, to be sure, hate with such passion that we would ever defy the law and assault our neighbors—or encourage others to do so. But in our horrified revulsion from some reported crime of intolerance, do we consider that the fault may in some part be our own? Simply by doing less than we might to implement our civilized notions of tolerance and respect for the law, we may be providing a permissive atmosphere in which intolerance may blossom into violence.

The Ku Klux Klan could never have flourished in the United States without the backing of large numbers of people who themselves would never adopt Klan methods. At every stage in the first century of its history the Klan has been an active agency for implementing what many people have believed in deeply. In other words, a "Klan spirit" has existed among a great many more people than have ever been active Klansmen. At different times this spirit has been directed against different groups; a good beginning point might be the harsh Puritan persecution of Quakers in the seventeenth century, not to mention the Puritan elimination of the local Indians. During Reconstruction, the Klan directed its campaign of violence against freedmen and Republicans. During the 1920's the Klan actively opposed Catholics, Jews, Mormons, and aliens, as well as Negroes. The Klan program of active hostility is as shifting as it is irrational; no group in the population is permanently immune from its attack.

A sober review of American history yields the unwelcome conclusion that the Klan spirit is a constant in our national behavior. At times it is quiescent, but it is not dead, only smouldering between eruptions. When, for a time, the Klan is relatively inactive, it is easy—and pleasant—to forget the violence the Klan once engendered;

[ix]

and even in its moments of great activity, men of good will possibly dismiss such behavior as an aberration. Stepped-up law enforcement, we assume, will crush the outburst; stronger laws will prevent any future revival. It goes against our grain to acknowledge the actuality of the Klan spirit, past and present, in the national ethos; it undercuts our cherished myths about ourselves and our country.

Men join the Klan, and defend its practices, out of deep personal conviction. Early leaders of the modern Klan—Ed Clarke, Colonel Simmons, Hiram Evans—were obviously cynical; but if for such men the Klan existed as a machine for making fortunes, the rank and file of the members were ordinary men, of the sort easily persuaded that America is in grave danger of subversion. Granted that some Klansmen have been sadistic, or "authoritarian personalities," the greater number have been impelled by a genuine, if misdirected, sense of patriotic duty. They have embraced the programs of hatred outlined for them by their cynical leaders as the means of saving the country. Not to act, in the face of the threat posed, allegedly, by identifiable minorities, could readily seem like cowardice, or even like treason to the nation's best ideals.

The original Klan evolved almost at once from a purely social club into an active terroristic group. It was motivated by a conviction that federal efforts to give freedmen the rights of American citizenship were in violation of the Constitution and of divine plan. The larger number of white Southerners, even when they deplored the Klan violence, argued that it was justified by the greater crimes committed by the federal authorities. The Klan was only doing what the regional majority wanted—preserving the American way of life as white Southerners defined it. Americans elsewhere had a different definition, but their commitment to the struggle was weaker, and much less durable. As popular support waned in the North, the federal drive lost its momentum and finally collapsed.

One major lesson from Reconstruction is that a determined minority, convinced of the rightness of its cause, can defeat an effort backed by the national majority if that majority wearies of the struggle. The modern Klan, no less than the old, provides an outlet for resistance by a determined minority. When it reached its peak in 1924, with about five million members, the Klan was not much more dangerous than earlier or later, because most of these millions were incapable of sadistic behavior. The hard core that did not resign after the scandals of 1924 comprised a dedicated élite, indifferent to overwhelming public disapproval and viewing themselves as better judges of crime and punishment than the constituted authorities. They were just as sure of the rightness of their cause, and of the propriety of acting outside the law, as were the old Klansmen during Reconstruction. And although they lacked the glamor that some wives and daughters of Klansmen, and some novelists and historians, cast over the old Klan, they enjoyed the backing of a substantial fraction of the population, people who deplored their violence but accepted it as necessary for the preservation of the American way of life as they conceived it to be.

The chief indictment of the Klan, early and late, is on the grounds of its violence against individuals. Had it refrained from action, as Henry W. Grady once urged it to do, the Klan would have taken its place among the many other organized groups that collectively shape public opinion. Recently, some leaders of the fractured Klan —for it ceased to be a national organization during the 1940's—have experimented with propaganda, quite successfully. But the Klan is on the Attorney General's list of subversive organizations because it *does* resort to violence and does not confine its activities to the dissemination of "literature." Even if the modern leaders should deliberately decide henceforth to eschew violence and depend entirely on propaganda, provocation would probably lead to new eruptions of violence which the leaders, like Bedford Forrest in 1869, would be powerless to prevent. Events in recent months make this a virtual certainty.

In the early years of the modern Klan, Catholics, Jews, and aliens were higher than Negroes on the list of hated minorities. But with the resumption of federal action to extend civil rights, Negroes have regained their usual priority at the head of the list. It seems a reasonable statement that the one continuing, underlying principle of the Klan is preservation of white supremacy. The shifting Klan hostility toward other groups reflects the corollary that the Klan has sought always to preserve control by white Anglo-Saxon Protestants—a majority of the nation's population during Reconstruction, a minority since about 1880 (although its members do not realize their minority status). The America developed by that majority-turned-minority has yielded to quite a different America, much closer to the term used by Walt Whitman, "a nation of many nations," with a resulting rich diversity that is one of its great distinctions and a major source of its virility. But many Americans do not like the change and would do anything in their power to halt it, and to restore the America of the past. The hope is futile, but a concerted resistance campaign, with or without violence of the Klan variety, can serve to slow the evolution.

The Klan has been defended, during Reconstruction—and in the twentieth century—as doing more good than harm. The greatest "good" it has done, and is now seeking to do, is to preserve a cherished but obsolescent way of life, and to maintain a pattern of privilege for a waning minority. As long as the Klan thinks it is working for good, and as long as an appreciable number of Americans tolerate or applaud its activity, or look the other way from a desire not to become involved, the Klan will remain an American institution.

It is one contention of this book that Reconstruction history is still being taught in the nation's schools in a way that justifies white supremacy and the Klan as its most effective agent. Despite numerous scholarly books and articles by the current generation of historians, most of our school history textbooks maintain the interpretation established early in this century by authors clearly partial to Southern tradition and hostile to the Negro hope of attaining full equality. This traditional interpretation condemns the whole federal program of extending civil rights to the former slaves, and applauds the redemption of the Southern states from allegedly vicious misgovernment by carpetbaggers, scalawags, and Negroes in an unholy alliance. The textbook authors, like Southern editors during Reconstruction, deplore the Klan violence but condone it as a necessary evil producing a desirable end. Renewed or increased efforts to implement civil rights, in our time, will be impeded, and may even fail, as long as school children, year after year, are exposed to the same old story. A first order of business, for those who would like to banish Klan violence forever from the land, may not be to enforce new federal laws but to demand a revision of the Reconstruction chapters in history books used in our schools.

Such a revision is hardly the purpose of this book, but the author will be gratified if readers are stirred to examine the textbooks their children are required to use. Several chapters attempt to relate the Klan to contemporary developments, and especially to the various groups it came into contact with—the Freedmen's Bureau, the Northern teachers in the South, the carpetbaggers and the scalawags (terms that must be used despite their pejorative connotation), and the Negro freedmen who were at the center of the struggle even though some historians have denied it. The modern Klan, different as it has been in many ways, is generally described as maintaining, and as being maintained by, the popular myths that the old Klan, abetted by sympathetic historians and novelists and politicians, created and confirmed. It should be added that this volume is not intended as an exhaustive history of the Klan in its first century; such a work would run to many volumes. Whole states are neglected—Alabama, for a conspicuous example—in line with the topical principle.

A preface is the traditional place to express indebtedness to friends and colleagues who have loaned books and pamphlets, offered suggestions and leads, and read chapter drafts. If they are not named here, they will know why, but they will also know that I am grateful for their help and encouragement. Most of them live in a city whose government has thus far refused to establish a biracial commission, and where a letter of protest to the editor results in abusive telephone calls. Libraries are less vulnerable to this form of recrimination. Among those that have been helpful are the libraries of the Florida State University, Tallahassee; the University of Florida, Gainesville; the Louisiana State University, Baton Rouge; Duke University, Durham, North Carolina; the North Carolina Department of Archives and History, Raleigh; The University of North Carolina, Chapel Hill; Fisk University, Nashville, Tennessee; the University of Virginia, Charlottesville; the University of Kansas, Lawrence; the Virginia State Library, Richmond; the Wisconsin State Historical Society, Madison; the Hayes Memorial Library,

Fremont, Ohio; the Buffalo and Erie County Historical Society, Buffalo, New York; and the Library of Congress.

Finally I express my inexpressible debt to my wife.

W. P. R.

Tallahassee

CONTENTS

Contents

[xvi]

Contents

PROLOGUE

On April 6, 1865, the Confederate Congress named Robert E. Lee commander-in-chief of the Confederate Army, just in time for him to receive, on April 7, a message from General Grant asking him to surrender. Two days later, in a formal ceremony at Appomattox Court House in rural Virginia, Lee surrendered the 27,805 men in his command. General Joseph Johnston, commanding 31,243 men in North Carolina, signed a separate surrender on April 18, at Durham Station. These two armies, Lee's and Johnston's, comprised the bulk of what remained of the Confederate armed forces, and once they were out of action the Confederate States of America ceased to exist as an effective independent nation. Some guerrilla action prolonged the fighting in isolated parts of the South, but for all practical purposes the Civil War was over, almost exactly four years after the first shots had been fired at Fort Sumter in Charleston harbor.

Mustering out was informal. The war-weary Southern soldiers, singly or in casual groups, simply turned toward home, mostly on foot, with just two things to be grateful for: they were alive, and they had been permitted to keep their guns. The federal government might not have been so generous had Lee declined to surrender, but he really had no choice. His supply lines had been broken, and he could no longer feed the troops. This breakdown in logistics was only a symbol, however, of the larger fact that the Confederacy lacked the wealth, the manpower, and the war-making capacity to hold out any longer.

It is a soldier's business to fight, not to probe the reasons for the fighting. But if most of the Confederates looked forward to relaxing at home, and to remembering their days of glory—at Bull Run or Ball's Bluff, Antietam or Fredericksburg, Chancellorsville or Chattanooga—the stay-at-homes, always more militant about principles than the soldiers themselves, reminded them of battles still to be fought. Blackened cellarholes, and gutted sections of burned cities, and rails twisted into fantastic shapes, were stark evidence of the devastation where men had fought and where columns had marched; the long lists of the dead were more terrible proof of the cost of war. But of more immediate concern, in a region with an economy based on agriculture, were the unworked fields—unworked because the seceded states had lost their single most valuable asset, the forced labor of slaves. The four million Negroes were all freedmen now; Lincoln had freed them by decree, in the Emancipation Proclamation that he had issued on January 1, 1863, and the Union victory had made the action binding.

 Southern whites could ignore the Proclamation, and all the legislation of Congress, as long as they could maintain their military opposition to the United States. But with peace they were forced back into the nation they had sought to leave and were at the mercy of the federal government. It was vitally important which men controlled that government, and during the eight months left of 1865 after the surrender, it was quickly apparent that, with Lincoln dead, control was in the hands of the Radical wing of the Republican Party. Such men as Charles Sumner and Thaddeus Stevens took an extreme position about Negroes, insisting they were full citizens now and entitled to all the rights that white men in the South had long been accustomed to looking upon as exclusively their own. The strong-minded Radicals had never learned what Southern whites accepted as uncontrovertible truth, that Negroes were by nature inferior and not qualified for equality.

Southern principle was never more rudely trampled on than in the months just after the war when Congress rejected the constitutions submitted by the states as requisite to return to the Union. The Radicals in Congress, supported by general public opinion in the North, were indignant over the clauses restrictive of Negro freedom; if these first constitutions had been accepted, the freedmen would have been little better off than they were under slavery. New constitutions were demanded, more favorable to Negro liberty, and, when they were submitted, Congress approved them. By the end of 1865, the Southern states were all full members of the Union once more, but the restored state governments were offensive to most Southern whites. Republicans in the North and Southern whites could not both be satisfied; and the Republicans, for the moment, were in the saddle.

The South had better reason to secede in 1865 than in 1861, but secede it could not. Open, above-board resistance soon proved futile; the Radical Republicans were too strong. If Southern whites were to regain control of their own states and restore a semblance of the life that they had known and loved, some other means of resistance would have to be found. Negroes could not be permitted to vote, or hold office, or do any of the other things that were traditionally the privilege of the superior race. The one course of dishonor was abject surrender; if the only feasible alternative was subversion of constituted authority, it was justified by the outrageous Radical flouting of Southern principles.

Circumstance, then, virtually forced the returning Confederate veterans into a far-flung underground resistance movement to harass the Republicans, whether white or Negro, and to keep up the pressure until the Radicals in Congress should lose their control or tire of the effort of keeping the South in thrall.

This underground resistance we know, today, as the original Ku Klux Klan.

Chapter One

THE
BIRTH
OF THE
KLAN

Pulaski is a county seat (1960 population, 6,616) in southern Tennessee, about eighty miles south of Nashville and not far from the Alabama state line, in a region that one Tennessee writer once called "the dimple of the universe." Imbedded in the wall of one of its downtown buildings is a plaque that indicates the city's major claim to renown:

> KU KLUX KLAN
> ORGANIZED IN THIS,
> THE LAW OFFICE
> OF
> JUDGE THOMAS M. JONES,
> DECEMBER 24TH, 1865
>
> ─────────
>
> NAMES OF ORIGINAL ORGANIZERS
> CALVIN E. JONES   JOHN B. KENNEDY
> FRANK O. McCORD   JOHN C. LESTER
> RICHARD R. REED   JAMES R. CROWE

This plaque was unveiled on May 21, 1917, by the widow of Captain Kennedy, the last of the six founders to die.

Similar plaques in other towns, on the walls of college dormitories, preserve the memory of the "immortal six" (or five, or seven) who founded one or another of the Greek-letter college fraternities. The original purpose of the Klan differed little from that of the college groups: a handful of boys, fond of each other's company, seeking to give their friendship some permanent form with a variable admixture of mystery and exclusiveness. Events soon dispelled the similarity, for the Klan was subjected to none of the controls —fixed college regulations and faculty surveillance—that have kept the fraternities relatively harmless. But at the very outset, that day before Christmas in 1865, the six young Pulaskians had no apparent motive other than the purely social.

Most if not all of the six had been in Confederate uniform just a few months earlier. All wars are followed by economic and social disorganization, and the returning soldiers usually have the worst of it. It is easy to believe that in such a country town as Pulaski the boredom, after four years of devoted heroics in a cause that failed, was appalling for young Lester and Kennedy, Crowe and Reed, Jones and McCord. Jobs and money were virtually nonexistent: Confederate currency had been totally devalued with defeat, and the labor force that the region had relied on time out of mind could no longer, because of Emancipation, be compelled to work. Forming a club was almost the only alternative to unbearable tedium.

Little more was done on that "founder's day" than agree to organize and to divide into two committees, one to choose a suitable name, the other to consider such matters as rules, titles, and activities. John Kennedy had briefly attended Centre College in Kentucky, where he must have observed some of the details of fraternity structure. He recalled from his study of Greek the word *kuklos*, meaning a band or circle. (One account of the founding reports the presence of a visitor from Georgia who proposed "Clocletz," the name of a phantom Indian chief much feared by the Georgia Negroes; but this sounds fishy—and woefully unclassical.) James Crowe suggested splitting *kuklos* in two and changing the

[6]

final letter to *x*, yielding *ku klux*. Then John Lester, remarking that all six members were of Scottish descent, proposed that *clan* be added, spelt with a *k* for consistency; and he tentatively tried out the combination: *ku klux klan.*

During most of the nineteenth century, Sir Walter Scott was a favorite author in the South, though perhaps not quite so overriding a favorite as has long been supposed. It is not improper to credit him with a share of the Southern romanticism of chivalry, honor, pride—and resistance to what was conceived as tyranny from outside. The Ku Klux Klan was never based on the blood ties of ancient Scottish clans, but neither had the South been an independent country forced into subjection by a stronger neighbor, though some Southerners saw a parallel in the defeat of the Confederacy. Scott's fiction had helped to condition Southern readers to foster illusions of an idyllic past and of personal and regional superiority; illusions that military defeat, far from dispelling, established more firmly than ever. Defeated Troy has always been exalted over the Greek victors, and Trojan blood has been deemed a purer red; lost causes have a way of evoking this magic.

Just as the Confederacy itself stimulated nostalgic regret in subsequent times, the Klan, for the same people and the same reasons, had the power to create an enduring notion of essential nobility. Susan Lawrence Davis shared this thinking: her *Authentic History: Ku Klux Klan,* published in 1924, overflows with virtual Klan worship. The dedication leaves no doubt about her viewpoint:

To My Mother, Sarah Ann (McClellan) Davis, and the
Other Southern Women Who Designed and Manufactured
with Their Own Fingers the Regalia for the Ku Klux
Klansmen and the Trappings for Their Horses, and to
the Ku Klux Klan 1865–1877 Both the Living and the
Dead, This History is Gratefully Dedicated.

In recording the first hours of the Klan, Miss Davis refers with an almost palpable awe to John Lester's trial of the club's name as "the first time these words ever fell from human tongue."

[7]

In the same year that the Davis book appeared, Mr. and Mrs. William B. Romine of Pulaski brought out a pamphlet of thirty pages, giving a slightly different version of the founding. They agree with Miss Davis in praising the makers of the regalia, but give more details about it:

> As the Klan stood primarily for the purity and preservation of the home and for the protection of the women and children, especially the widows and orphans of Confederate soldiers, white, the emblem of purity was chosen for the robes. And to render them startling and conspicuous red, emblem of the blood which Klansmen were ready to shed in defense of the helpless was chosen for the trimmings. Also a sentimental thought probably was present in adopting the color scheme, as white and red were the Confederate colors. Be it said to the credit of the women of the South who designed and made with their own hands more than four hundred thousand of these Klan robes for both horses and riders, not a word was said by these women to any one about them and not one single secret concerning them was ever revealed.

The next meeting was held a few days after the first, not in the judge's office but in a house whose owners were away on an extended visit; they had asked Captain Kennedy to take care of the place. Miss Davis names the owners as Colonel and Mrs. Thomas Martin, but the Romine account locates this second meeting in the Spofford mansion, which in 1924 housed the Men's Club of Pulaski. In the course of the evening, James Crowe had the brilliant thought that costumes would heighten the mystery, and it seemed no breach of hospitality to raid the linen closet and requisition the stiff white sheets and pillowcases. After all, as Miss Davis remarks in her book, "masquerading was a popular form of entertainment in those days." There was equal propriety, apparently, in borrowing horses from a nearby livery stable. After using more of Mrs. Martin's (or Mrs. Spofford's) sheets to disguise the horses, the six original Klansmen mounted and rode slowly and in silence through the streets of Pulaski, amusing passersby with grotesque gestures.

The cream of the jest was to listen next morning, with secret delight, to the comments of friends and relatives who had seen their parade. One unexpected result, reported by various observers, was that the superstitious Negroes had not been amused by the spectacle, but, instead, had taken the riders for ghosts of the Confederate dead. What had been conceived as a lark to relieve the general tedium took on a sudden new dimension; if idle Negroes could be frightened so easily, perhaps they could be persuaded to resume work, and something like the prewar balance could be restored—the plantation system that kept the Negroes subservient and at work, producing the income that white men had been accustomed to. (The Romines recorded that parading was not begun quite so early as the second meeting, and followed, instead of preceding, the decision to try to frighten Negroes back to work.)

The novelty alone would have attracted applications for membership, but the possibility of intimidating the freedmen no doubt accelerated the growth of the Pulaski Klan. It was fun with a serious purpose to rouse a Negro at night, ask him for a bucket of water, and pretend to drink it all without a pause; it took only a simple apparatus, hidden by the Klan regalia, of funnel and rubber tube and pouch. Then, with a loud smacking of the lips, the Klansman could say, "That's the first drink I've had since I was killed at Shiloh." It was equally good sport to bid a Negro shake hands and to extend to him from under the sheet a skeleton arm or one made of wood. A third stunt is reminiscent of Irving's headless horseman: a false head, commonly an outsized gourd with a mask attached, could be removed and offered to a Negro to "hold for a while." The ex-slaves, most of them without even rudimentary education, were quite susceptible to these frightening maneuvers and the countless refinements devised by Klan members throughout the South.

One early decision by the founders in Pulaski seems to have been generally followed by the Klan everywhere: new members were not to be sought. But there was seldom any need to proselytize, for "Southrons" learning about the Klan were commonly eager to join. A member, discovering that a friend was interested, could easily think of ways to tell him when and where to go for further information. Sometimes a member would sound out a friend by expressing an interest in joining himself; if the friend showed the right attitude, they would agree to go to the meeting together. By March 1866, the Pulaski Klan had a permanent "den" of its own, Dr. Ben Carter's cyclone-damaged house on a hill at the edge of town.

The would-be member, alone or with his Klansman friend, approached the den after dark, where he was challenged by an outer guard (called Lictor), who blew a whistle to summon a courier (Night Hawk). Blindfolded, the applicant was led into the den, where the Grand Turk put a series of test questions to him. If his responses were not satisfactory, he was taken outside and dismissed. If the answers were right, the order was given to drape the "royal robe" over his shoulders, place the "regal crown" on his head, and strap around his waist the "sacred sword-belt." He was then told to repeat, phrase by phrase as read to him, the Ku Klux oath. In addition to containing the usual vows never to reveal the signs, symbols, grip, password, or secrets of the order, the oath forbade him ever to reveal his membership and pledged him to abstain from alcoholic beverages as long as he remained an active member. When the oath was completed, the blindfold was removed and the new member saw in the altar (a mirror) that his robe was a donkey skin, his crown an old torn hat bedecked with donkey ears, and his sword-belt a common saddlebelt. At this point seriousness gave way to good-natured horseplay for as long as it could be kept up.

Applicants considered too young were led out of the den and left sitting on a log; sooner or later they would give up, remove the blindfold, and steal sheepishly home. An occasional "undesirable" was rolled down the hill in a barrel. Exposure, whether by boys or by members not quite the right sort, was to be avoided at all costs. The risk became more serious later on, when Klan and federal agents came into direct conflict, and when scattered acts of violence began to damage the public image of all Klansmen. The original secrecy adopted by the founders in Pulaski set a precedent that other dens found easy to follow and increasingly worth preserving.

The six founders were too few in number to provide a full complement of den officers. There was no Grand Scribe at first. The original den leader, Frank McCord, was called Grand Cyclops; his chief lieutenant, known as Grand Magi, was Captain Kennedy. Crowe was chosen Grand Turk, a kind of marshal or master of ceremonies. Calvin Jones and Captain Lester were Night Hawks, or couriers, and Richard Reed was the first Lictor, or outer guard. New titles were invented for the next few members admitted; after that, new members were called Ghouls.

The titles have little in common except a suggestion of weirdness. The one title that seems out of place is "Lictor." In Roman antiquity a lictor attended upon a magistrate, bearing the fasces before him and executing his sentences of judgment against offenders. Coincidentally, the Klan chose for this officer a title related to the symbol of authority adopted in the twentieth century by Mussolini's Fascists.

> **WHAT DOES IT MEAN?**—The following mysterious "Take Notice" was found under our door early yesterday morning, having doubtless been slipped there the night previous. Will any one venture to tell us what it means, if it means anything at all? What is a "Kuklux Klan," and who is this "Grand Cyclops" that issues his mysterious and imperative orders? Can any one give us a little light on this subject? Here is the order:
>
> "TAKE NOTICE.—The Kuklax Klan will assemble at their usual place of rendezvous, "The Den," on Tuesday night next, exactly at the hour of midnight, in costume and bearing the arms of the Klan.
>
> "By or of the Grand Cyclops. G. T."

One of the earliest—possibly the first—newspaper story on the Klan was this one in the Pulaski *Citizen* on March 29, 1867. The editor of the *Citizen* was the Grand Geni of the local Den.

Few Klan members on the den or local level have been so well known as the Pulaski founders; the aura that gathers about the heads of all founding fathers precludes anonymity. As a group, from the biographic evidence, they seem to have been men of good character and well qualified for the positions in public life that they later achieved. When men in other towns sought to form dens, the Pulaskians assumed the responsibility of approving their applications, but with the rapid spread of the Klan this practice soon became only a formality and was eventually abandoned.

The Pulaski den did take every care to supervise closely the first applicants. These were in nearby Athens, Alabama, where Northern schoolteachers had been shaking the very foundations of Southern tradition by treating their Negro students as human beings on a level with themselves. Colonel Lawrence R. Davis of Athens asked his old friend Captain Lester for advice, and the notion of a Klan den was the obvious answer. No such practical purpose had attended the creation of the Pulaski den; it is significant that with the organizing of the very first new "chapter," regulation—meaning active measures to preserve the old racial relationships—was the acknowledged motive. The Pulaskians, if they wished to preserve their own original purpose as a strictly social group, could have withheld approval. It is more reasonable to suppose that they quite willingly accepted for the Klan the practice of intimidating Negroes and had no reluctance about encouraging like-minded groups elsewhere to adopt the same practice. The Pulaski Grand Cyclops, Frank McCord, joined Captain Lester in administering the oath to the fifteen charter members at Athens. A good site had been selected—"The Cove," a natural amphitheater deep in the woods about three miles out of town. After the ceremonies, the maintaining of white supremacy was discussed, and it was decided to make this the chief purpose of the Ku Klux Klan.

A week later, also at "The Cove," a large number of Athenians were added to Den No. 2. There could have been little time for the horseplay following the formalities, as at Pulaski, for these were men with a grim purpose. They had been incensed by, as Miss Davis, the Colonel's daughter, reported, the bold attempt of one of the Northern teachers "to associate openly with negro men, thus offending the Southern people in their helplessness to legislate against such an evil condition."

Perhaps, if confronted with such a crisis, the Pulaski den might not have been content with silent night parades and with crude practical jokes to frighten Negroes. At Athens, the Negro who had been seen riding in public with the bold Northern schoolma'am was taken to "The Cove." He was shrewd enough to explain to the assembled Klansmen that he was only obeying the white woman's command. If his life was spared, he said, he would swear never again to ride with a white woman; and he promised to tell all his friends to give up any notion of social equality with whites. The Klan dismissed him with a light punishment: he was merely ducked in the icy spring at the bottom of the amphitheater and sent home, wet and shivering.

Even under the close surveillance of officers from the Pulaski den, the Athenians added the new dimension of physical punishment. As the Klan spread, it was increasingly impossible for Pulaski members to supervise the proceedings, and the autonomy each new den enjoyed led to a wide variety of attitudes and practices. Some crime worse than riding with a white woman could easily seem to merit more severe punishment. Within a year there were hundreds of local groups with the same name, the same titles and ritual, and the same over-all purpose, but exhibiting a wide range of behavior, from little more than horseplay to the boldest flouting of established law and order.

Members favoring restraint would quite naturally be distressed by reports of violence elsewhere, for excesses committed by any den reflected on the entire Klan. It was all very well to say that bogus Klans perpetrated the most heinous offenses, but with no central authority to extend control over all the dens, who could say which ones were genuine and which were bogus? The secrecy confounded the problem: as long as Klansmen concealed their identity, what proof could be offered that "genuine" members did not commit any given atrocity?

For just such reasons the more responsible dens, at Pulaski and elsewhere, decided to hold an organizational meeting early in 1867 in Nashville, Tennessee. Local legend, which in the absence of more concrete evidence is all we have to go on, fixes the time as April and the place as Room 10 in the newly completed Maxwell House. By a coincidence in timing, Congress had just passed the Reconstruction Act over President Johnson's strong opposition, dividing most of the South into five military districts and giving the commanding generals great authority, even over the judiciary. If the Radical Republicans had deliberately set out to infuriate white Southerners and encourage resistance, they could hardly have devised a better method. In any event the Klansmen who gathered in Nashville sensed a particular urgency to plan effective countermeasures.

General George W. Gordon, who at the time was practising law in Pulaski, accepted the assignment of drafting a "Prescript," a formal statement of basic principles. It is surprisingly brief, four sentences only: a preamble and three other sections. "We recognize our relation to the United States government, the Constitutional laws thereof, and the Union of the States thereunder." So states the preamble. The first section specifies the objectives: protection of the weak and the innocent, the relief of the injured and the oppressed, and the succoring of the unfortunate, especially the widows and orphans of Confederate soldiers. The other two sections commit the Klan to support and defend the Constitution, to assist in the execution of all Constitutional laws, and to protect the people from invasion, from unlawful seizure, and from trials by other than their peers "in conformity with the laws of the land."

The effects of these statements, high-sounding and innocuous as they may seem, will be illustrated in later pages; it is enough to say here that "invasion" covered the activities of the military governments and the agents of the Freedmen's Bureau (which the federal government had established to help the former slaves), that "peers" meant Southern whites, and that the former slaves were not viewed as being among the weak, the injured, the oppressed, and the unfortunate, or among those qualifying for protection.

The convention also adopted an independent and much longer statement defining the Klan as "an institution of Chivalry, Humanity, Mercy, and Patriotism," describing its general structure, giving titles to the larger territories and their officers, and prescribing den procedures in some detail. Ten questions that were to be put to each applicant for membership tell us more about the Klan rationale than may have been intended. The expected answers affirmed opposition to the Radicals currently dominant in Congress, to the Grand Army of the Republic, to Negro equality with whites, and to the Union League, a non-governmental society which the Klan viewed as the chief instrument for promoting that equality. In addition, the new member was required to adhere firmly to the principle of "a white man's government" and to seek early restoration of local state sovereignty. The final question was: "Do you believe in the inalienable rights of self-preservation of the people against the exercise of arbitrary and unlicensed power?" The assembled delegates may have been the better element of the Klan, uneasy over reported excesses and sincere in their hopes for moderation, but this question, and the answer expected, endorsed the right to resist the federal mandate; for in Klan thinking, which has survived the original Klan, the application of federal force against regional tradition and practice has always seemed, to many Southerners, arbitrary and unauthorized by the Constitution, if not expressly in violation of that document. There is, in other words, no hypocrisy in swearing allegiance to both the Constitution and the Union, and then defying the federal government and certain federal laws. It is fundamentally a matter of how one interprets the Constitution, and in the classical Southern view it was the North that had violated its spirit, and the South that was upholding it.

Once the set of questions had been posed and answered satisfactorily, at night and against the background of flaming torches, an official charge was to be read to the new recruit. According to this document, the Klan had been formed "to regenerate our unfortunate country and to relieve the White Race from the humiliating condition to which it has lately been reduced in this Republic. Our main and fundamental objective is the MAINTENANCE OF THE SUPREMACY OF THE WHITE RACE in this Republic. History and Physiology teach us that we belong to a race which nature has endowed with an evident superiority over all other races, and that the Maker, in thus elevating us above the common standard of human creation, has intended to give us over inferior races a dominion from which no human laws can permanently derogate." The closer another race approaches the black African, "the more fatally that stamp of inferiority is affixed to its sons, and irrevocably dooms them to eternal imperfectibility and degradation."

America was founded by the white race and for the white race, the reasoning continued, and any effort to transfer control to the black race was an obvious violation of the Constitution and of divine will. No white man could submit to such encroachments "without humiliation and shame." Social equality must therefore be forever barred as a step to political equality and to intermarriage and "the production of a degenerate and bastard offspring. . . . We must maintain the purity of the white blood, if we would preserve for it that natural superiority with which God has ennobled it." Negro rights were to be recognized and protected, with firmness and liberality; but the whites must retain the privilege of determining what those Negro rights were, for asking Negroes what they considered their rights to be, would be representing the political equality the Klan was sworn to prevent.

The formal structure of the Klan was relatively simple: each state was designated a Realm, ruled over by a Grand Dragon; each congressional district a Dominion, ruled by a Grand Titan; and each county a Province, under a Grand Giant. The entire area where the Klan had members was named the Invisible Empire. Robert E. Lee, in declining an invitation to accept the supreme command, is reputed to have written to the convention that his approval must be "invisible," a word that may have suggested the general name. Lee's approval extended to the second choice, Nathan Bedford Forrest, who accepted the honor at Nashville and served as the only Grand Wizard in the original Klan's history. It should astonish nobody to learn that many of the other major officials—Grand Dragons, Grand Titans, Grand Giants—were also former high-ranking Confederate officers. But their connection with the Klan was not learned until later, for in accepting amnesty at the end of the war they had sworn to obey all federal laws and never again to oppose the federal government.

With dens springing up in all parts of the South, with a national organization achieved, principles enunciated, and procedures systematized, the Klan was now ready to make itself an invisible empire indeed, an underground government opposing at every level the efforts of a federal government which it conceived as arbitrary and in violation of the Constitution. Within a little more than two years, General Forrest officially disbanded the Klan—his part, according to a not very reliable rumor, of a verbal agreement between him and President Grant. It seems more reasonable to suppose that the official dissolution of the organization was for window dressing only, to provide even greater invisibility. The Klan was much too useful as the agency of Southern white resistance for local dens to obey Forrest's order if it was sincere, and most of the violent incidents occurred after the order was given. To give up the Klan, just then, would have been tantamount to abandoning the principle of white supremacy, which few loyal sons of the South could conceive of doing.

Chapter Two

WHITE SUPREMACY

"Our Main and Fundamental Objective Is the MAINTENANCE OF THE SUPREMACY OF THE WHITE RACE *in This Republic."*

Out of the proceedings of the organizational meeting at the Maxwell House in Nashville in April of 1867 came the Prescript of the Ku Klux Klan, together with a set of ten questions which every would-be Klansman had to answer in the affirmative, and a formal concluding charge to initiates that contained the sentence quoted above, capitals and all. In other official pronouncements of the original Klan, and in formal statements issued by the revived Klan, the same objective is prominently asserted with only slight changes in wording. It is usually followed by a sentence or two attributing the superiority of the white man and the inferiority of the Negro to divine intention. The Maker, according to the Nashville convention, "has intended to give us over inferior races a dominion from which no human law can permanently derogate."

The Klan's dedication to the principle of white supremacy is obvious enough, but it is hardly less obvious that the Klan did not invent white supremacy. If it invented anything, it was a method of doing illegally what the great majority of Southern whites, in the difficult days after the Civil War, desperately wanted to do but found they could not do through legal measures. The Klan could not have been the effective force it was without the overwhelming support of the Southern whites, or without the cloak of secrecy under which it could operate with little fear of detection. Some of the "better elements" of Southern society publicly deplored the worst Klan violence, but their sense of outrage stopped short of exposing individual Klansmen and prosecuting them as criminals. Public opinion *could* have suppressed the Klan, but it didn't. The Klan, whether or not its methods were pleasant to contemplate, was doing what people wanted—preserving white supremacy.

It was not uncommon for Southerners of "the better sort," such as President John Leland of the Female College at Laurens, South Carolina, to deplore Klan violence and then proceed to put the federal actions in a far worse light. However wicked the Klan might be, to loyal Southerners it was not as wicked as the vindictive self-seeking Radicals in Congress and their agents in the South, who humiliated the local whites by setting above them a race known to be inferior. This reasoning is found so often and is expressed so consistently and unequivocally, that it is impossible to doubt the sincerity of the protesting Southerners. The books they sometimes wrote gave voice to firmly held regional views that must be understood if we are to give the Klan its due.

Americans can be proud of the speed with which minority groups have passed through the three stages in the process of assimilation. Every group in our population—with one conspicuous exception—met initial hostility from older Americans, survived this hostility into the mid-ground of tolerance, and then passed to the final stage of full acceptance. If we were to concentrate our attention on the initial hostility, we would have to acknowledge a good many blemishes in our self-image as a tolerant, generous, hospitable people. The Puritan hatred of Quakers, written into harsh legislation in the seventeenth century, is only a notorious early example of intergroup conflict that has recurred often in our history. But many

This costume was worn by a Klansman of an early Den in Nashville, Tenn. The black calico robe was trimmed with white. A strip of red cloth marked the mouth. The buttons were tin. *Wide World Photo*

[20]

groups gained full acceptance so long ago that it is possible for their members to forget the early troubles.

Much of the original hostility rose out of differences between old and new groups; differences that in time either wore away or became familiar parts of the national diversity. Massachusetts has long since abandoned its persecution of Quakers because the religious differences separating Puritans and Quakers became unimportant—or not important enough to produce physical persecution. German and Irish immigrants, who first arrived in appreciable numbers a little more than a century ago, met violent discrimination, but their descendants are today so well assimilated that they have produced two of our most recent Presidents, Eisenhower and Kennedy—and the latter, as a Catholic, represented a religious group that has had to endure the extremes of hostility. These examples could easily be multiplied; collectively they yield a record of rapid assimilation that has been remarkable—so remarkable, indeed, that the one great exception is an anomaly difficult to understand.

Negroes are no recent addition to the population, with unfamiliar traits that arouse the suspicion of older inhabitants. They have been here almost as long as any white group, and much longer than most. They differ from all other groups in having been brought here by force and in having been kept in servitude for a long period. But they have had their freedom for a hundred years, during which time they have not opposed being assimilated. What they most want, in fact, is the full acceptance that other minorities have achieved. This is the only civilization they know or want to know as theirs. Many other non-whites—Orientals, East Indians, American Indians—have found general acceptance; the continuing rejection of Negroes cannot be due to their skin color alone.

One explanation is that human beings, from some deep psychological urge to feel superior, welcome the presence of a group they can view as inferior. In Europe, where countries are small and close together, the need is met by neighbors with differing languages and customs; the United States is too large for that, and only in small border regions are Americans provided with "inferior" neighbors to look down upon—Mexicans in the Southwest, French-Canadians in northern New England. The American Indians are well distributed, but most of them are segregated on reservations; besides, they are too few in number. Negroes, roughly a tenth of the population, are even more widely scattered in the nation though with varying density, and nowhere are they physically separated from the whites except in the most local sense; they comprise an ideal group for whites to feel superior to.

In parts of the country where they have been most numerous, Negroes were so long deprived of the privileges available to all whites that, by the time of the Civil War, they were demonstrably inferior—in education, achievement, social status, and opportunity. Despite notable exceptions, most of them are still inferior in these same ways. And because they are, it is fatally easy for whites to suppose that the inferiority is the Negro's own fault, the result of innate incapacity. It is also very easy for whites to accept their advantage over the Negroes as a normal and inescapable part of "the way things are." Even whites who are favorably disposed toward Negroes help to maintain the differential in relative advantage simply by not ever taking the final step in the process of assimilation—full acceptance of Negroes as equals. Tolerance is obviously better than hostility, but it is a neutral virtue at best. Tolerance permits the open-minded white to enjoy the very same advantage over the Negro that the most rabid segregationist demands.

Another possible explanation is that the adverse image of the Negro has been nurtured for a longer time and more deliberately than the image of any other minority. Slaveholders were no different from other white Americans—no more vicious in nature and with no less human decency. But their very ownership of slaves made them seek to justify slavery, sometimes by citing passages in the Bible, more often by assembling evidence that Negroes were beings essentially inferior to themselves. If they needed precedent, they could have pointed to the Puritan rationale concerning the Indians: a series of troublesome minor wars hardened the Puritan hearts and yielded, toward the end of the seventeenth century, the explicit theory that Indians were savages without souls and suitable objects of extermination. The Southern slave-owners wanted their slaves alive, not dead, but the extreme view among them was close to the Puritan conclusion: Negroes were not really human beings, but members of a lower biological order. Less extreme but more widely held was the opinion that they were human, all right, but measurably and forever lower than whites on the human scale. Evidence supporting such views is still being assembled and published; what it proves is not Negro inferiority, but the persistence of the wish to justify the white advantage.

Wanting the presence of an inferior group to feel superior to is often accompanied by the notion that one's own race or nation is especially favored by God. Since every race or nation has something distinctive, it is always possible to prove—to one's own satisfaction—that one's own race or nation enjoys divine favor. Even great adversity can be and has been interpreted as a sign of this special interest: "God punishes those he loves."

But success gives greater support than adversity to a self-image of superiority. In American history the high point of national arrogance may have been the years just before and after the turn of this century, when Albert Beveridge, senator from Indiana from 1899 to 1911, was voicing eloquently what many Americans loved to hear. On April 27, 1898, speaking in Boston at a meeting honoring the memory of General Grant, he said that Grant "had the prophet's seer-like sight which beheld, as a part of the Almighty's infinite plan, the disappearance of debased civilizations and decaying races before the higher civilization of the nobler and more virile types of men." On September 16 of the same year, in Indianapolis, cheers and applause punctuated another Beveridge speech: "The opposition tells us we ought not to rule a people without its consent. I answer, the rule of liberty, that all just governments derive their authority from the assent of the governed, applies only to those who are capable of self-government." Then, after his election to the United States Senate, Beveridge turned his maiden speech to that body into a ringing eulogy of the "Nordic" peoples: "God has not been preparing the English-speaking and Teutonic peoples for a thousand years for nothing but vain and idle self-contemplation and self-admiration. No! He has made us the master organizers of the world to establish system where chaos reigns. . . . He has made us adepts in government that we may administer government among savages and senile people."

If this sounds like the Klan announcement at Nashville in 1867 that the Maker "has intended to give us over inferior races a dominion from which no human law can permanently derogate," it does not mean that Beveridge was a Klansman; it suggests, instead, that the Klan has not been alone in claiming exclusive divine approval. This is easy to believe in a society that encourages each of its members, especially in early childhood, to assume a direct personal interest on the part of God. It is almost bred in our bones, and is among the things that each child must unlearn if he is to make a reasonable adjustment to a society as diverse in its origins as ours. The more cosmopolitan the child's environment, presumably, the sooner he is faced with the probability—which he may, of course, reject—that *his* family, *his* church, *his* kind of person, does not have God's exclusive interest. Individuals in very homogeneous sections may be spared the shock of this discovery, especially if the divine favor assumed by one group has become a regional ideology deliberately fostered and even reflected in local laws. For the irreligious, meanwhile, the racist dogma can exist without a religious base, or can even be a substitute for religious belief.

"Racism," to quote anthropologist Ruth Benedict, "is the dogma that one ethnic group is condemned by nature to congenital inferiority and another group is destined to congenital superiority. It is the dogma that the hope of civilization depends upon eliminating some races and keeping others pure. It is the dogma that one race has carried progress with it throughout human history and can alone ensure future progress. . . . Racism is essentially a pretentious way of saying that 'I' belong to the Best People. For such a conviction it is the most gratifying formula that has ever been discovered, for neither my own unworthiness nor the accusations of others can ever dislodge me from my position. . . . It avoids all embarrassing questions about my conduct of life and avoids all embarrassing claims by 'inferior' groups about their own achievements and ethical standards."

More than a century ago, John Stuart Mill said, "Of all vulgar modes of escaping from the consideration of the effect of social and moral influences on the human mind, the most vulgar is that of attributing the diversities of conduct and character to inherent natural differences." To which Jacques Barzun adds, "It is a vulgar error, not only because it thrives and is abroad among the people, often unaware of itself, but always charged with hatred and hypocrisy; it is also a vulgar error because it denies individual diversity, scouts the complexity of cause and effect, scorns the intellect, and ultimately bars Mind from the universe of created things."

It is doubtful whether Senator Beveridge was aware of scorning intellect, or of offering any slight to Americans who were not Anglo-Saxon or Teutonic in their derivation. Although the Anglo-Saxons —that is, people descended from the original English migrations —became a statistical minority sometime in the 1870's, they had been the majority for so long, and were so solidly entrenched in wealth and power, that it was very easy for them to think of themselves, in 1900 and for many years later, as the majority they no longer were in fact. The myth hangs on stubbornly, indeed, that the real Americans are white, Protestant, Anglo-Saxon, and long in the land; groups with a hyphen, such as "Polish-American," or without one, such as "the Finns in Michigan," fall somewhat short of the ideal, however satisfactory their assimilation.

In a moment of imperialistic fervor, when the bulk of the population could echo Rudyard Kipling's notorious contempt for "lesser breeds without the law" and could endorse the notion that the United States had the right to take over other peoples, as the virile races of Europe had been doing for some time—at just such a moment the American people put themselves nakedly on exhibit as victims of a racial myth. Success was the proof of divine favor, and the time was at hand to carry out the Almighty's infinite plan for the disappearance of debased civilizations and decaying races. That some Americans were recent transplants from the debased civilizations, and that others belonged to decaying races, hardly mattered, for the simple reason that these were not the *real* Americans. So, at any rate, went the myth.

To the general American sense of Anglo-Saxon superiority was added, in the South, a particular commitment to white supremacy and Negro inferiority. The Southern whites in this most homogeneous of our regions have always been overwhelmingly Anglo-Saxon; and the Negroes have always been the one significant minority. In the early years of the nineteenth century the sense of guilt at owning other human beings persisted even when slavery grew much more profitable than it had ever been before; but the increasing profits reduced the hope expressed by Jefferson's generation that the institution would soon disappear. Without that consoling assurance, as Oscar Handlin remarks in *Race and Nationality in American Life,* "the Southerners could not bear to acknowledge that their society harbored within it an ineradicable evil. The only alternative was to deny that slavery was an evil."

But simple denial meant little. It became increasingly important, especially when Northern Abolitionists stepped up their attack, to construct a positive theory, one that showed slavery to be an actual good—for the slave himself, for the Southern economy, and for the nation at large. Evidence was ample: Northern mills needed the raw cotton that could be harvested only by Negro labor; without slavery the South would turn into a desert, a drag upon the rest of the nation; and slavery gave the Negroes the benefits of civilization. The few free Negroes in the South were dismissed as worthless; and in the West Indies and Canada, where slavery had already been abolished, both the Negroes and the economy had degenerated—so said the Southern theorists.

In their zeal the apologists for slavery sometimes went too far, as they did in describing the Northern freedmen as universally depraved, criminal, and unstable. Slave-owners might believe invented statistics showing that Northern prisons and mental hospitals and poorhouses were crowded with Negroes, but residents of places where these institutions were located recognized the fictitious nature of the assertions. Another mistake in Southern strategy was in describing the Northern Abolitionists as despicable men—a characterization that particularly offended Northerners who held certain enemies of slavery in great respect: Samuel Sewall, for his tract dated 1700, "The Selling of Joseph"; John Woolman, the Quaker who issued two essays, in 1754 and 1762, both entitled

Some Considerations on the Keeping of Negroes; de Crèvecoeur, the transplanted Frenchman, who devoted the ninth of his *Letters from an American Farmer* (1782) to the evils of slavery; and Benjamin Franklin, whose last public act was signing a memorial to Congress urging the abolition of slavery, and who within a month of his death in 1790 wrote a brilliant ironical essay, "On the Slave Trade." Northerners might disapprove strongly of Abolitionist neighbors, but they could not accept "despicable" as an adjective suitable for Whittier, Lowell, and Emerson. Besides, if opposing slavery made a man despicable, what would become of the reputations of such Southerners as Washington, Jefferson, Patrick Henry, Madison, and Monroe?

Not all Abolitionists were eminent, of course. In the foreword to his *Theodore Weld: Crusader for Freedom*, Benjamin P. Thomas has this to say: "All sorts of men enlisted in the abolition ranks: quiet men and ranters, broad-minded men and narrow bigots, passive resistants and direct actionists, respecters of law and order and some whose sole allegiance was to 'a higher law,' exhibitionists and men of humble modesty. Eccentricity was prevalent among them, but their one common and emblematic quality was unselfish consecration to a high ideal. They were dangerous, to be sure, dangerous to all institutions and concepts that denied a portion of mankind its natural birthright." Eminent or not, Abolitionists could be considered despicable only in the context of an absolute belief that slavery was divinely ordained and that opposing it was heretical.

This belief existed, however, and it was supported by Biblical passages—for the Bible was written in an age when all societies held human beings in bondage. Divine sanction of slavery was just as easy for white supremacists to accept as any other part of the classical Southern position. John Leland, in his book *A Voice from South Carolina*, referred to Abolition being urged "even in the Sanctuary of God," as if nothing could be more shocking than Northern clergymen ignoring the scriptural sanctions of slavery and the demonstrable inferiority of the Negro. True religion and white supremacy, for a good many Southerners, were not only compatible, they were virtually identical. A white Mississippian, on trial in

1964 for the murder of a Negro leader, said virtually that in court: "I believe in segregation just like I believe in God."

The Southern theorists overlooked no line of reasoning, all of it familiar to students of racism. Much evidence was assembled to prove the Negro's innate inferiority. Not only were Negroes supposed (by whites) to be more ignorant than white men; they were also said to lack the capacity for any but the most rudimentary education. They had never created any great culture, certainly none to be compared with Anglo-Saxon achievement. They lacked even elementary notions of virtue; one man estimated that it would take many generations of training to inculcate in Negroes the moral sense of the white man. And Negroes had none of the Anglo-Saxon genius for self-government—a genius that not even other white men quite shared. Even more obvious evidence lay in the physical appearance of Negroes: the broad flat nose was considered a clue to a slothful mind, and the dark skin a defect in color matched by worse defects in character. The very docility of most slaves was viewed as lack of the spirit that made white men superior. On the human scale, Anglo-Saxons were at the top, Africans at the very bottom.

Negro inferiority became so firmly established in Southern theory that a superior Negro was not considered possible. A free Negro was an offense to Southern decency, since beings as inferior as Negroes did not deserve to be free like whites. But a Negro who was both free and visibly superior was particularly infuriating, since he was living proof of an impossibility. In one of the most memorable passages of *Huckleberry Finn,* Mark Twain caught the essence of this fury. Huck's good-for-nothing father is speaking:

Oh, yes, this is a wonderful gov'ment, wonderful. Why, looky here. There was a free nigger there from Ohio—a mulatter, most as white as a white man. He had the whitest shirt on you ever see, too, and the shiniest hat; and there ain't a man in that town that's got as fine clothes as what he had; and he had a gold watch and chain, and a silver-headed cane—the awfulest old gray-headed nabob in the state. And what do you think? They said he was a p'fessor in a college, and could talk all kinds of languages, and knowed everything. And that ain't the wust. They said he could *vote* when he was at home. Well, that let me out. Thinks I, what is the country a-coming to? It

[28]

ONE VOTE LESS was the title of this Thomas Nast cartoon in *Harper's Weekly* on August 8, 1868. The cartoon was aimed at the Democrats' platform, which called for repeal of the Reconstruction Acts.

was 'lection day, and I was just about to go and vote myself if I
warn't too drunk to get there; but when they told me there was a
state in this country where they'd let that nigger vote, I drawed out.
I says I'll never vote ag'in. Them's the very words I said; they all
heard me; and the country may rot for all me—I'll never vote ag'in
as long as I live. And to see the cool way of that nigger—why, he
wouldn't 'a' give me the road if I hadn't shoved him out of the way.
I says to the people, why ain't this nigger put up at auction and
sold?—that's what I want to know. And what do you reckon they said?
Why, they said he couldn't be sold till he'd been in the state six
months, and he hadn't been there that long yet. There, now—that's
a specimen. They call that a gov'ment that can't sell a free nigger till
he's been in the state six months. Here's a gov'ment that calls itself
a gov'ment, and lets on to be a gov'ment, and thinks it is a gov'ment,
and yet's got to set stock-still for six whole months before it can take
a-hold of a prowling, thieving, infernal, white-shirted free nigger, and—

At this point Pap tripped over a tub of salt pork, and his mono-
logue took a colorful new turn.

Twain no doubt exaggerated for effect, but white supremacy as
the Klan strove to maintain it, and as Southern white thinking
overwhelmingly asserted it, was total: the most worthless white
man was held to be innately superior to the finest Negro. Where
segregation is enforced today, the same reasoning holds, although
it is hardly as tenable in logic as it was during slavery. Too many
Negroes today hold college degrees, even doctorates, and have
been notably successful in all fields of activity, for reasoning men
to cling to this notion; but the white supremacist is not guided
by reason. He is guided instead by a theory carefully developed
more than a century ago to justify slavery.

Some slave-owners, on religious grounds, could never quite accept the notion of Negro inferiority as a result of racial degenera-
tion. If all sons of God are one in God, not even attributing the
Negro race to Cain could overcome the doubt. The Christian doctrine of human brotherhood, bolstered by basic democratic dogma,
stood in the way of a clear conscience. But somebody offered an
explanation that removed the difficulty. Negroes were said to have
evolved along a line distinctly separate from that which produced
the white race and that culminated in the noble Anglo-Saxons;

white and Negro were biologically distinct species. Once this could be accepted, all *men* could be free and equal, brothers in Christ, and of one blood. This argument was an alternate means of reaching the definition of Negroes as nonhuman.

This view found only limited acceptance among the devout, but it had a particularly strong appeal for the less educated whites. It never worked its way into official Klan statements, which in general were very literate, the work of men of culture; but in its more violent practice the Klan showed less respect for Negro life than for the well-being of a horse or a dog. With the hardening of racism in the nation, manifest in the revived Klan after 1915, the notion that Negroes are subhuman or, rather, not human at all, seems to have grown more virulent. An extreme example, one that makes the fictional diatribe of Huck Finn's father seem mild, occurred in 1963, shortly after four Negro children were killed in the bombing of a church in Birmingham. At a Klan meeting just outside the city limits of St. Augustine, Florida, a Klan agitator from outside the state spoke as follows:

My friends, I want to share with you something of the history, the glorious history, of the Klan. The Klan was born out of bloodshed, out of a real need to protect the Southern white man from the carpetbaggers—the Jew Carpetbaggers. You know, of course, that the carpetbaggers was Jews, and they come down here and teamed up with the Niggers and tried to take away everything that the white man had. But they learned that the white man would not take all this lying down. He organized. He organized into Klans. He rose up to defend his honor and his interests. And, I'll tell you that to this day, the Jews, the Niggers and all the rest of the colored people are not afraid of anything else, but they are afraid of the Klan. . . .

Now, some of you say, "But Jesus was a Jew." That just goes to show you how these cotton pickin', half-witted preachers has fooled you. Jesus wasn't no Jew, he was a white man. I'm speaking for God, and you'd better hear what I say. . . .

Not long ago, a man from the F.B.I.—you know what that is, the Federal Bureau of Integration—came by to talk to me. . . . "Now, you don't really advocate violence, do you?" And I said, "The hell you say. The Niggers has declared all out war on the plan of God, and on God's family, the white man." They said to me, "Do you know who bombed the church in Birmingham?" And I said, "No, and if I did, I wouldn't tell you."

But I'll tell you people here tonight, if they can find those fellows, they ought to pin medals on them. Someone said, "Ain't it a shame that them little children was killed." Well, they don't know what they are talking about. In the first place, they ain't little. They're 14 or 15 years old—old enough to have venereal disease, and I'll be surprised if all of 'em didn't have one or more. In the second place, they weren't children. Children are little people, little human beings, and that means white people. There's little monkeys. There's little dogs and cats and apes and baboons and skunks and there's also little Niggers. They're just little Niggers. And in the third place, it wasn't no shame they was killed.

Why? Because when I go out to kill rattlesnakes, I don't make no difference between little rattlesnakes and big rattlesnakes, because I know it is the nature of all rattlesnakes to be my enemies and to poison me if they can. So I kill 'em all, and if there's four less Niggers tonight, then, I say, "Good for whoever planted the bomb! We're all better off."

Such vehemence and virulence may merely prove how low the modern Klan has sunk; yet it is a logical extension of a theory deliberately developed to justify slavery before the Civil War and of the restrictions put on the freedmen in the first postwar constitutions. Slavery wasn't the only pattern, it is evident, for implementing white supremacy. The more literate modern defenders of white supremacy—including some governors, state supreme court justices, and Congressmen—do not descend to excluding Negroes from the human family and do not join a small minority of extremists in advocating a return of slavery. But they do support discrimination as codified in state and local laws, and they do attack federal efforts to destroy such legislation. Whether knowingly or not, they use the timeworn arguments familiar during Reconstruction to justify limited freedom for Negroes and to support the Klan in its active resistance. To paraphrase Orwell in *Animal Farm*, to such people all Americans are free and equal, but some are freer than others, and more equal. The obvious clue, for the objective observer, is the reference to federal attacks on "the citizens of the South" as if all those citizens were white; Negroes are simply counted out.

When Congress rejected the first postwar constitutions and forced the creation of new documents more in line with the national intention concerning the freedmen, and when it then proceeded to

WHITE LEAGUE INTIMIDATION.

ONE of the means employed by the White League in the intimidation of Republican voters at New Orleans we give above. The following is an extract from the letter which accompanied it :

"I was on duty in New Orleans on the night of November 3, when it was reported to me by a captain of police that during the morning incendiary and threatening documents of various kinds had been distributed over the city by the White Leaguers. On my asking him to get me a sample copy, he handed me the inclosed."

When we reflect that employers in Louisiana formed leagues that pledged themselves to discharge every negro laborer who did not vote for the Democratic ticket, that others are said to have driven their workmen before them to the polls, that the secret menaces of the White Leaguers, armed and powerful, may well have terrified every Republican voter whether white or black into submission, it seems extraordinary that so many Republicans were so courageous as to vote at all.

The White League, a variant of the Klan, distributed handbills bearing this symbol. This was published by *Harper's Weekly* on November 28, 1874. The "2 x 6" were the dimensions of a coffin.

enact laws punishing Southern white resistance to the federal program, collision was inevitable. The question was just how free the freedmen were to be; and this question still exists to divide the nation. Southern whites fought back with every available weapon, and when legal measures failed, the Klan sprang to the defense with its tremendous advantage of being able to ignore legality.

Along with the employees of the federal government, a good many other Northerners moved south after the war, chiefly of two sorts: businessmen and teachers. The businessmen, despite the almost universal Southern denunciation of Northerners, were not molested by the Klan. All that the businessmen were doing was making money for their Southern and Northern partners. But the teachers, who seldom got more than $500 a year from their church and private sponsors in the North, were undermining the structure of Southern theory at a vulnerable point—the notion that Negroes were incapable of any but rudimentary education. The familiar explanation that the Klan was organized to oppose the hated federal program breaks down at just this point: the second den, formed at Athens, Alabama, and a great many other dens, responded not to Freedmen's Bureau activity but to the behavior of idealistic young Northern teachers who accepted Negroes as equals and thus flouted all that Southern whites held dear. The teachers, unlike the Bureau agents with their supporting troops, were particularly vulnerable.

Defenders of the Klan could always say that the trend toward greater violence drove the better elements out of the Klan and left it in the hands of the least responsible men, the riffraff, the reckless young men with no community standing to put in jeopardy. The suspicion survives, however, that the Klan offered an alternate method of resistance for the same leading citizens who had previously learned the futility of legal resistance. The secrecy that was essential to success makes it hard, if not impossible, to determine whether, or to what extent, the membership was essentially riffraff or Southern gentility; no doubt the proportion varied from place to place. But whatever its makeup, and however its membership shifted, the Klan has always had its ardent defenders, whether contemporary apologists, or authors of romantic Southern fiction, or staid historians of the period just after Senator Beveridge led the nation on its worst imperialistic binge. Beveridge and his notions have been generally repudiated, but the writings of this group of historians have done much to convince the nation of the rightness of the Southern theory and, as a logical corollary, the rightness of what the Klan was striving to uphold.

Of numerous scholars who could be named as responsible for giving authoritative support to the Southern interpretation of history, five deserve special notice. It may or may not be significant that all five were either born in the South or educated in Germany, or both. The oldest, John W. Burgess (1844–1931), was a native of Tennessee; his parents owned slaves. Educated in Germany, he was so impressed by the German method of scholarship that he used it as model for his pioneering department of political science, at Columbia; and it is not astonishing that he bracketed the Teutonic and Anglo-Saxon peoples as the greatest the world has ever known. James Ford Rhodes (1848–1927), second oldest of the group, was born in Cleveland, son of a prosperous coal magnate. After studying in New York, Chicago, Paris, and Berlin, young Rhodes spent some time in the South—in Georgia, North Carolina, and Tennessee—for his father's business. Later he joined his brother-in-law, Mark Hanna, in creating a coal and iron empire, and was able to retire at the age of thirty-seven to devote the rest of his life to the writing of history. Next in age was Woodrow Wilson (1856–1924), and after him William A. Dunning (1857–1922), New Jersey-born and German-educated, who influenced several generations of graduate students at Columbia. The youngest of the five was Walter L. Fleming (1874–1932), born in Alabama, a graduate of Auburn and Columbia, and a professor first at Louisiana State and later at Vanderbilt.

All five of these scholars assumed the inferiority of the Negro, though not all of them expressed the assumption with the vehemence with which Burgess condemned Congress for its monumental mistake in giving Negroes the vote. Rhodes, for example, in Volume VI of his monumental *History of the United States*, speaks of the freedmen as being "Three and a half million persons of one of the most inferior races of mankind," and later, after a lengthy quotation from Louis Agassiz about the native inferiority of Negroes, remarks in a footnote, "This I am informed is a pretty general view of ethnologists." Scholars honestly convinced of the inferiority of the Negro race would be less than honest if they interpreted Reconstruction history other than they did; but their very eminence confirmed the "classical" Southern interpretation, which can be accepted only if Negroes are proved to be inferior—an assumption overwhelmingly repudiated by science in our time.

It may seem reasonable that men born before slavery was abolished should accept the notion of Negro inferiority; but Fleming, youngest of the five, born nine years after the end of the Civil War, went as far as any of the others in approving the Klan. In *The Sequel to Appomattox,* published in 1921 as Volume 32 of Yale's *Chronicles of America Series,* he had this to say (pages 258–59):

> The work of the secret orders was successful. As bodies of vigilantes, the Klans and the Councils regulated the conduct of bad negroes, punished criminals who were not punished by the State, looked after the activities of Northern preachers and teachers, dispersed hostile gatherings of negroes, and ran out of the community the worst of the reconstructionist officials. They kept the negroes quiet and freed them to some extent from the influence of evil leaders. The burning of houses, gins, mills, and stores ceased; property became more secure; people slept safely at midnight; women and children walked abroad in security; the incendiary agents who had worked among the negroes left the country; agitators, political, educational, and religious, became more moderate; 'bad niggers' ceased to be bad; labor became less disorganized; the carpetbaggers and scalawags ceased to batten on the Southern communities. It was not so much a revolution as the defeat of a revolution. Society was replaced in the old historic grooves from which war and reconstruction had jarred it.[*]

As read by younger scholars of "revisionist" leanings, the adjective "white" must be inserted before "people" and "women and children" in this remarkably revealing passage. But the most astonishing sentence is the last, which makes no pretense of hiding the author's satisfaction that the Klan restored society "in the old historic grooves."

[*] From *The Chronicles of America.* Copyright Yale University Press. Sole distributors United States Publishers Association, Inc.

Of the five scholars named above, the most prestigious was Woodrow Wilson, by virtue of his election as the twenty-eighth President of the United States. His dissertation, written for his Johns Hopkins doctorate in 1886, was on *Congressional Government*. After brief periods of teaching at Bryn Mawr and Wesleyan, he moved to Princeton in 1890, as professor of jurisprudence and political economy. In 1901 he brought out his impressive, multi-volume *History of the American People;* it helped him become president of Princeton the next year.

As a Virginian and a staunch Democrat, Wilson was not enthusiastic about the Republican Party of the 1860's; he called it a child of slavery, pointed to its lack of a tradition of leadership in normal times, and measured its weakness by the ease with which the Radicals captured it during Reconstruction. The graft among the Radical members of Congress and Grant's cabinet officers was reason enough to discredit the party, its program, and its philosophy; by extension, it cast a cloud of general suspicion on all the Northerners in the South during the period. No conservative Virginian, with or without a doctorate and a Princeton professorship, could accept the Radical doctrine or view with other than repugnance anything the Radicals did.

Wilson followed the classical Southern line of reasoning when he spoke of the slaves. As Union armies approached, ever-increasing numbers of slaves deserted their masters in the bland faith that the federal government intended first to free them and then to take care of them. "They had the easy faith," Wilson wrote, "the simplicity, the idle hopes, the inexperience of children." He seems not to have considered the possibility that the slaves did not so much desert their masters as that the masters, because of worsening economic conditions and the advancing Union armies, deserted them along with their plantations. Nor did he mention the moot question of whether they really *were* slaves, since in theory at least the Emancipation Proclamation had freed them. Instead, he said that "idleness bred want, as always, and the vagrants turned thieves and importunate beggars. The tasks of ordinary labor stood untouched; the idlers grew insolent, dangerous; nights went anxiously by, for fear of riot and incendiary fire."

With the war's end, Wilson continued, Southern legislatures took "such measures as English legislators had been familiar with time out of mind. . . . The greater part of [their legislation] was paralleled by statutes of labor and vagrancy still to be found in the statute books of several of the northern states." He did not mention the crucial difference, that in the South these familiar laws applied only to Negroes. The Southern whites, however, were frustrated by the Freedmen's Bureau, whom Wilson described as men "fond of using arbitrary power very masterfully, and glad upon occasion to use it for the utter humiliation of the southern white men with whom they dealt." He did admit that some Bureau agents were men of probity, but he intimated that the Radical leaders in Washington encouraged their employees to be corrupt and vindictive, since such behavior would serve their own purpose of keeping the Southern whites impoverished and humiliated. The Bureau, backed as it was with federal power, suspended Southern laws at will, according to Wilson, and "practically made the law which should in fact govern the negro and determine his relation to his master."

So Wilson must sincerely have thought; and his way of thinking has persisted for the sixty years since he wrote. In 1939 a historian of the Ku Klux Klan, Stanley Horn, spoke of the friction in Mississippi and elsewhere as "being intensified by the pernicious activities of the Freedmen's Bureau and the Loyal Leagues [the latter being an alternate name applied, chiefly in the South, to the Union League]." It is high time to take a fresh look at the evidence and stop parroting such partisan assertions as if they were once and for all time proved true.

Woodrow Wilson at least admitted that race relations played an important part in Reconstruction. Some historians virtually ignored the Negro in their insistence that the Civil War and its aftermath were essentially a struggle between Northern industrialism and Southern agrarianism; it is a phase of the economic interpretation of history that we associate with the name of Charles A. Beard. But as one of the revisionists, Bernard Weisberger, has recently remarked, "Reconstruction confronts American writers of history with things which they prefer, like other Americans, to ignore—brute power and manipulation, class conflicts, race antagonism." To suppose out loud that the Civil War and Reconstruction had anything to do with the status of the Negro was, for many years and in many quarters, to risk being branded as naive. Yet to disregard the slavery issue and the question of how free the freedmen were to be is tantamount to giving silent approval to the almost universal nineteenth-century conviction of the Negro's innate inferiority. Historians who choose to ignore the struggle over the Negro and the morality of one group maintaining its historic advantage over another group may reasonably be charged with giving scholarly sanction to the perpetuation of racial discrimination.

Ignoring the question of slaves and freedmen, in other words, plays directly into the hands of today's white supremacists, who, whether or not they know anything about history, echo the primary premise of the Ku Klux Klan—that Anglo-Saxons are by nature better citizens and entitled to more privileges than men of inferior breeds lacking the genius for self-government. The "Black Codes" spelled out clearly the differential in privilege that Southern legislators, immediately after the Civil War, believed necessary and justified; and they also reveal how extremely difficult it was for any Southern Negro, free or slave, to be anything but inferior in fact as he was in Southern theory. The notion of White Supremacy was etched so deeply in Southern white thinking that it produced legislation clearly in violation of federal laws. Then, when the military governors suspended this racial legislation as obviously unconstitutional, Southern whites in large numbers accused the governors, and the federal government, of insulting Southern honor and of deliberately trying to humiliate the South.

The suspension of the new state constitutions could be effective only so long as the South was under military government. The Ku Klux Klan, operating outside the law, could disregard the suspension and systematically enforce the spirit of the constitutions. As soon as military government was removed, it was an easy matter for Southern whites to reapply the restrictive practices, if not at once in specific state legislation—most Jim Crow laws date from as late as the 1890's—at least in ordinary practice. Reconstruction may have been, as some historians have insisted, a continuation of the titanic struggle between industry and agriculture; but the grassroots struggle, as most whites and Negroes observed it or took part in it, was closely concerned with the question of just how free the freedman was going to be.

The Black Codes or, more precisely, the pattern of discrimination they symbolized, were at the heart of the struggle. On one side were the military officers, the Freedmen's Bureau, the Union League, the missionary and benevolent societies whose quiet work with the freedmen has been given little historical recognition, and all the other contemporary groups and individuals actively concerned with improving the lot of the newly freed Negroes. On the other side, no less actively working to maintain the traditional racial differential, was the Ku Klux Klan. The friends of the Negro had the advantage of federal power and public opinion outside the South, but the Klan had greater advantages—operations in total secrecy, the ability to ignore the forms of legalism, and the support of the great

Harper's Weekly optimistically saw Grant's election in 1868 as a death blow to the Ku Klux Klan. The cartoon was published on November 14, 1868.

majority of the Southern whites. Just as the defeat of the Confederacy might have been predicted at the outset of the Civil War by a dispassionate weighing of the war-making potential on the two sides, it might have been predicted in 1865 that the peace would be won by the Klan—or by the South of tradition with the Klan as its active instrument. The losers were the Southern Negroes, the Northern representatives who were forced to retire from the field, and the national progress toward ideal democracy.

The twentieth-century Klan greatly broadened the range of hostility, including with Negroes such other enemies of true religion and true patriotism as Jews, Catholics, and recent immigrants. It revived the old Klan's insistence that *real* Americans were white, Protestant, and of native origin. It differed in being national instead of regional—although it must be admitted that even the old Klan had a certain amount of Northern support. All sections of the country, throughout our history, have had "dirty hands" concerning the Negro in America; the Ku Klux Klan has not been the only villain in the dark drama of race relations.

The Klan in its way and the Northern agents in their quite different way were equally intent during Reconstruction on solving what has long been called "the Negro problem." It has certainly been a problem for the Negroes, but it might better be relabeled "the white problem," since it was created by whites and has been maintained by whites. The Negroes did not ask to be brought from Africa; it was white men who brought them by the shipload, never asking their consent, and it was white men who sold them to the highest bidder like any other imported commodity. Once the Negroes were here, white men defined their status; it was white men, not Negroes, who decided that anybody with at least one Negro great-grandparent was legally a Negro and subject to the same restrictions as an African of unmixed blood. The mixtures, meanwhile, resulted chiefly from white aggressiveness, unless it can be assumed that Negro women in large numbers forced their favors upon their white masters. White men, to an extent their great-grandsons prefer not to believe, saw nothing immoral in having slave concubines or, subsequently, in disowning their mulatto offspring—especially when the law, made by white men, forbade the recognition of such children.

Some Southern spokesmen even argued that this concubinage was good, since it kept prostitution at a minimum in the South. The attribution of racial mixtures to Union soldiers during the Civil War is, incidentally, a prime example of guilt transference.

Under slavery, white men saw no advantage in educating slaves beyond the most rudimentary levels; and the attitude carried over into the widespread Klan opposition to the schools set up by the Freedmen's Bureau and by Northern philanthropy during Reconstruction. Southern whites were positive that Negroes were incapable of education; but even if they were educable, advanced schooling would only make them dissatisfied with their lowly assignment of agricultural labor and harder to keep in their place, a place determined by the whites. A free Negro was an anomaly in an economic system that was based on slave labor, and the rules by which the whites hedged in free Negroes gave them hardly greater freedom than the slaves enjoyed. After the war and emancipation, the Southern whites felt they had to extend the same restrictions to all Negroes, and even argued that these restrictions were for the Negroes' own good. Old habits die hard. One of the principal sources of resentment toward the Northern "invaders" was their contention that Negroes were people like anybody else, to be treated like other people. White supremacists knew better.

White supremacists still know what they want and what they don't want. They have changed their tactics but not their firm belief that whites are innately superior to Negroes and therefore deserving of greater rights and privileges. At the centennial of the Klan, the principle it fought to maintain was again being challenged. The modern Klan, a thing of shreds and patches, seems unlikely to serve, like the old, as the chief instrument of regional resistance, chiefly because few Southerners would endorse the extremes of violence and terrorism that gave the old Klan its victory. But it is the old Klan, not the new, that inspires continued resistance and the hope, however dim, of a second victory, routing the federal government so completely that for another seventy-odd years it will be unable to regroup its forces.

Chapter Three

THE
KLAN
IMPEACHES
A
GOVERNOR

When we consider the acrimony engendered by many gubernatorial contests and the many rascals and incompetents who have been elected, it is astonishing how few governors have ever been removed from office by impeachment. William Woods Holden of North Carolina was the first, in 1871. He was neither incompetent nor, except in the eyes of his enemies, a rascal. His removal, at a time of inflamed partisan tension, may best be ascribed to Klan determination to redeem the state for white supremacy—a determination so desperate that whatever the charges against him, the verdict would have been "guilty." At the trial before the state senate, his lawyers were barred from introducing testimony about the Klan violence that had prompted his actions. His conviction is a conspicuous example of the Klan's success in evading its own just punishment and making its enemy pay. Not until 1935 was Holden's reasonable certainty of the Klan's guilt confirmed as fact.

Born in 1818 in Orange County, Holden was a printer's devil at ten and, by twenty-five, the owner-editor of the *North Carolina*

Standard, published in Raleigh, the state capital. Previously a Unionist Whig, he was denounced as a turncoat when he took over the *Standard.* It was only the first of several major shifts in position that encouraged the enduring impression that he put expediency above fixed principle. He made the *Standard* the chief Democratic organ in the state and, for a quarter century, one of the most powerful newspapers that North Carolina has ever had. In 1850, after sixteen years of Whig control, the Democrats finally won the governorship; for the part he played, Holden was rewarded with the state printing contract. In his editorials he preached the most advanced secessionist doctrines. But when he lost his bid for governor in 1858, his ardor for the old-line Democrats began to cool. Elected as a delegate to the secession convention, he voted with the majority to secede, but within three years he was prominent in the peace movement and openly opposed both Jefferson Davis and Governor Zebulon Vance.

This wartime conduct was favorably regarded in Washington. At the war's end, President Johnson removed Vance and named Holden provisional governor, the first to be appointed in the South. It was a brief assignment, limited to calling a convention of loyal men to draft a new state constitution. But the document that resulted was so hostile to the spirit of Negro freedom and equality that during 1866 and 1867 Holden was often in Washington trying to have it overthrown, as it finally was in 1868. Whenever he was at home, he was busy as president of the state's Union League, an office that proved an excellent steppingstone to the governorship, which he won on the Republican ticket in 1868. His detractors insisted that he won only with the help of the 80,000 Union Leaguers and the less numerous members of other secret Republican societies, such as the Red Strings and the Heroes of America.

No less an authority than Bedford Forrest attributed the formation of the Ku Klux Klan to the "insolence" of the Union League. Whether or not the League deserves so much credit, it was certainly a principal target of the Klan. It had been organized during the war by two prominent Northerners, Henry W. Bellows, pastor of New York's First Unitarian Church, and Stephen Colwell, a wealthy

Philadelphia ironmaster and railroad director, who was also chairman of the Joint Commission of Freedmen's Aid Societies. Originally, the League's purpose was to rally popular support for the government's war effort, but when peace came its energies were redirected to stimulating interest in Republican principles. It was logical for the League to expand its operations southward, where a vast new electorate had been created and stood in need of instruction in the rights and duties of citizenship. Each Southern state was organized as a Council, with a hierarchy of local and regional divisions and officers. If one sought to prove the validity of General Forrest's assertion, supporting evidence would include the similarity of the rituals used by both League and Klan, and the fact that both were actively committed to influencing elections. Their most obvious difference was that the League never tried to conceal its existence. Negroes joined in large numbers, attracted by the ritualism and flattered at being invited to join a white man's club.

The League and the Klan appealed to quite different sets of emotions and loyalties. The Klan stirred up an atavistic lawlessness—defiance of external authority that we associate with the clans of Scotland in their long resistance to English power. Racial pride and a fierce devotion to regional tradition were more obvious causative factors in the Klan's growth and popularity.

Negroes shared none of these, but their own compulsions were just as strong. Club life, like the bearing of arms, had always been denied them as slaves; with emancipation, their essential gregariousness led to the formation of a great number of secret societies. They would be unlikely to forget, moreover, that Southern whites had fought for the right to keep them in slavery, while Northern whites had set them free; and the resulting deep sense of gratitude to the Union found a good outlet in the League and its ceremonies. In the meeting hall a central altar displayed a Bible and copies of the Declaration of Independence and the United States Constitution. The formal opening prayer asked divine protection for all "loyal people" against "foreign foes and domestic traitors." Candidates for admission, each with one hand on the open Bible, repeated the oath of membership, which bound them to support the Declaration and the Constitution, to help maintain freedom, to foster education, to practise friendship and charity, to vote for men sympathetic to these purposes and to the League, and, of course, never to divulge the League secrets. The closing ceremony included exchange of the secret signs of the order, chiefly the four L's: Liberty, Lincoln, Loyal, and League (the last two providing the name often used for the organization, Loyal League).

Southern believers in white supremacy were alarmed, in 1867, when the League reversed its former rule against bearing arms and began to form military companies, drilling frequently, parading, and posting guards at meetings—a practical necessity if the meetings were to be safe from surprise Klan attacks. The right to bear arms, it should be remembered, was one of the privileges of the superior race, and its extension to the inferior race was viewed as an insidious effort to level mankind and even to raise the Negroes to a dominant position. People given to this kind of thinking got into the habit of attributing every new crime to the League; actually, there was no significant increase in crime, except that committed by the Klan itself, during the Reconstruction period. But the Klan, and people who supported it and gained by its activities, were capable of extreme illogic. Most Klan victims were not criminals, despite the Klan's pious claim that it existed to punish crime. The Klan also asserted that it was a guardian of morality, but very few of its actions were related to immoral deeds. As for any need of an extra-legal organization to punish either crime or immorality, only in counties where the Klan disrupted orderly government did the courts have any difficulty in punishing offenders. And the special courts established by the Freedmen's Bureau were not lenient toward accused Negroes, although their alleged leniency was used as one of the justifications for the Klan's resort to violence.

Whether or not the carrying of guns in Union League drills and parades actually inflated Negro ego to the point of insolence, the guns were very seldom fired at whites; the certainty of swift and terrible punishment was a strong deterrent. But, in the view of conservative whites, burning a barn was as terrible a crime as rape or murder and as deserving of the ultimate punishment—if it was a Negro who did the burning. Governor Holden, however, had a bad habit of pardoning Negroes who he felt had been unfairly tried and convicted. One way to obviate the pardons was to eliminate the offenders. Two Negroes accused of burning three barns in Orange County, on a single night in 1869, were hanged by the Klan before they could be arrested. Two lives for three barns seemed a reasonable equation.

The Klan's capacity for deceit was virtually limitless. Editors and politicians who were subsequently proved to have been Klansmen themselves derided the very notion that a Klan existed. On February 24, 1870, the Greensboro (N.C.) *Patriot* declared that "this Ku Klux cry is all a humbug." Two nights later, in neighboring Alamance County, the Klan hanged a Negro leader. What the general public probably could not realize was how elaborate the pattern of deception was and how many facets it had: magnifying Negro crime while denying that a Klan existed, shifting the blame for Klan violence upon its victims, or upon the Republicans for encouraging Negroes to violence, denouncing equality as an "infidel and unfounded assumption in the Declaration of Independence," and declaring not human rights but "the possession and protection of property" to be "the chief concomitant of civilization." Then, when it was no longer possible to deny the Klan's existence, editors stoutly argued that it should continue to operate as long as the Union League was committing its terrible crimes, and glorified it as an agency for upholding the law, punishing miscreants, discouraging crime, and protecting property, white women, and racial purity.

If this magnificent pattern of deceit had been only a contemporary device for a specific political purpose, it might have taken its place among other curiosities of history. But its very success at the time and its usefulness later in keeping North Carolina safe for white supremacy gave it the patina of apparent truth. As recently as 1939, one historian of the Klan wrote that Governor Holden "subjected the state to three years of misrule and oppression until he was impeached in 1871." This is of course what the Klansmen wanted voters to believe in the 1870's; it is a remarkable tribute to the effectiveness of their propaganda that some people still believe it.

It is not too difficult, however, to see why recent writers have accepted the conservative interpretation. In addition to the general histories of the South published around the turn of this century, the most complete and detailed study of the state during Reconstruction gives scholarly authority to that interpretation. Not a Southern publisher, moreover, but Columbia University brought out, in 1914, as Volume LVIII in its "Studies in History, Economics and Public Law," J. G. de Roulhac Hamilton's *Reconstruction in North Carolina*. Hamilton was Alumni Professor of History at the University of North Carolina. In Chapter Twelve, "The Ku Klux Movement," he declared that the South "became a veritable hell through misrule which approximated anarchy. Called into existence by this state of affairs, the Ku Klux lifted the South from its slough of despond by the application of illegal force which overthrew Reconstruction and ultimately restored political power to the white race. In the process, it furnished protection to the oppressed, but . . . in the end [it] fell into the control of reckless spirits who used it for private vengeance rather than public punishment." By that time, however, the Klan's purpose had been largely accomplished; women could go outdoors "without the accompaniment of a deadly terror," property was fairly safe again, "and the supremacy of the white race and of Anglo-Saxon institutions was secure."

Starting with such a premise, it is hardly to be expected that Hamilton would describe Governor Holden as a great American. The premise suggests a deadly struggle for mastery between defenders and opponents of white supremacy, with the defenders the heroes fighting for right, and the opponents the villains diabolically seeking to destroy what was right. The premise also equates Negro equality with Negro domination, as if any reduction of the time-honored white advantage over the Negro meant subjection for the whites. The momentary majority of Negroes in certain state legislatures has become the prime horrifying object lesson for white supremacists, who seem to assume that if Negroes should somehow gain control they would impose on the whites the same restrictions that the whites have imposed on the Negroes. But not even in the darkest hours of Reconstruction, when white supremacy was most seriously threatened, did Negroes ever hold the upper hand in the South. No Negro was ever elected governor of a state, and Negro leaders were never independent of their white colleagues. It was never a question of white versus Negro control, but rather a question of which group of whites would be masters. In North Carolina, moreover, it was a struggle between native groups of whites, for the state was exceptional in having few Northerners in the cast of its Reconstruction drama.

As soon as Holden was elected, he resigned the League presidency, explaining that a governor should not continue to hold so partisan an office. He also announced that he was resigning his active editorship of the *Standard*. A good many members of the League either did not learn of these actions or preferred not to believe them, for they continued to regard Holden as their president and the *Standard* as his mouthpiece and theirs too. Some Democrats also doubted the good faith of his resignations.

One of Holden's first official actions as governor was to issue, on October 12, 1868, a proclamation condemning subversion of civil authority and warning that intimidation of Negroes would not be tolerated. The intimidation, however, continued, chiefly in the form of whippings. In 1869 the legislature, with its Republican majority, made it a felony to go about masked and in disguise. The law had no more effect on the Klan than the proclamation. In January 1870, however, a bill with real teeth in it was passed, authorizing the governor to declare a state of insurrection in any county where the civil authorities proved unable to protect its citizens. The Klan supposed it was doing just that; but the citizens it was intent on protecting were a different set from those that Holden and the legislators had in mind. The bill also authorized the use of military force to reduce the insurrectionary conditions. Holden promptly established a state militia; but his enemies, who never missed an opportunity to discredit him, insisted that its initials N.C.S.M. stood not for the "North Carolina State Militia" but for the "Negro, Carpetbag, Scalawag Militia."

This 1870 legislation was known as the Shoffner Act, for the man who introduced it: T. M. Shoffner of Alamance County, in the north-central part of the state about midway between Durham and Greensboro. As might have been expected, Shoffner's Klan neighbors—including the sheriff and all his deputies—vowed to kill him. As one man reported: "They are going to suppress Shoffner's writ of *habeas corpus* tonight." The crowning touch of the plan they adopted was to ship Shoffner's body to the governor. But the scheme went awry because one of the Klansmen put friendship ahead of his solemn Klan oath and hid the intended victim until he could get him out of the state. Shoffner moved to Indiana.

Foiled in its attempt to kill Shoffner, the Klan sought and found another victim—Wyatt Outlaw, Negro head of the Union League in Alamance County. On the night of February 26, 1870, they forced their way into his house, took him to the courthouse square in Graham, and hanged him from a tree. On his breast, when his body was found the next morning, was this sign: "Bewar, ye guilty, both white and black." The Klan spread the story, which the people in Alamance, at least, did not believe, that Outlaw had once fired into a Klan column riding through Graham. Why such an act justified killing him would be comprehensible only to those with a Klan mentality. His real crime, quite obviously, was swinging Alamance into the Republican column in the 1868 election by getting out the Negro vote. A violent sequel to the hanging was the elimination of a half-wit named Puryear, who had happened to witness the midnight scene and talked about it next day. He disappeared suddenly and some weeks later was found in a mill pond with a rock tied to his neck.

Caswell County, just north of Alamance and bordering Virginia near Danville, was the only other North Carolina county where Republican strength was growing. These two counties, as a direct consequence, were the setting for the worst Klan violence in the state. In Caswell, between April first and the middle of May, 1870, the Klan whipped or scourged twenty-one men, both white and Negro, and killed two others. One of those killed was a Negro, Robin Jacobs. The other was white, John Walter Stephens, Caswell's state senator and Republican leader. At the time of his murder, he was serving as one of Holden's detectives, trying to collect evidence of Klan activity.

Professor Hamilton lent his authority to the legend, which has no basis in fact, that Stephens handed out matches to Union Leaguers with the remark that one small match could burn an entire barn. In actuality, Stephens was unusually effective in restraining

This red robe was worn by a Klansman in North Carolina in 1870. The horned hood was one of the early variations in Klan regalia. *Courtesy of the Buffalo and Erie County Historical Society*

the Negroes from violence. He had so much faith in them and in his ability to control them that he had actually pledged his life for their good behavior. After a series of warnings, however, he took out extra life insurance and armed himself with three pistols.

The insurance paid off, but not the pistols. Stephens was disarmed and killed in the Caswell County courthouse. He did not share Shoffner's luck of having a Klan friend to whisk him out of danger.

Several prominent citizens were subsequently arrested, but none of them was indicted; no witnesses stepped forward to describe what they had seen or heard. Elsewhere in the state Holden, with fair success, sent trusted lieutenants, men of high character, into each county to talk quietly with local leaders and thus build up public opinion against violence. Only in Alamance and Caswell Counties did this plan totally fail; there, grand juries did not indict, and outrages mounted. By June 1870, when the toll for the state reached thirteen murders and twenty-two known whippings, Holden decided to make use of the Shoffner Act: He declared these two counties in a state of insurrection and ordered Colonel George W. Kirk to raise a regiment and to make arrests as needed.

Kirk, who was living in Washington at the time, had been one of the men President Johnson had considered for provisional governor in 1865 before he chose Holden. A native of Tennessee, Kirk had commanded a Union regiment in the war and had earned the hatred of many North Carolinians. Holden ran off five hundred handbills, calling upon Kirk's old regiment—the Third North Carolina State Volunteers—"to aid in enforcing the laws, and in putting down disloyal midnight assassins. . . . The horrible murders and other atrocities committed by rebel K.K.K. and 'southern chivalry,' on grayhaired men and helpless women, call in thunder tones on all loyal men to rally in defence of their state." Kirk used the handbills, apparently, only to announce his intentions to North Carolinians; he recruited most of his force in eastern Tennessee. Some Republicans joined the horrified Democrats in protesting Kirk's appointment, but other Republicans applauded it. Dr. J. J. Mott, a top official of the Western North Carolina Railroad, told Holden that Kirk was the best man he could have named. "And by the Eternal God," Mott wrote, "I say deluge the state in blood from one end to the other rather than our people should suffer again the treatment of the last six months." The Democratic press, in expected contrast, vilified Kirk as a "bushwhacker" and Holden as a scoundrel. It was a time of strong language and strong feelings; and Holden believed it was a time for strong actions by a strong man.

Kirk led his men to Company Shops (now Burlington), which served thereafter as their base. On July 15, 1870, he arrested three prominent men at Graham and refused to release them on bail, despite writs of habeas corpus issued by the state's chief justice, Richmond M. Pearson. The Shoffner Act, admittedly, did not authorize a refusal to honor writs of habeas corpus. But Holden, in a letter to Pearson, defended the refusal on the ground that as governor it was both his right and his duty to use whatever means he thought necessary to suppress civil strife. "I am satisfied," he wrote, "that the public interests require that these military prisoners shall not be delivered up to the civil power." On July 23, after a series of legal thrusts and parries, Pearson delivered a lengthy opinion that closed with these words: "I have discharged my duty; the power of the judiciary is exhausted and the responsibility must rest on the Executive."

In the meantime Kirk had moved on to Yanceyville, county seat of Caswell County, where he arrested several men for the murder of Stephens. This was on July 18, two weeks before the state election. Holden's enemies were indignant; the arrests, they charged, were politically inspired, to discredit the Democrats and to keep the Republicans in power, and were part of a grand strategy that embraced the declaration of a state of insurrection, the forming of a punitive regiment, and the appointment of Colonel Kirk to command it. It did not occur to them to say that the Klan had deliberately staged its violence just then because it *was* so near the election, fully expecting that Holden, never a man to refrain from a fight, would react exactly as he did. He thus helped the Democrats more than his own Republicans by a simple boomerang effect. The election, on August 4, was an overwhelming victory for the aroused Democrats, who elected five of the state's seven members of Congress and won heavy majorities in both houses of the state legislature.

On August 5, while he was still confident of Republican victory, Holden blundered into arresting his archenemy, Josiah Turner, editor of the Raleigh *Sentinel*. Turner, an ardent spokesman for the conservative Democrats, would have been opposed to Holden in any case, but he bore a personal grudge. Holden, as provisional governor, in 1865 had recommended against Turner's pardon. Holden had judged Turner's journalistic opposition to the Union, during the Civil War, treasonable beyond the possibility of pardon when the war was over. Turner's extreme violence of language would have been hard for even the mildest of governors to overlook; and Holden was not noted for mildness. Consider, for example, Turner's brief editorial in the *Sentinel* for August 2:

LIES LIKE A THIEF

The governor has been lying on us for twelve months; his profligate son and organ lies on us to-day by calling us a Ku Klux. If we are, why don't the pumkin-faced rascal arrest us? We defy and dare him to arrest.

And the next day Turner's editorial column began with a letter:

TO GOVERNOR HOLDEN

Gov. Holden:—You say you will handle me in due time. You white-livered recreant, do it now. You dared me to resist you; I dare you to arrest me. . . . Your ignorant jacobins are incited . . . by your lying charges against me that I am King of the Ku Klux. You villain, come and arrest a man. . . .

Yours with contempt and defiance—*habeas corpus* or no *habeas corpus.*

This was more than Holden cared to take; despite advice not to, he gave the order to Kirk, who arrested Turner and confined him in the very room where Stephens had been killed. Democratic indignation rose several more notches.

The next day Holden was startled to learn that a federal judge named Brooks, acting with dubious authority, had issued a writ for the release of all the prisoners held by Kirk. An urgent appeal to Washington brought the disconcerting reply that President Grant, hitherto a strong supporter of Holden's policies, refused to intervene, on the advice of Secretary of War Belknap. The *Standard* editorially mourned the defeat of the Republican Party in North Carolina and blamed it on "Not the Democrats, the Whigs, the Conservatives, but the CONSTITUTIONAL UNION GUARDS, the WHITE BROTHERHOOD, and the INVISIBLE EMPIRE. Their weapons have not been arguments or eloquence; but the SCOURGE, the KNIFE, and the ROPE." (The Union Guards and the White Brotherhood were Klan-like groups so closely associated with the Invisible Empire that all three groups acknowledged the leadership of a single man in Chapel Hill; the different names were really a dodge to permit Klansmen to swear, without committing perjury, that they did not belong to the Ku Klux Klan. All authorities, whether approving or opposed to the Klan, have treated the three groups collectively as the Klan in North Carolina.)

On November 10, Holden declared the insurrection in Caswell and Alamance Counties at an end; there was little else he could do, for all the prisoners had been freed as a result of legal maneuvers that he was powerless to halt. Eleven days later, the hostile new legislature convened, and among its first actions the House of Representatives voted to impeach Holden on eight counts. The trial, by the state senate, lasted from February 2 until March 23, 1871; Holden was found guilty on six of the counts and was removed from office. He had able lawyers, who based his defense on the legality of proclaiming insurrection in counties where justice was being thwarted by violence and conspiracy; but the partisan nature of the trial is shown by the senate's refusal to admit as evidence the Klan violence that was the very heart of the defense. The prosecution argued that Holden had not proved the existence of a conspiracy; and of course it belabored the point, which could not be denied, that he had refused to honor the writs of habeas corpus. He was also held responsible for the inhuman treatment which Kirk's prisoners had reported, such as suspension by the neck to extort confessions. (People who doubted that the Klan existed could hardly be expected to know that these atrocities were pure Klan invention.) Holden was too much of a fighter to avoid removal by resigning, as a later North Carolina governor did when he in his turn was impeached—for the Holden trial made impeachment popular in the next few years. It must have been apparent to Holden that conviction was a foregone conclusion from the moment that the legislature refused to seat several duly elected Republican members, thereby gaining the two-thirds Democratic majority needed to convict. The verdict included disqualification henceforth from any state office; but Holden served as Raleigh postmaster, appointed by Grant, from 1873 to 1881.

Colonel Kirk and his second in command, a New Jerseyite named Bergen, were both jailed. Kirk, with the help of some money from Holden, managed to get out of the state; he subsequently joined the police force guarding government buildings in Washington. Bergen stayed longer in jail, accused of the worst mistreatment of his Klan prisoners. Later he remarked, with justifiable bitterness, that his reward for his services to Holden was six weeks' pay and ninety-four days in jail.

It is probable that the state would have gone Democratic in 1870 even without Holden's provocative behavior. Only 4,000 more Democratic votes were cast than in the previous election, but about 12,000 fewer Republicans voted. The Klan had done an excellent job of intimidating the Negroes. Whether the Democratic legislature would have impeached Holden under any circumstances is somewhat less certain; a weak governor would have posed no insuperable problems to a legislature heavily dominated by the opposing party. But Holden's very strength roused his opponents to mount a particularly strong campaign, and one that was skillfully designed to turn all the blame against him. He was virtually certain that the Klan was guilty of violence in opposing him, specifically in the murder of Stephens, but he wasn't given a chance to prove it. The vote to convict was along party lines. In effect, he paid the highest political penalty for not being able to prove guilty men guilty.

Democrats had been incensed by Kirk's arrest of prominent citizens at Holden's orders: "Good and honest conservative citizens of our state," as one editor put it, could not have done so horrible a thing. It was the crassest sort of insult to suggest that prominent citizens were Klansmen, if it were conceivable at all that the Klan was involved. If leading citizens ever *had* belonged to the Klan, moreover, it was generally believed, then and later, that they had withdrawn long before 1870 in protest against the mounting violence. But on December 12, 1872, a Negro servant named Patsie Barton in a sworn statement repeated a detailed account of the Stephens murder as he had overheard Frank Wiley, a former Caswell County sheriff, tell it to a friend. In addition to Wiley, the names included a prominent landowner, another planter who was a graduate of the University of North Carolina, a current Democratic candidate for office, a respected coachmaker, a former Confederate captain, and a member of a socially prominent family.

Barton's statement was mere hearsay, however, and without corroboration would have carried little weight in court. Besides, Negroes were not supposed to know the difference between fact and invention. But when a certain Captain John G. Lea died in 1935, an affidavit he had written in 1919 was opened; it had been left sealed in the files of the North Carolina Historical Commission. Its nine typed pages make it too long to reproduce here in full, but in condensed form it offers both a factual record by a principal participant and an insight into the mental workings of one Klan leader.

A cover page, bearing the signatures of both Lea and a witness to his signing, informs us that he wrote this "true story" at the request of the Historical Commission. Just after General Lee's surrender at Appomattox, in April 1865, the narrative opens, "a bummer named Albion Tourgee, of New York, from Sherman's army, came to Caswell County and organized a Union League." Tourgee named W. A. Stephens (*Stevens,* as spelled in the deposition) and Jim Jones justices of the peace. Both actively stirred up the Negroes against the whites. Jones freed a Negro accused of stealing a hog owned by one Captain Mitchell, an act of such flagrant partisanship that Lea began organizing a Ku Klux Klan. Elected organizer for the county, he established dens in every township. A first order of business was whipping Jim Jones and running him out of the county.

Stephens was charged with much worse activities: burning a hotel in Yanceyville, a row of brick stores, and two barns full of curing tobacco. Actually, two Negroes were accused, but both said that Stephens had ordered them to set the fires. The Klan thereupon gave

Stephens "a fair trial before a jury of twelve men," found him guilty, and sentenced him to death. He was tried, of course, *in absentia.*

The Klan soon had an opportunity to execute the sentence, when the county's Democrats met in the courthouse at Yanceyville to prepare a slate of candidates for the coming election. "I had ordered all the Ku Klux Klan in the county," Lea recalled, "to meet at Yanceyville that day, with their uniforms under their saddles." Ex-sheriff Wiley "beckoned to Stevens and carried him down stairs, and Captain Mitchell, James Denny and Joe Fowler went into the room and Wiley came out. Mitchell proceeded to disarm him (he had three pistols on his body)," but he balked at killing him. Wiley hurried to Lea and demanded action: " 'You must do something; I am exposed unless you do.' Immediately I rushed into the room, with eight or ten men . . . he asked me not to let them kill [him]. Captain Mitchell rushed at him with a rope, drew it around his neck, put his feet against his chest and by that time about a half dozen men rushed up. . . . Stevens was then stabbed in the breast and also in the neck by Tom Oliver, the knife was thrown at his feet and the rope left around his neck. We all came out, closed the door and locked it on the outside and took the key and threw it into County Line Creek. I may add that it was currently believed that Stevens murdered his mother while living with him."

The larger part of Lea's statement concerns the subsequent "Kirk-Holden war," as historians have dubbed it, and the Klan's success in averting suspicion and in driving the hated Union League leaders out of the state. When Lea, Captain Mitchell, and ex-sheriff Wiley were tried before the state supreme court, the prosecuting lawyers, Lea boasted, "never did prove that there was a Ku Klux Klan in Caswell County."

Nor could Governor Holden prove, in his impeachment trial, what the Klan leader in Caswell County admitted, without the slightest trace of remorse, half a century later.

One sequel must be added, since it shows the value of electing a legislature with a majority on the right side. In December 1872, a federal grand jury indicted sixty-three Klan members in Alamance County for various felonies, and eighteen for murder, including the murder of the Negro Union League leader with the striking name of Wyatt Outlaw. As in the Stephens affair in Caswell County, many of the men indicted were from the best families. Fearing the possible results and unable to quash the indictments, the county Democrats got the legislature to repeal the law, retroactively, under which the indictments were drawn. On second thought, it seemed a good idea to make similar grand jury action impossible in the future; and the legislature obligingly passed a new law granting amnesty and pardon for crimes committed on behalf of any secret organization. Members of Negro secret organizations, however, were specifically excluded.

Chapter Four

SOUTH CAROLINA: THE LAWLESS TEMPER

As in other Southern states, the first postwar constitutional convention in South Carolina produced a document so contrary to the overwhelming public sentiment in the North that Congress rejected it and insisted on a second convention, one that would be more sympathetic toward the notion of making citizens of the newly freed slaves. While this second convention was meeting, the conservative whites of the state held a convention of their own and issued a proudly defiant declaration: "The fact is patent to all," they asserted, "that the Negro is totally unfitted to exercise the highest function of a citizen. . . . We protest against this subversion of the social order, whereby an ignorant and depraved race is placed in power over the virtuous, the educated, and the refined." The whites of South Carolina, the declaration continued, would "never acquiesce in Negro Equality or supremacy."

So strong a statement carried the threat of active resistance to the Radical plan for Reconstruction, as reflected in the new constitution. The Ku Klux Klan did not materialize as the instrument of this resistance, however, until 1867, when R. J. Brunson was sent to organize dens in the state. A member of the original den at Pulaski and thereby automatically a man of prestige, Brunson had very good success. He stayed about two months, using Rock Hill, near the North Carolina line, as his base of operations. By the time he left, dens were established in all the western part of South Carolina, and Rock Hill was an acknowledged hotbed of Klan activity. In the lower sections of the state, particularly in the coastal regions where Negroes outnumbered whites but were held under close discipline, the Klan never made much headway. It was the "up-counties" of the piedmont, where white men viewed Negroes as potential competitors in the labor market, that were the most fertile soil for the Klan.

Klan activity in South Carolina had two peaks. The first was late in 1868, in predictable reaction to a revised state constitution adopted that year, one with stronger provisions for ensuring Negro voting. York, Laurens, Anderson, Edgefield, and Abbeville Counties all had numerous Klan incidents, mostly in the form of warnings to Negroes not to vote. The second and much more violent peak followed the election in the fall of 1870, when the success of Republican candidates was proof that Negroes in large numbers had not been sufficiently frightened away from the polls. York and Laurens again earned notoriety, along with Union and Spartanburg Counties. President A. W. Cummings, of Spartanburg Female College, kept a running score of incidents in Spartanburg County alone: from election day in October 1870 until July 15, 1871, his tally of individuals positively known to have been victims of Klan aggression of all sorts came to 227. The strongest action was directed against members of the state militia: four of them, all Negroes, were killed. Cummings estimated that of 2,300 white men eligible to vote in the county, 1,800 belonged to the Klan.

The most widely publicized Klan action in South Carolina occurred at Union Courthouse in December 1870. An itinerant whiskey salesman named Matthew Stevens, a one-armed Confederate veteran, had sold some drinks to a group of Negro militiamen who had stopped him on the highway. Emboldened by the alcohol, they had kept insisting on more until Stevens, in alarm, tried to get away. A scuffle ensued, and he was killed. Soon afterward, several militiamen were arrested and lodged in the Union County jail. A circuit judge named Thomas, from a different judicial district and probably a Radical, sent a writ of habeas corpus to the sheriff, ordering him to remove the prisoners to Columbia the next day, to thwart possible mob violence. The sheriff ignored the order. Two nights later men in the familiar Klan disguise took two of the Negroes from the jail and hanged them. Within less than a week an even larger group of Klansmen, estimated at four or five hundred, took seven more from the jail and hanged them too.

The number of victims would alone make this a significant Klan exhibit, but a sign posted on the courthouse bulletin board gives it an even greater significance. Since the Klan was committed to acting in total secrecy, many and perhaps most acts of violence can be attributed to it only by reasonable conjecture, but on this occasion it clearly identified itself. The sign read:

TO THE PUBLIC
K K K
TAKEN BY HABEAS CORPUS

Once again we have been forced by force to use *Force.* Justice was lame, and she had to lean on us. Information being received that a "doubting Thomas" . . . had ordered guilty prisoners from Union to the City of Columbia, . . . this thing was created; otherwise it would never have been. We yield to the inevitable and inexorable, and account this the *best.* "Let not thy right hand know what thy left hand doeth" is our motto. We want peace, but this cannot be until Justice returns. We want and will have Justice. . . .

It is quite possible that the Union sheriff could not have removed his prisoners if he had tried, for it was local opinion that if they were taken to Columbia they would be freed on "straw bail." By a variety of irony fairly common during Reconstruction, two other militiamen were subsequently arrested, tried, and executed as the actual guilty persons.

Acts of violence such as this mass lynching, in various parts of the South, prompted Congress to pass what came to be generally known as the "Ku Klux Acts" of 1871. Designed to enable federal law-enforcement officials to deal more effectively with the "Invisible

Empire," these acts were anathema to Southerners who hoped to preserve white supremacy and who viewed the Klan as the one best means of preserving it. But to Amos Tappan Akerman, a native of Georgia who in 1871 was Attorney-General of the United States, the "Ku Klux Acts" were a virtual godsend. Two letters Akerman wrote that fall, now in the library of the University of Virginia, amply express the views of the man chiefly responsible for maintaining law and order in the land. The first letter, dated November 9, 1871, is addressed to B. D. Silliman in Brooklyn, N.Y.:

> Every day's information reveals more and more of the extent and ferocity of the unlawful combinations in that part of the country. To-day I learn that in one county of South Carolina two hundred and fifty persons have made confession of their connection with the Ku-Klux. A judge of one of the State courts, who is very kindly disposed towards his Ku-Klux neighbors, writes to me a remonstrance against the action of the United States government, and unwittingly lets out the fact that from fifteen hundred to two thousand of his neighbors have absconded. Of course none but the guilty would flee, and if that number have run away, in addition to those in prison and those released after confession, it is manifest that the local law is utterly unable to cope with the criminals. Indeed it seems to me that it is too much even for the United States to undertake to inflict adequate penalties through the courts. Suppose that we have from five thousand to ten thousand cases, (and I have no doubt that at least the former number and perhaps the latter could be brought to light) we have the judicial force to try only a small fraction of the number. Really these combinations amount to war, and cannot be effectually crushed on any other theory. But I am chronically garrulous on the Ku-Klux, and therefore will force myself to stop. . . .

The second sample is from a letter that Akerman wrote to William M. Thomas of Chester, South Carolina, on November 22:

> One of the worst features of the lawlessness in the South is the cunning with which it veils itself and endeavors, sometimes successfully, to impose even on intelligent men in its immediate neighborhood. You have apparently been, to some extent, the object of its devices; but, unless I greatly deceive myself, you will learn soon, if you have not learned already, how powerful, how depraved, and how savage is the organization which the Government of the United

States is endeavoring to suppress. Ultimately, these measures will promote the peace and prosperity of the South. The present medicine is harsh, but needed to overcome the disease. If the disease were allowed to run its course, it would render society intolerable for many years to come. If the lawless temper, which now prevails, is strengthened by exercise, it would not long confine itself to its present political direction, but would be exercised to the disturbance of society, and to the injury of good citizens for other objects.

Five months later, at the end of March 1872, the law enforcement arm of the federal government cracked down on South Carolina, making some five hundred arrests in a number of communities. One of the men arrested was John Leland, Ph.D., president of the female college in Laurens, who later described the experience in an angry book. Through his words we are able to visualize what happened in Laurens and, with minor variations, in other county seats of the piedmont region. The day chosen was a Sunday, when people rose later than usual and were likely to be at home. Two federal columns—infantry from the east, cavalry from the west—converged on the town, methodically hunted up the men named in warrants, and took them into custody. The charges were commonly "conspiracy and murder." The general situation was serious enough, in the opinion of the officials directing the operation, to justify the suspension of the writ of habeas corpus as authorized in the "Ku Klux Acts." This meant, for President Leland and the others rounded up, that they could not go free on bail; it was, in effect, a revocation of one of the most cherished of all our civil rights.

Many of the arrested men were prominent citizens—lawyers, clergymen, physicians, business leaders, and others presumed to be the moulders of public opinion. The very fact that they were arrested under the "Ku Klux Acts" conveyed the impression that they were active Klansmen, which many of them indignantly denied, no one more indignantly than Leland. All the men were taken to Columbia, the state capital, for detention while awaiting trial. Fifty-five were eventually sentenced to terms in prison—five who pleaded guilty and fifty who were tried and convicted.

It is quite probable that President Leland was as innocent of overt criminal action as he insisted when, in 1879, he brought out *A View from South Carolina*. While he was in prison in Columbia, he remembered that one of his college classmates, at Williams, was now Justice Fields of the Supreme Court; and he wrote him a long letter detailing the circumstances as he saw them. Fields co-operated handsomely: almost at once a court order arrived, freeing not only Leland but the entire Laurens contingent. But instead of feeling any particular gratitude, Leland smarted over the insult to his prestige and poured his venom, undiluted after seven years, onto the pages of his book, making it one of the strongest indictments of federal "misrule" during Reconstruction.

Leland had been indicted for his alleged part in conspiring to overthrow the Radical control of Laurens during the election of October 1870. Just what happened at that time is difficult to reconstruct with any assurance. The local Radical leader, Joe Crews, had seen fit to make a show of force with the Negro militiamen quartered just outside the town, to discourage anti-Radical violence, although the conservative whites construed the action in quite a different light: sheer insolence, they thought, and also a device for covering up the means that Crews intended to use to win the election. During the day somebody accidentally discharged a gun in the courthouse square, and a small riot followed. Nobody was hurt; it was not a very serious situation, relatively speaking, but it soon came to be known as the "Laurens Riot." Next morning four men were found dead, on the outskirts of town—three Negroes and one federal employee. There were no clues to the killers, whom Leland assumed to be ruffians from some other county.

"And just here," Leland wrote, "the writer of these pages can assert, without fear of successful contradiction, that there never has been a Ku-Klux organization in the county of Laurens, either before, during, or since the riot of 1870." He thought it undeniable that such secret conclaves did exist in some counties of the state, and that sometimes they were guilty of "flagrant acts of lawlessness and outrage." But he added that nobody deplored the violence more than the better elements of the communities. He further insisted that the Klan, where it did exist, was necessary as a defense against the heinous acts of cruelty and tyranny committed by the

Freedman's Bureau and the Union League. An example he gave would no doubt have been instantly recognized as cruel and tyrannical by all right-minded Southern gentlemen: a group of Negro men, standing by the roadside, had uttered snide remarks about some white ladies riding by in a carriage, and had uttered them in tones loud enough for the ladies to overhear them.

If the Klan elsewhere—and it was a familiar habit to insist that it existed *only* elsewhere—became overzealous, it was, in Leland's opinion, because the better elements had withdrawn from membership and had left it in the hands of "those lawless and reckless spirits, to be found in almost every community." Even so, he thought the Klan had been unduly magnified and its outrages amazingly multiplied.

The "Laurens Riot" takes up only a small part of Leland's book. The lengthy first section is an able review of the classical Southern interpretation of history. The fact that such a man—graduate of a New England college, holder of a doctor's degree, and president of a college—would subscribe to this interpretation should be convincing evidence that it was not irresponsible rhetoric. Leland went a little further than most Southern theorists in one respect: the Abolitionist fanaticism, he wrote, swept a regional President into office in 1860, leaving South Carolina no honorable course except to secede. And he was particularly bitter about the terms "rebellion" and "insurrection" applied by Northerners to this act of withdrawal, which he considered entirely justified.

In his next chapters Leland presented the postwar conditions in South Carolina as men sharing his views no doubt honestly saw them. Confederate soldiers returning home after Lee's surrender were told of the insolent behavior of Sherman's troops, stealing, burning, deliberately ruining fine carpets and furniture, shooting domestic animals for spite or for sport. Columbia and Charleston had both been burnt, if not *by* the federal troops, then at least because they were there. Plantations whose owners had been forced to flee had been seized by their former slaves, and the Freedmen's Bureau had encouraged the Negroes to keep them. The Bureau, in Leland's opinion, was "a mere swindling machine in the hands of sharpers," who enriched themselves by assessing outrageous fines for trumped-up charges. The federal agents enforced their decisions by bayonets carried by the colored Massachusetts regiments, which had been recruited from Sea Island Negroes, lowest of the lowly in breeding and intelligence. Free men with the merest iota of Southern honor could not co-operate with the Bureau scoundrels or the military commanders, especially after Congress rejected the original postwar state constitution and, in December 1865, restored the "conquered territory" status. Henceforth, in Leland's sarcastic opinion, the commanding general was the governor, edicts from army headquarters the legislature, military tribunals the judiciary, and the Freedmen's Bureau the municipal government.

Men like Leland could see nothing but pure vengeance and the wish to humiliate in the congressional rejection of the first postwar constitution. Fear of a great Negro insurrection had prompted the delegates to surround the freedmen with a set of controls so strict that slavery was hardly worse. To let South Carolina thus thwart

Frank P. Blair, the Democratic candidate for Vice President in 1868, charged that the Freedmen's Bureau was guilty of "military despotism." This was how *Harper's Weekly* commented in a cartoon published on October 24, 1868.

the intention of the federal government would have been to nullify the Union victory; it was something not only the Radicals in the United States Senate but also the great majority of Americans outside the South could not possibly have found acceptable. It is open to question, however, whether fear of insurrection was the real reason for the repressive legislation. In the extensive congressional inquiry into the Ku Klux Klan in 1871, witness after witness testified to the docility of the former slaves. The very first witness was the brilliant James L. Orr, who had been governor of South Carolina from 1865 to 1867. He told the congressional committee that it was a "matter of surprise that the negro has not become more insulting, exacting, and domineering than he has," considering his group memory of slavery and his sudden freedom; white men forced into slavery and as suddenly freed would not have behaved so well. The only explanation Orr could offer was the moral power of the white over the Negro that had developed during the more than two centuries. As for insurrection, he pointed out that slaves had never been armed, while every white man between sixteen and sixty was thoroughly familiar with guns and owned at least one.

Orr was a remarkably successful politician, serving as state legislator for four years and as Congressman for ten, from 1849 to 1859; he was so well regarded that in 1857 he was elected Speaker of the House. Better than most Southerners he understood Northern motives, and he was shrewd enough to realize when it was expedient to accommodate the North. He vigorously opposed the secessionist sentiment, but in the showdown he was a signer of the secession ordinance. He served as a member of the Confederate Senate until the fall of Richmond, and he was the first elected postwar governor of South Carolina. But his efforts to soften the Black Code and his willingness to co-operate with the federal army officers were viewed as compromise, and he lost the confidence of the state's Democrats. When his term as governor ended, he joined the Radical Party and was elected a circuit judge in his native Anderson County. A little more of the expediency that was charged against him would have spared his state, and the South in general, much of its wretchedness during Reconstruction.

It was no doubt typical of Orr to deprecate the fear of Negro insurrection. A different kind of fear was that Negroes, if given the vote and allowed to run for office, would dominate government at all levels wherever they outnumbered the whites. Almost as if they wished to prove this possibility, the great majority of South Carolina whites boycotted the elections that were conducted under the revised, Radical-sponsored constitution. Of 46,882 whites registered in 1868 and eligible to vote, 42,354 refrained; of 80,550 registered Negroes, only 14,132 refrained. Some counties with actual majorities of white registrants sent Negroes to the legislature. A familiar Southern assertion, that whites in large numbers were deprived of their political rights, or "politically disabled," because of their war activities, does not explain the "black and tan" legislatures so often cited by historians to show the horrendous results of federal interference; the white boycott of the South Carolina elections was deliberate and the election of a Negro majority to the legislature was the boycott's logical consequence.

Orr, as a seasoned practical politician, saw what had happened much more clearly than President Leland, who put all the blame on the Radicals. In Leland's opinion, the Radicals could gain and keep control of the state only by denying the vote to as many whites as possible while encouraging as many Negroes as possible to vote—and vote Republican. "Hence, these thick-skinned and heartless, but hungry and zealous partizans, known as carpet-baggers, were the very instruments [the Radicals] needed for this cruel work of sowing suspicion, enmity, and even deadly hatred between the two races." The next step in Leland's logic was to suggest that Klan counteraction to such vile and vicious behavior was entirely justified. It may be significant that Leland was in 1868 a candidate for the office of state superintendent of education but lost to a Radical from New England, J. K. Jillson; it was the same election in which the state head of the Freedmen's Bureau, Robert K. Scott of Ohio, was elected governor. Jillson served for nine years and accomplished a great deal for education in the state, particularly in winning general acceptance of the notion of schools for all children. But Leland dismissed him as a contemptuous opportunist. Leland was perhaps most irritated by the ominous note in Jillson's first public statement after being elected: "The education of *all* children of *all* classes and castes is indispensable to the highest and best welfare of the community." Dangerous thought, that.

Unlike the constitution-makers who in 1865 expressed fear of a Negro uprising, Leland insisted that racial amity prevailed during and after the war until the Radicals callously stirred the Negroes to hatred of the Southern whites. Judge Orr went further, declaring that the Negroes never stopped being docile and tractable. Leland attributed the corruption of the new legislatures to the ignorance and gullibility of the Negroes, but Orr insisted that the corruption was equally evident among the white members, and hinted that for every man accepting a bribe there must be another man offering it. Leland and Orr also differed in the kinds of corruption they saw, Leland expressing horror at the ten-dollar gold pens given to each legislator, and the calendar inkstands costing twenty-five dollars, and the soaring costs of printing ($35,000) and of supplies ($200,000 a year, with $68,000 of it for stationery alone). The more experienced Orr measured the corruption in terms of the millions of dollars of state debt incurred to pledge support of railroad bonds. Both kinds of corruption have been used *ad nauseam,* along with the composite photographs of the "black and tan" legislatures, to indict Radical Reconstruction in South Carolina. But the corruption in the state capital was nothing compared with events in the North—Boss Tweed, the Crédit Mobilier, the Whiskey Ring, and the sale of army post traderships by Grant's Secretary of War. For this was a time of gross public immorality in many parts of the country, not just in South Carolina. Moreover, blaming that state's share on the incompetence of the Negro members of the legislature has not been tenable since 1932, when Francis B. Simkins and Robert H. Woody, in their *South Carolina During Reconstruction,* showed how superior the Negro members were to the white members—something that men like Leland assumed to be impossible.

Governor Scott, soon after he took office in 1869, established a state constabulary to keep order and help enforce the will of the state legislature and the federal government. Leland naturally viewed its purpose differently, as an instrument for assessing fines and fees for the enrichment of carpetbaggers. He may not have known that Congress had appropriated no funds for the Freedmen's Bureau, which could operate only on the fines and fees. His portrait of the typical Radical leader may well have been drawn from Joe Crews of Laurens, the one Radical he had occasion to observe. It is a familiar process of "reasoning": "Joe Crews is a Radical. Joe Crews is a vile, vicious man. All Radicals, therefore, are vile, vicious men."

Crews wasn't quite as bad as Leland thought, but Judge Orr agreed fairly closely with Leland's opinion. Answering questions put to him by Congressmen at the Klan hearings, Orr singled out Crews as a conspicuous example of the venal, vindictive Radical at his worst. He had failed at business, out of sheer incompetence, and bore a grudge toward people who were successful; now, with a little authority, he enjoyed the chance to retaliate. It was reported and widely believed that he urged Negroes to seize and burn the crops, now that they had the power. Judge Orr, after saying he knew personally of no instance of a white man provoking Negroes to rise against the whites, cited Crews as a single exception, and repeated what had become a familiar anecdote, of Crews at one Negro meeting mentioning the low cost of matches—only five cents a box. Leland, who stayed at his desk all day during the Laurens riot but reported events as if he had seen them, spoke of Crews repeatedly voting his Negroes at one ballot box after another and then, when the polls closed, ignoring the ballots and merely writing down the results he wanted on pages torn from "a greasy memorandum book."

Judge Orr (like Leland in denying the existence of the Klan in his own county, but positive that it existed in Leland's) agreed that most Klan activity was the work of "reckless young men" of slight local stature. "I think," he testified, "the better portion of the community are responsible for these acts no further than that they do not use their influence, both morally and in actually enforcing the law. I think that is where the fault lies with them." Guilt by inaction, the failure of local men of influence to require and enforce respect for the law, may have had some bearing on just who was arrested in Laurens that spring morning in 1872. But Leland seems never to have felt any responsibility.

At one point in his book Leland puts first among President Grant's evil deeds his "trampling on the time-honored rights of the great Anglo-Saxon race." This would have been welcome news to the Angles and Saxons in twelfth-century England, forced to wear iron neck-rings to indicate their lowly status; somebody forgot to tell the conquering Normans that the Anglo-Saxons were a great race, with time-honored rights. And somebody forgot to include, among readings required for American school children, Daniel Defoe's "The True-Born Englishman," which makes a farce of the racial purity imputed to the great migrations from England in the seventeenth century.

Farcical or otherwise, the relevance of assumed Anglo-Saxon superiority to the success of the Ku Klux Klan can hardly be exaggerated. If a white South Carolinian in 1870 had been taught since earliest childhood, as his father and grandfather had been taught before him, that "the great Anglo-Saxon race" had time-honored rights over men of races assumed to be inferior, what could possibly happen to make him think otherwise? Military defeat could hardly alter his thinking; it might, indeed, only confirm it, on the principle, so often cited by the most vigorous defenders of the "chosen people" concept, the ancient Israelites, that God punishes those he loves. The only other race the typical white Southerner ever saw in large numbers was the Negro, and the inferiority of this group was obvious—in education, in economic standing, in political experience, in social graces—because it was the nature of the slave system to preserve this inferiority. If the premise of white supremacy is firmly established throughout a large region, if it is shared by all the whites who attend school and church together, and who conduct normal social and business dealings with each other day after day, any external challenge to the premise would be certain to rouse resentment. And any overt efforts to destroy the premise by forcing the extension of familiar privilege to the generally inferior group would almost certainly prompt energetic counteraction. White supremacy was simply something that Southern whites *knew;* it was nothing to be trifled with, or changed by agents of an external power, in this case the federal government. Resistance to the federal effort was, accordingly, defense of the principle closest to Southern white hearts; and not to resist was treasonable to the South. No wonder the "best people" acquiesced in the Klan's illegal activity and encouraged it by not condemning it or bringing its leaders into the courts. No wonder, also, that the "best people," along with the rest of the Southern whites, were unable to see any excuse for the federal agents or for the teachers sent south by Northern churches; helping Negroes close the time-honored gap was an affront to Southern principle, something that any red-blooded white Southerner had to resist, by legal means if possible, by illegal means when the legal steps failed. The chief illegal means was the Klan.

President Leland wrote nothing that had not already been asserted by the rump convention of 1865; both, quite clearly, were expressing the views of the majority of South Carolina whites. Nor was this a narrowly contemporary opinion during a time of inflamed passions. In 1902 the political scientist John W. Burgess, in his influential *Reconstruction and the Constitution*, charged Congress with "a great political error, if not a sin, in the creation of this new electorate. . . . The claim that there is nothing in the color of the skin from the point of view of political ethics is a great sophism. A black skin means membership in a race of men which has never succeeded in subjecting passion to reason, has never, therefore, created any civilization of any kind." It may be wondered whether Burgess thought the Klan violence, and the silent approval given to it by the "better elements" in Southern society, illustrated the subjection of passion to reason.

Three years later, in 1905, the Rev. James H. McNeilly read a paper at a convention of the Presbyterian Ministers' Association of America; it was subsequently printed with the title *Religion and Slavery: A Vindication of the Southern Churches*. After praising the traditional stand of Southern Presbyterians not to meddle with the civil and political status of Negroes, McNeilly blamed well intentioned outsiders for sowing "the seeds of distrust and of strife between the races." Negroes, he observed, had a firm awareness of their innate inferiority, while their immorality was of a degree that only generations of the strictest moral training could overcome. The South, if it had been left alone, would have worked out her problems, he thought, to the point where "the two races, white and black, would have lived together in perfect harmony, with the white man occupying the dominant position and the negro willingly subject." This was of course reasoning after the event, but McNeilly was right, for after the federal government abandoned its campaign the South *did* work out her problem, with the whites dominant and the Negroes subject—but not quite "willingly."

Judge Orr, in his congressional testimony, was openly dubious about any effective federal means of controlling the Klan—or any other group, organized or unorganized, that took the law into its own hands. Sending troops into a community where trouble had occurred did serve to bring quiet or at least to reduce the violence; but the Klan could merely transfer its activities to other places. Besides, the troops were strangers, unfamiliar with the lay of the land; men who knew every lane and field could easily avoid being captured even by the most determined soldiers. To the question, "Has the law, in any instance you know of, been executed against the Klansmen," Orr replied, "No, sir; the trouble is to find who they are. If the people know, they are afraid to disclose their knowledge." Later in his testimony he was asked whether organized groups shouldn't be treated as public enemies. He agreed that they should, but reverted to the problem of identification. "It will have to cure itself," he remarked. "I am very nervous, occasionally, about its leading to retaliation and violence."

Over the years, as the possibility of punishment became increasingly remote, Klansmen who could not have been identified in the 1870's admitted that they had "ridden with the Klan." By the mid-1890's, after the Supreme Court's "separate but equal" dictum (in the celebrated case of Plessy *v.* Ferguson) reflected an apparent federal acquiescence in the pattern the Klan had fought to preserve, old Klansmen became objects of veneration, and the solemn oath of perpetual silence lost its binding power. It turned out that in a good many Southern counties during Reconstruction all the officials who were not Radicals were Klan members. Except where Radicals were strong enough to be elected sheriff, county judge, and clerk of the court, enforcement of the law against the Klan was simply out of the question.

In "Civil Disobedience" Henry Thoreau listed three possible courses open to men opposed to their government: submission without protest, submission while protesting and doing everything possible to change the law or redirect the government's course, and disobedience at once. For himself, he chose the third, and proceeded to "invent" passive resistance.

The Klan—presumably in total ignorance of Thoreau, except perhaps as a notorious Abolitionist—chose none of these, unless its course is viewed as a variation of the third with "active" substituted for "passive." But whether a variation or a fourth possible course, it is the one that John Brown chose at Harpers Ferry, and many another rebel, famous or infamous, against what is viewed as intolerable injustice. The list of such active rebels, in this country, would have to be headed by Thomas Jefferson.

So far so good. And the believers in white supremacy (today more often called "racists") do not hesitate to cite the notable models. But most Americans see a great difference between rebellion honorably and openly mounted—the Revolutionary War, for example, or the Southern secession—and clandestine violence of the sort used by the Klan: the donning of robes and masks after dark to track down a Northern schoolteacher or a Freedmen's Bureau agent or an "uppity" Negro to warn or whip or hang from the nearest tree. Most Americans have a word for this fourth alternative: *criminal.* Yet the Klan used this alternative with notable success, demonstrating its effectiveness against agents of a federal policy deemed intolerable by the majority of Southern whites, and confirming lawless resistance as an instrument for implementing local sentiment. The events in South Carolina proved how successful the resort to criminal action could be, then or at any future time. This may be the central, enduring part of the Klan's legacy to America.

1864.   1868.

'TIS BUT A CHANGE OF BANNERS said this *Harper's Weekly* cartoon of September 26, 1868. The cartoon reflected the Republicans' charge that the Democratic presidential and vice presidential candidates, Seymour and Blair, were linked with the Klan and the veterans of the Confederate Army.

Chapter Five

THE WAY OF THE SCALAWAG

The *Shorter Oxford Dictionary* defines "scallywag" or "scallawag" as a disreputable fellow, a good-for-nothing, scapegrace, or blackguard. In trade union slang the term meant a man who would not work; it was also used for undersized or ill-conditioned cattle. However it was applied, it carried a resounding pejorative connotation that made it, for conservative Southern whites, wonderfully suitable for a native son who joined with the hated Republicans in their Reconstruction program. The spelling was altered—to "scalawag"—but not the general meaning. It would be a classic understatement to say that the way of the scalawag was hard.

Scalawags fared variously. In Mississippi the most prominent scalawag was probably James Lusk Alcorn, who in 1869 was the first governor elected under the Reconstruction constitution. A wealthy plantation owner in the flood-rich Delta, Alcorn had been a Unionist Whig before the Civil War, which was entirely natural since the Whigs were the wealthiest and best educated element in the state. When, after the war, they found they could not regain their former power, some of them joined the Democrats, but more of them, as men of property, turned to the party dominated by business interests. As governor, Alcorn soon discovered that he was in the middle, politically, and couldn't win. Although he was a convert to the Republican Party, he alienated its Radical members by being unable to accept Negroes as social equals; but his advocacy of voting rights for the freedmen drew violent denunciation from the Democrats, who called him an open enemy of his race and a traitor worse than Benedict Arnold. Defeated in his bid for a second term, Alcorn retired to his Delta plantation and dreamed of a revived Whig Party. His successor, Adelbert Ames, being from Maine, could not be accused of treason to his region; he was only a carpetbagger, not quite so low as a scalawag in the Southern white's scale of values.

Not all scalawags could thus retreat to wealth; for some, there was no exit. One of the luckless was Judge Chisolm, of Kemper County, the Klan's number one victim in Mississippi, whose story will be told shortly. Governor Alcorn and Judge Chisolm, each in his own way and at his own level, were seeking to give the freedmen something better than most Southern whites thought they deserved.

In 1860 there were 773 Free Negroes in Mississippi as compared with 436,631 slaves, but the Free Negroes had little more freedom than the slaves. They had to have written permission to move from one county to another. They could not own firearms. They could not testify in courts except in cases involving only Negroes or mulattoes. Like the slaves, they could not gather in groups of more than five to teach or to learn how to write—a severe deterrent to education. They could be whipped if found guilty of small offenses; whites were never whipped for the same or worse offenses. They could not vote, own land, enter military service, serve on juries, or enter into business contracts; and of course they could not intermarry with whites. When, later, white Southerners spoke of restoring or preserving the great Southern tradition, a significant part of it was this historic legalized discrimination between themselves and the Negroes, whether slave or free.

If white Mississippians considered strict control of the few Free Negroes necessary before the war, how much more important it must have seemed to them after the war when all the Negroes were free! The convention called to frame a new constitution, in the late spring of 1865, after lengthy debate adopted the following resolution regarding slavery:

> The institution of slavery having been · destroyed in the State of Mississippi, neither slavery nor involuntary servitude otherwise than in punishment of crimes whereof the party shall have been duly convicted shall hereafter exist in this State; and the Legislature at its next session, and thereafter as the public welfare may require, shall provide by law for the protection and security of the person and property of the freedmen of the State, and guard them and the State against any evils that may arise from their sudden emancipation.

This has a fine ring, as resolutions commonly do. In October a general election was held, and the new legislature convened about two weeks later. The members for the most part had not suffered at the hands of the Negroes during the war, but knew them as docile, tractable, obedient to command, though inclined to idleness and shiftlessness, and unreliable concerning agreements. So said the Committee on Laws, which added that the lawmakers must deny the freedmen certain privileges for the good of the freedmen themselves. At the time, fear of a Negro insurrection was minimal; of much more immediate concern were the crops which the Negroes, as slaves, had planted and cultivated, and which now were almost ready for harvesting by the same Negroes, as freedmen. Since the state's economic well-being depended on continued Negro labor—the only labor force competent for the job—it must have seemed reasonable not to leave the outcome to chance or to Negro willingness to work without coercion. It was seriously argued in this legislature, and we must suppose as seriously believed by both the representatives and their white constituencies, that no question of freedom was involved, and that the sole purpose of the laws passed was to prevent the idleness that might jeopardize the state's economy.

A few features of the laws adopted by this session improved the lot of Mississippi's Negroes. Couples cohabiting as husband and wife were henceforth to be considered married, and their issue legitimate. They could now be competent witnesses in civil cases between whites and Negroes, and in criminal cases if crime was alleged against a Negro's person or property. But these few concessions were outweighed by the restrictions put upon residence, movement, and labor. Beginning in January 1866, every Negro would be required to have a legal home or employment, evidenced by either a license from the mayor of a town or a member of the Board of Police, or by a written contract for labor. If the contract was for more than a month, it had to be written in duplicate and attested. A Negro leaving his job before the expiration date of the contract forfeited his pay for the entire period; furthermore, if he thus violated his contract, it was the duty of a civil officer, and the privilege of any private citizen, to arrest him and return him to his employer. For this service the arresting individual was entitled to five dollars, plus ten cents a mile for each mile traveled, the sum to be deducted from the arrested Negro's subsequent wages. Appeal was possible, to a Justice of the Peace and then to the county court, but no further. Anybody found guilty of persuading or attempting to persuade a Negro to violate his contract could be fined and sent to jail.

The apprentice regulations are also interesting. Twice a year, in January and July, civil officers were required to report to the probate court every Negro under eighteen whose parents could not or would not provide for him. The probate court then had the duty of ordering the clerk to apprentice such a minor to some suitable person, who had to give bond to the state that he would furnish him with sufficient food, clothing, and medical attention, and teach him to read and write. The master could inflict punishment, though not of a cruel or inhuman sort. There were detailed rules governing runaways. In general the apprentice system was modeled upon indenture laws of Northern states, with the signal difference that in Mississippi it applied only to Negro youngsters.

Once the Negro reached the age of eighteen, he had to contend with regulations concerning vagrancy, a condition defined as including not only lack of visible means of support but also disorderly and lascivious conduct, and associating with whites on terms of social equality. A Negro found guilty and unable to pay the fine of fifty dollars would, upon completion of his ten-day jail term, be forced to work for whoever offered the shortest term of service in return for paying the fine.

Jesse Thomas Wallace, whose *History of the Negroes of Missis- sippi from 1865 to 1890* earned him a Columbia doctorate in 1928, concluded that "these laws provided that all penal and criminal laws of the Mississippi code of 1857 punishing crimes and mis- demeanors by slaves, freedmen, free Negroes, and mulattoes were re-enacted against Negroes except as to manner of trial and punish- ment changed by law." In other words, the freedmen after 1865 were put under regulations no less strict than those applied be- fore the war to Negroes of any status. Assuming sincerity on the part of the legislators, it is easy to imagine their indignation when the War Department immediately decreed that the provisions would be recognized only if they were applied equally to whites and Negroes. Since the rationale of this re-enacted Black Code was to keep the Negroes working and not to discriminate against them as a race, a demand that the provisions apply equally to whites must have been puzzling, to say the least. The legislators quickly iden- tified the Freedmen's Bureau as the principal force seeking to nul- lify their intentions, and the stage was thus set for a struggle that could end only with total defeat for one side or the other.

A Freedmen's Bureau circular, dated August 8, 1865, was par- ticularly offensive; it stated that where local courts did not ac- cept Negro testimony, cases in which Negroes were parties would henceforth be tried by courts set up by the Bureau itself. No such courts, of course, had ever been known in Mississippi; they flouted all traditions of proper judicial procedure, as Mississippians con- ceived it, and constituted an insult to the judges, lawyers, and clerks of the local courts, who had their own notions of legal pro- prieties. The Bureau annoyed the native whites in various other ways, including the employment of Negro troops to enforce its own orders and those of the War Department. These troops were never *all* Negro, but even a few Negroes in a regiment constituted an insult. It was ludicrously simple for Mississippians, both black and white, though for totally different reasons, to believe that the federal troops were quartered in the state deliberately to humiliate the local whites.

Since the self-interest of the whites in Mississippi opposed at every point the purpose of the federal government and its agencies, collision was inevitable. Newspaper editors throughout the state, overwhelmingly Democratic, used every known device, and invented new ones, to attack the unwelcome "do-gooders." One Republican paper did exist, in Pontotoc—*Equal Rights*. Its editor, Colonel W. R. Flournoy, before the war had been the largest slaveholder in northeastern Mississippi. Vernon L. Wharton in *The Negro in Mississippi 1865–1890* (1947) calls him "essentially a humanitarian" who was motivated by "deep Christian convictions," but the general opinion during Reconstruction is echoed by James W. Garner, in his *Reconstruction in Mississippi* (1901), who wrote that Flournoy "enjoyed the distinction of being the most extreme and obnoxious radical in the state." It was to be expected that, sooner or later, the Klan would attack him, but on the night of the raid Flournoy escaped by jumping through a window. There was shooting, and one of the raiders was mortally wounded. A bystander removed the wounded man's mask to make his breathing easier, and took him to the local jail, where he gave a false name— that of his brother who had been killed at Shiloh—and admitted that the purpose of the raid was to kill Flournoy.

Some of the Democratic editors consistently denied the presence of the Klan in the state, while others defended its activities, no matter how violent. The Jackson *Clarion* did both, though at different times. On December 13, 1870, it doubted editorially that such an organization had members in the state, but on March 21, 1877, it explained the Klan's formation as a natural result of the "instinct for self-preservation." Some editors blamed Klan activity on Alabama Klansmen who crossed the state line. Since the worst violence developed in the counties bordering Alabama, this may have been in large part true. The statement, however, also reflects a common tendency to blame outsiders for any Klan violence.

What has been called the "Chisolm Massacre" is an excellent illustration of both the violence that was virtually endemic in the eastern counties of Mississippi and the methods used by the Klan and defended by the Democratic editors. William Wallace Chisolm was born in Georgia in 1830 but at the age of sixteen moved to Mississippi with his parents. In 1858 he entered public life by being elected magistrate (the equivalent of justice of the peace) for his township. Two years later he was elected probate judge—hence the name usually given him, Judge Chisolm—and held office until 1867. His enemies later asserted that he owed his long tenure in office to the Negro vote, which, as Kemper County's leading Radical, he controlled. No doubt he got all the Negro votes that were cast, but before 1865, when no Negroes voted, he seems to have been held in consistently high regard by the white voters even though they knew he was a Union man.

The sheriff was usually named Gully—one of a numerous tribe which took good care of its members. When John W. Gully was sheriff, he had appointed fourteen of his kin as deputies. But with the advent of military government after the war the Gullys were shorn of their power. In 1869 Judge Chisolm's brother, John, was elected sheriff; Chisolm himself became first deputy sheriff and also tax collector. Earlier, as judge, he may well have worked out an accommodation with the Gullys, as his enemies later declared; the only alternative may have been open war. But now he had no need to work with them. If their resentment at being "outs" after so long being "ins" led to a show of force, Chisolm must have felt that the federal troops would provide whatever support he might need. The Gullys' enmity, however, was soon only a small part of the opposition that developed toward Chisolm. Being a declared Radical was hard for Democrats to swallow; but being an efficient tax collector was unforgivable.

The taxes that it was Chisolm's duty to collect were chiefly for the support of schools. As early as 1803 Congress had authorized the creation of public schools in the entire area south of Tennessee and had stipulated that every sixteenth section (square mile) of land be set aside for school purposes. In Mississippi, however, nothing had happened; no public schools were established until 1865, by which time the sixteenth sections could not even be located.

For whites with enough money, there were private schools. The rest of the white population got along quite happily without education. Why, suddenly, just when the state was economically close to ruin, did the federal government insist upon setting up a system of public education? The plan was viewed with suspicion as one more insult devised by the vindictive Radicals in Washington to humiliate the defeated citizens.

The correlation between the lack of schools and the violence during Reconstruction need not be explored here. William Faulkner has said all that needs saying about the strain of violence in rural Mississippi—and most of the state *is* rural. What matters is that in 1865 property owners were faced for the first time with the duty of paying for public schools—schools for Negro children as well as for white. Negro ownership of taxable property was negligible; the prewar Black Codes had seen to that. This meant that the whites were asked to carry the entire burden of taxes for the support of schools. No tax collector, whatever his political label, could have been both efficient and popular.

There are numerous ways of expressing dislike. Kemper County, located on the Alabama border about midway north and south, expressed it with greater violence than most other counties in Mississippi. In a two-year period, 1869–71, thirty-five Negroes were known to have been killed, and Negro whippings were an almost nightly occurrence. White men were killed less often—or perhaps we should say they were killed only when the Klan deemed it absolutely imperative.

On one occasion federal troops were sent into Kemper County to restore order. They arrested a man named Ball, but he escaped and made his way to Texas. Somewhat later he returned, but he was so careful to avoid all his former Klan associates that they decided he was planning to turn state's evidence, and they killed him. Following a script that was often re-enacted, two Negroes were promptly arrested and charged with Ball's murder. One broke out of jail and fled the county; the other was tried and acquitted. Not all Negroes charged with Klan murders were so lucky.

On May 26, 1871, Klansmen entered the plantation owned by ex-Governor R. G. Powers in search of a Negro, Matt Duncan. The white superintendent ordered them to leave, and in the ensuing scuffle one young Klansman, George Evans, was shot to death. He was secretly buried by his father, who attributed his death to eating too many oysters and sardines. Matt Duncan's offense was reporting the wanton killing of a little Negro boy, who had been drawn and quartered and thrown into a swamp. One wonders whether the widows and daughters of Klansmen, honoring the memory of their husbands and fathers, ever had the slightest awareness of the most horrible Klan crimes.

These Mississippi Klansmen were arrested by federal authorities in 1871 for the attempted murder of an entire family. The sketch, published in *Harper's Weekly* on January 27, 1872, was from a photograph.

The dismal record of Klan violence in Kemper County was capped by the elimination of Judge Chisolm in 1877. He had managed to survive politically; he was elected sheriff in 1873 for a two-year term, and in 1876 he was the Republican candidate for Congress. Klansmen badgered him at party rallies and intensified their hate campaign by serenading him for two nights just before the election. Late on the night of November 3, just as the family was preparing to retire, a cannon was discharged, breaking several windows. The Klansmen kept up a shouted barrage of indecencies until two in the morning. The next night the demonstration was even louder. A band blared out "The Bonnie Blue Flag," the Confederate "national anthem," and "Dixie," the Klan theme song, which is today a symbol to Negroes of white supremacy arrogance. In the election Chisolm was defeated, as all Republicans were that year in Mississippi; but a federal grand jury indicted thirty Klansmen for violating the Enforcement Act, which guaranteed candidates freedom to campaign. The state press, loftily ignoring the Klan interference with Chisolm's campaigning, vilified the indictment as the "most inhuman and uncalled-for act of tyranny and oppression ever perpetrated upon a free people."

The indictment led to nothing, for when the next court session opened in March 1877, it was discovered that all the records had been stolen. Some eighty-five criminal and forty civil processes were thus lost. Judge Chisolm and his seventeen-year-old daughter Cornelia had spent the winter in Washington, returning home on March 29. On that very day the former sheriff, John Gully, was found dead near the Chisolm home.

About a month later, a warrant was issued charging Chisolm and five other men with the murder. The actual killing was attributed to one Ben Rush—who later proved that he had been in Arkansas at the time of the murder. Chisolm, his conscience clear, went to the county jail in De Kalb, where the current sheriff had considerately loaded the guards' guns with blank cartridges. A co-defendant, John Gilmer, never got as far as the jail: on the way he was shot in the head and killed, despite a heavy guard. Two Negroes, named in the indictment as witnesses of Gully's murder, were taken to the woods and savagely beaten to ensure that they would keep their mouths shut.

The strategy was working perfectly; it went awry for only one of the two-hundred-odd Klansmen who had gathered at the jail to mete out their kind of justice: Chisolm managed to shoot him dead when the mob stormed the door of his cell. Johnny Chisolm, aged thirteen, had his arm shot off while helping his father and shortly after was killed. Cornelia was wounded several times, as was the judge. Mrs. Chisolm, who alone was not hit by a bullet, got her husband home only by making the Klansmen think he was dead. When they learned he was still alive, they laid siege to his house. A few friends and relatives were courageous enough to stand by him. Doctors came by roundabout routes. The Governor dropped in and told Mrs. Chisolm, "I have no power to do anything at all. I think it is doubtful whether a jury in [Kemper] county will ever convict any of the mob." (He was right.) Chisolm died on May 13, Cornelia two days later. They were buried by relatives, next to Johnny, in sight of two churches but with no clergyman brave enough to read a funeral service.

On the first anniversary of Judge Chisolm's death, a memorial service was held in the Metropolitan Church in Washington, with Bishop Haven of Atlanta giving the eulogy. And in Clinton County in northern Pennsylvania one J. C. Sigmond donated a plot in Cedar Hill Cemetery for a Chisolm monument which remains to this day a curiosity of the region. But what kept the incident alive was a book, *The Chisolm Massacre,* published in 1878. Its author, James M. Wells, was an internal revenue agent and a close friend of the Chisolm family; he had been one of the loyal group who had held the Klan at bay while the Judge and his daughter lay dying. It was his bitter conclusion that "the people of the South are governed by passion and prejudice more than by reason or law."

Whether Wells was right or wrong depends, of course, on the particular reader's predisposition. Mississippians did not like the book much; the next year James Lynch of West Point, not far from De Kalb, published an answer: *Kemper County Vindicated.* He made no effort to prove Chisolm's guilt in the Gully murder, but he attributed Chisolm's death to Chisolm himself, for being a notorious Radical. That, one gathers, was for Lynch the greatest of crimes. Democratic editors in the state, who had long been openly hostile to Chisolm, stepped up their campaign of vilification after his death. One point they kept reiterating was that Johnny and Cornelia had been shot by accident; neither they nor Mrs. Chisolm had had any right to be at the jail to help the judge. The same editors saw no reason to question the right of the Klansmen to be there, or their right to besiege the Chisolm house prior to election day and after the gory scene at the jail.

At one point in his angry book Wells remarks: "Let a negro be accused of a crime against one of his own race, even, and his punishment, after the most extreme interpretation of the law, will be swift enough; . . . the will of a single white man is sufficient to procure the arrest and summary punishment of a negro at any time." For true believers in white supremacy, such a remark must have been puzzling: Why would anyone think that a member of a race known to be inferior should be given the same rights in court as a white man? That some white men—outsiders—thought justice should be color-blind, and that they should invade the South with this doctrine and set about imposing it despite the long-established regional tradition, was more than puzzling—it was infuriating, and it was used to justify the Klan's illegal methods of opposition. But even worse was a born Southerner like Judge Chisolm siding with the intruders in their unwarranted efforts to educate Negroes and to gain for them equality under the law.

How people think is all, no doubt, a matter of conditioning. Let members of a college fraternity in a white university call out the fire department at two in the morning and steal fire axes from the truck while the firemen hunt for a nonexistent blaze, and the incident is laughed off as typical high spirits. Let other college students, in the same Southern city but from a Negro campus, volubly protest segregated moving picture theatres, and they are hauled off to jail by the score and fined a total of $48,000 in a trial in which a defense plea of high spirits draws a rebuke from the bench. If in the 1960's the double standard of justice still prevails in some parts of the South, how much more justifiable it must have seemed during Reconstruction, when slavery was a fact of the very recent past and when the tensions of civil war had not begun to relax! From the Northern point of view, and in one book, Chisolm was a martyr to the cause of extended democracy. From the Southern point of view, and in another book, he was a traitor to his region and to its sacred ideal of white supremacy and his death was his own fault.

In Kemper County, as in the South at large, the federal effort to eliminate the double standard was defeated, largely by Klan action backed by the overwhelming regional adherence to white supremacy. Recent renewal of the same federal effort, after several decades of quiescence—and apparent acquiescence—runs head-on into the same firmly planted belief, though today it is often cloaked in a hocus-pocus of the sanctity of private property, an obvious fraud when it is applied only against Negroes. Negro "inferiority" is far less obvious today than in the 1860's and 1870's; too many Negroes have overcome all obstacles in rising to eminence in every sort of occupation, for innate inferiority to be any longer seriously argued as justifying differentials in rights. The Klan *did* succeed in making white supremacy the unwritten law, even though its implementation, virtually unchallenged by the federal government, clearly violated national laws. The modern Klan's adherents, however, are not merely claiming to be enforcers of white supremacy. They claim to be patriots fighting Communist infiltration of the federal government. The old Klan, for all its faults, at least had the guts to say that white supremacy was its reason for being.

Chapter Six

THE KLAN AND THE NORTHERN TEACHER

In 1839 a group of slaves aboard the slaver *Amistad* managed to kill her captain. The importation of slaves had been outlawed by Congress in 1808, and this fact no doubt influenced the Supreme Court's decision to free the *Amistad* slaves after lower courts had found them guilty of murder. Another influence upon the Court was the so-called "Amistad Committee," composed of prominent citizens who volunteered to help with the legal defense. Seven years later this committee became the nucleus of the American Missionary Association, which undertook mission work both at home and abroad but focused its attention on the Southern Negroes. By 1866 the AMA had 353 teachers in the South and an annual budget of close to $400,000. Two years later it had 532 teachers at work. It founded several colleges for Negroes, including Fisk University in Nashville, Tennessee, Hampton Institute in Virginia, and Atlanta University in Georgia. Operated chiefly by the Congregationalists, the Association also drew support from the Free-Will Baptists and the Dutch Reformed.

The AMA was the largest church-related group fostering the

education of former slaves and their children. Other groups, supported by single churches, included the Freedmen's Aid Society
of the Methodist Episcopal Church, the Friends' Association of
Philadelphia and Its Vicinity for the Relief of the Colored Freedmen, and the Home Mission Society (Baptist), which founded
Shaw University in Raleigh, North Carolina, and Benedict College
in Columbia, South Carolina.

Other aid societies were organized without church affiliation.
The New England Freedmen's Aid Society, first of several regional
groups with virtually the same name, sent twenty-two teachers
South in 1865 and seventy in 1868. Maintaining one teacher, the
Society estimated, cost $500 a year. In 1862, New York and Phila-
delphia each established a National Freedmen's Aid Association.
All these nonsectarian societies united in May 1866 to form the
American Freedmen's Union Commission, which in that year could
boast of operating 359 schools scattered through all the Southern
states except Texas. The Commission received considerable help
from abroad, especially from England, France, Germany, and
Switzerland.

The Freedmen's Bureau was grateful for all these private activities. The 1868 report of the Secretary of War recorded a total of
2,295 teachers in schools for Negroes in the South; but 990 of these
teachers were local Negroes, and some of the remaining 1,305 were
Southern whites. Of a total of 1,831 schools, 1,325 were sustained
wholly or in part by the freedmen themselves, who owned 518
buildings—many of them churches—used for school purposes. In
the tabulation of money supplied, the federal share was just over
a million dollars, compared with an estimated $700,000 provided
by Northern church and secular groups, and $360,000 provided
by the freedmen themselves. It is amply evident that the major
source of both money and teaching personnel was private, and
that the government's share was limited to financial help for projects
already begun and chiefly promoted by nongovernmental agencies,
thus contradicting the charge sometimes made by white Southerners that the teachers were agents of the Radicals who controlled
the federal government.

If the estimated cost of maintaining one teacher in the field was $500 a year, hope of monetary reward was not the dominant motive of the teachers who volunteered their services. The chief motives were piety and humanitarianism, in varying proportions. Teachers sent by church groups were encouraged to add religious instruction to the strictly educational; the Freedmen's Union Commission told the teachers whom it subsidized to avoid religion in the classroom. This was one of two controversies splitting the Northern societies; the other was whether schools should be integrated. There was less disagreement concerning the infusion of political propaganda into the curriculum.

A typical school day opened with prayers, scripture reading, and a song—"John Brown's Body," perhaps, or "Battle Hymn of the Republic," or "Marching through Georgia." Sometimes a catechism was included, such as the following, which was given for the benefit of Northern visitors at a mass gathering in Richmond:

Are you glad you are free?
  Yes, indeed.
Who gave you your freedom?
  God.
Through whom?
  Abraham Lincoln.
Is Mr. Lincoln dead?
  Yes.
Who is your President?
  Johnson.
Are you glad you have schools and teachers?
  Yes.
Do you want these friends who are here today to go North and send you more teachers?
  Yes, indeed!

Negro youngsters particularly liked to sing "We are free":

> *Free! We are free! With a wild and joyous cry*
> *We children in our gladness shouting far and nigh!*
> *Free! We are free! Oh, let the tidings fly,*
> *We are free today!*

Probably more effective, however, than either the songs or the catechisms was the informal classroom discussion of current politics, with the teacher pointing out that it was Northerners, and Republicans in particular, who were most concerned about the welfare of the freedmen. All such departures from the normal curriculum of the three R's, spelling, and geography quite naturally irritated the Southern whites, partly because most of them were Democrats, but more because they feared the results of indoctrination in social equality.

The Northern teachers usually went home when their appointments ended, but some stayed for the rest of their lives. A few joined the Reconstruction state governments, most often in departments of public instruction. One of them, Justus K. Jillson of Massachusetts, was elected Superintendent of Public Instruction in South Carolina in 1868. His election automatically made him a "notorious Radical"—at least that is what President Leland of Laurens Female College called him in his angry book. Leland, incidentally, was Jillson's unsuccessful Democratic opponent in the election.

Very few of the Northern teachers had any actual contact with the Radical state governments, but in Southern white reasoning the way they implemented their idealism identified them with the Radicals. With almost no exceptions the teachers were resented as "radicals and social equality propagandists," according to a Freedmen's Bureau agent in Albany, Georgia, in 1868. At best they were tolerated, but toleration often gave way to open opposition and even, for the male teachers, violence. Like the agents of the Freedmen's Bureau, they were prime targets of Klan operations; but unlike the agents, who could depend on the protection of federal troops, since the Bureau was under the War Department, the teachers were especially vulnerable.

It took considerable courage to be a Northern teacher in the Reconstruction South. A simple stroll down a village street could become unpleasant. Southern ladies showed their contempt with a jerk of the head, and white schoolboys shouted ribald remarks. One teacher in Lexington, Virginia, reported that she was habitually greeted by white college students at her boardinghouse as a "damned Yankee bitch of a nigger teacher." She was luckier than some teachers, however, for many could not find anybody willing to provide room and board, or even to sell them food. Many, unable to find space in white hotels or private homes, lived with the families of their pupils; it was a familiar frontier practice, immortalized in such books as *The Hoosier School-Master,* but in the South it earned a special degree of contempt unlike anything ever experienced by a frontier teacher. The smaller the community, the worse the ostracism, which helps explain why the most successful Negro schools were in larger places such as Charleston and Memphis.

One determined teacher set up housekeeping in an abandoned slave cabin. She told congressional investigators: "For any family to receive me would be to incur the ridicule of the community." White Southerners who were not themselves averse to taking in such pariahs as boarders or roomers shrank from the odium the gesture was certain to bring upon them. When owners rented houses to Northern teachers, they commonly charged exorbitant rents. A teacher who simply could not find a place to eat and sleep could not stay—which was exactly what a good many Southern whites wanted.

The very few white Southerners who approved of education for the Negroes wanted it limited to elementary levels and to segregated schools. The popular novelist and journalist J. T. Trowbridge, in the course of an extended tour of the South just after the Civil War, visited numerous Negro schools and "did not hear of the white people taking any interest in them. . . . Such of the citizens as do not oppose the education of the black," he observed, "were generally silent about it. Nobody said of it, 'That is freedom! That is what the Yankees are doing for them!'" The self-sacrificing labors of the Northern teachers and the indifference or hostility of the local whites reminded Trowbridge forcefully of the stereotyped assertion that "The Southern people are the Negroes' best friends."

Trowbridge, without intending to do so, provided one possible reason why Southern whites did not visit the Negro schools. The pupils, he could not help noticing, were a visible reminder of what he called the "bleaching" of the race. In one school in Vicksburg, with eighty-nine pupils, only three were of pure African stock.

The Klan and the Northern Teacher

In a Mississippi school there were forty-six blacks and twenty-three mixed; in a third, thirty blacks and seven mixed. "The younger the generation," he concluded, "the lighter the average skin; by which curious fact one perceives how fast the race was being bleached under the 'peculiar' system of slavery." The racial purity that the Klan pledged itself to preserve was possible in slave times only by disowning the natural results of concubinage.

It is curious, when viewed in retrospect, that the Southern whites seldom if ever paused to consider that the Northern teachers might write to their families back home. Perhaps, in their overriding resentment toward members of their own race who did not share their belief that the Negroes should be kept "in their place," they could not conceive that the teachers came from families with any claims to social respectability. The letters home, with their hair-raising reports of "Southern barbarism" witnessed at first hand, and telling of the general poverty and backwardness of the region as compared with the North, were almost certain to neutralize the carefully nurtured Southern self-image of cultured gentility. Of course, the Confederate soldiers had discovered that men on the other side were not the ogres of the propaganda; but the stay-at-homes, especially the women, apparently never did get rid of the notion that all Northerners were wicked and "common."

It has always been the practice in the South to establish one's social position by citing relationships with prominent families; and the Northern teachers could cite no such relationships. The fact that their families were reputable in their own states meant nothing in a society that was both aristocratic and provincial. Most of the teachers, moreover, were better educated than the Southern people who snubbed them, but not even graduation from college meant as much as did a tie with an old Southern family. The Klan's solemn claim of being a chivalric order rang hollow to the mothers and fathers in the North who read the letters, sad or angry, that the idealistic young people wrote.

Christianity, or rather its institutionalized form in America, seems as susceptible as any other human institution to local concepts and prejudices. Southern Methodist clergymen, as Ralph E. Morrow reports in *Northern Methodism and Reconstruction* (1956), shunned Methodist clergymen from the North as if they were counterfeiters or horse thieves. Methodist Bishop Thomas Bowman, formerly the president of DePauw University, said as late as 1875, "My wife has not enjoyed the privilege of speaking with a [Southern] white woman in over two years." And one Southerner remarked, concerning Northern Methodists in the South, "There is no use of a hell if such damn rascals are not sent to it."

The Northern teachers were among the most idealistic of their generation, and they were almost invariably pious, with the fixed habit of attending church on Sunday. But the regional brand of Christian fellowship made such attendance a severe test of courage. An initial visit might be followed by a curt note extending a cordial unwelcome. Men, apparently, were somewhat less openly hostile than their wives, who, as one Northern teacher reported from Wilmington, North Carolina, greeted them not with the smile and handclasp traditional for strangers but with "the scornful curl of the lip, the brushing away of the dress for fear of contamination, the raising of the finger to touch the *black* ribbon of the hat, thus telegraphing to one another: 'The nigger teachers have come.'"

Charles Wallace Howard, a Presbyterian minister who edited an agricultural paper, *The Plantation,* and was vice president of the state agricultural society, no doubt spoke for many of his fellow Georgians when he testified before the congressional committee investigating the Klan: "There is a very different condition socially in the estimation placed upon Northern and Southern women at the South. . . . Our women are not inclined to look favorably upon Northern ladies who come here, so far as their social relations are concerned. . . . They just let them alone. They do not disturb them. I know nothing of the Northern females who come to teach colored schools; never spoke to them. They were rigorously excluded from society."

To Albion Tourgée, who was perhaps the Klan's number one opponent, the rigorous exclusion of the Northern teachers from society was both incomprehensible and hateful. Like his fictional hero in *A Fool's Errand,* Comfort Servosse, he knew many of the young ladies who had moved to the South to teach in Negro schools, and he declared "that he had never known a like number of ladies, more accomplished, pure and devoted than the 'females' at whom the South sneers. They were usually the daughters of well-to-do families who, inspired with a genuine missionary spirit, determined to give a year or two to the work of enlightening a race whose history had awakened their intensest sympathy. Their social standing at home was uniformly good and in many instances conspicuously so. The daughters of farmers, merchants, college professors and clergymen of the highest eminence were to be found in their ranks." The Klan, to its credit, Tourgée observed, never molested these girls.

Most of the Northern teachers, both men and women, were young, and many of them were students or recent college graduates. In a list of a thousand-odd whose homes have been located, twenty-five were from Oberlin, an Ohio college notorious in the South because it was the first in the nation to admit women and Negroes. Apart from Oberlin, however, the list shows that the teachers were virtually from everywhere: from Michigan and Massachusetts, Ohio and New Hampshire, Wisconsin and Indiana, Quebec and Oregon, Illinois and New Brunswick, Iowa and Nebraska, Delaware and England, New Jersey and Connecticut, Maryland and Pennsylvania, Hawaii and Nova Scotia, Maine and Minnesota, Rhode Island, the District of Columbia, Vermont, Virginia, New York. They came from big cities—Boston and Chicago, New York and Baltimore, Toronto and Cincinnati, Portland and Hartford, Cleveland and Pittsburgh; and from smaller cities—Montpelier, Angola, Fall River, Fort Wayne, Carbondale, Tarrytown, Yarmouth, Nashua, Keokuk, Corning; and from college towns—Ann Arbor and Hillsdale and Kalamazoo in Michigan; Granville and Oberlin in Ohio; Brunswick, Maine; Rockford, Illinois; Beloit, Wisconsin; and from hundreds of villages—Four Corners, Ohio; Piano, Illinois; Jericho Center, Vermont; Amo, Indiana; Hickory, Iowa; Goodale's Junction, Maine. There were Abbotts and Aldriches, Bakers and Booths, Clarks and Cranes, Days and Fosters and Hamiltons, Howards and Hosmers, Lanes and Mitchells, Palmers and Pierces, Stevensons and Warrens, Wilsons and Withingtons and Wrights. There were only a few with other than familiar English names: there were two Cardozos, an O'Riordan, a Peduzzi, a Rosencrans, a Warfel, and, in the Z's, a Zachos, two Zelies, and a Zoll. The great majority, clearly enough, were from the dominant element in American society—middle class, Protestant, of English descent—exactly the same class that dominated society in the South. Newer groups in the North that by 1870 collectively outnumbered the "Anglo-Saxons" were not yet economically in a position to send their children to college or to help pay their way south to teach, or even to spare them from the joint enterprise of keeping the family solvent. Possibly the greatest cause of resentment among Southerners was the fact that the visitors *were* of their own social class—that is, if they ever made the effort to find out that much about them.

Some of the teachers, like some of the Northern clergymen, met the hostility with Christlike resignation; others fought back with open defiance; a few quit and went home. Ralph Morrow tells of one teacher sent to Virginia who "sadly turned her face homeward for no other reason, she said, than a few months of being 'cheered, whistled, groaned, crowed, squealed, and hissed at.'" Other teachers fared worse but stuck it out. One, also in Virginia, reported, "Men bandied rude, insulting jests at my expense, and coupled my name with curses. . . . Even from the children I heard . . . 'She's nothing but a damned nigger teacher.'"

If women teachers were never directly molested by the Klan, which left their persecution, as it were, to the population in general and especially to the "ladies' auxiliary," the men teachers were not so lucky. In the great majority of Klan incidents the only evidence was supplied by the victims—if they lived. Corroborating evidence almost never existed. But even the relatively small proportion of incidents in which the Klan communicated with the intended victim or published warnings in newspapers and broadsides yields a substantial number of documents, many still extant, that conclusively prove Klan activity. Sometimes even names were given, although this was contrary to the cherished Klan secrecy.

The warnings were often so illiterate that a teacher might be inclined to shrug them off with a laugh. One teacher in Georgia received this message:

You are a dern aberlition puppy and scoundrel if We hear of your name in the papers again we will burn your hellish house over your head cut your entrals out.

The K K s are on your track and you will go to hell in four days if you don' mind yourself, mind that you don't go the same way that G.W.A. went some night

Yours in hell

The "G.W.A." referred to was G. W. Ashmore, a prominent Georgia Radical who had recently been murdered in Jonesboro.

Another teacher, employed by the AMA, received a more literate and colorful Klan greeting in 1868:

1st quarter, 8th Bloody moon—Ere the next quarter be gone! unholy teacher of the blacks, begone, ere it is too late! Punishment awaits you, and such horrors as no man ever underwent and lived. The cusped moon is full of wrath, and as its horns fill the deadly mixture will fall on your unhallowed head. Beware! When the Black Cat sleeps we that are dead and yet live are watching you. Fool! Adulterer and cursed Hypocrite! The far-piercing eye of the grand Cyclops is upon you! Fly the wrath to come.

Ku Klux Klan

The curious clause "we that are dead" suggests the device, often successfully used to frighten ignorant Negroes, of pretending to be the ghosts of Confederate soldiers killed in battle.

One Klan letter, sent to a man named Schneider who taught a Negro school in Warren County, Mississippi, explains in considerable detail how the Klan operated:

HEADQUARTERS K.K.K. March 3, 1871.

Mr. S:—As it is customary for our order never to attack any one without telling him the cause and giving him fair warning, we wish to say, that having had your case before the order at its last meeting, you were found guilty of certain misdemeanors by a unanimous vote.

Charge 1. Associating with negroes in preference to the white race as God ordained. Guilty.

Charge 2. For being instrumental in the removal of one of our fellow citizens from the office of justice of the peace in the county and beat where you reside and placing a carpet bagger, negro, and scalla-wag in his stead. Guilty.

There was one other charge, but there being a few dissenting votes on this—not guilty.

It is an established rule of the order never to give a man more than three days to leave the county, but taking into careful considera-tion your situation and the size of your carpet bag, we have con-cluded to extend the time to five days; at the expiration of said time, we will wait upon you if you are in the county. Hoping that you will view the subject in a sensible light and leave, as we always dislike to use harsh means, our object being to purify our state, and we commence our work on scallawags and carpet baggers first.

Yours, etc.

A wronged and outraged Mississippian
and chief of the Ku Klux Klan.

Letters of this sort exist by the hundred in the files of the Ameri-can MissionaryAssociation and other groups that fostered the edu-cation of freedmen. Their very number, indeed, has discouraged scholars from the formidable task of cataloguing them and analyz-ing them methodically. Until this is done, it can be only a reason-able conjecture that the most extensive Klan harassment of North-ern teachers occurred in Mississippi.

The conjecture is reasonable because Mississippi had the worst record of public education in the South. Not until 1919, in fact, did the state legislature provide for universal public education, the last state in the Union to do so, 116 years after Congress had re-served every sixteenth section of the state's land for school pur-poses. The Mississippi whites had never paid any taxes for the sup-port of schools until the Radical state and county officials imposed them in the late 1860's. The usual Southern opposition to the education of Negroes was therefore, in Mississippi, compounded by resentment at paying taxes never before imposed. Somewhat more than in other Southern states, the school question loomed large in the political struggle; but it was the teachers who became the chief victims of the resentment.

In Louisville, seat of Winston County, some thirty-six masked riders visited the white teacher, a Mr. Fox, and forbade him to continue his contract. They also sought Peter Cooper, the Negro teacher of the local Negro school, but not finding him at home, they burnt his clothes and his trunk and made off with $24 in cash. Within a few months the Klan succeeded in closing eleven schools in that county, by burning the schoolhouses and intimidating the teachers. It apparently did not occur to the Klansmen that school-burning would only increase the cost of education; they must have believed they could totally prevent the schools from operating and thus bring relief from the school tax they found so hateful.

In Lowndes County a Negro Congregational preacher who also taught school was "ku-kluxed"; after a warning delivered by a band of about a hundred men in disguise, he abandoned his school. But the Klan was not satisfied: a second night visit had the purpose of ordering him to stop preaching. There were enough preachers in the county without him, he was told. He refused to quit, how-ever, and for some reason was not again molested.

One notorious Klan action in Mississippi, widely reported and discussed throughout the nation, was the whipping of Colonel A. P. Huggins, Superintendent of Schools in Munroe County. While on a tour of inspection in March 1870, he stopped for the night at the house of a friend named Ross, a prominent Democrat. About ten o'clock, awakened by a call at the gate, he saw the premises crowded with men in white robes. He declined an invitation to step outside; and Ross ignored a request to force him out. The Klansmen then threatened to set the house afire, and Huggins, unwilling to let his friend suffer such a loss, went to the gate. The leader announced to him the decree of a particular den that he should leave the county within ten days and thus relieve the people from further taxes. His chief offense, he was informed, was collecting taxes to keep the Radicals in power. His reply was that he would leave the county when he chose, and not before. He was no doubt very angry, but so were the Klansmen, and they outnumbered him a hundred to his one (the Klan never did run any risk of being overpowered). Huggins was taken a quarter of a mile down the road and given seventy-five lashes with a stout leather stirrup strap. Whipping, it should be understood, was a punishment never given to Southern whites, but often enough meted out to convicted Negroes.

Some counties in Mississippi saw more violence than others; Kemper County was among the worst. In a two-year period, 1869–1871, thirty-five Negroes were known to have been killed within this county, and Negro whippings were an almost nightly occurrence. In August 1873, two years after the congressional investigation of the Klan, a schoolhouse was burned and its teacher, Charles Robinson, was staked to the ground and threatened with death if he did not leave the county; having no wish for martyrdom, he left a couple of days later. The Klan, in theory at least, was officially disbanded by order of Bedford Forrest in January 1869, and the Democratic minority of the congressional investigating committee discounted testimony about Klan violence after that date as the work of spurious Klans. But the principal effect of the disbandment order was to free local dens from even the loose control that the Maxwell House organizational meeting, in April 1867, had been able to establish. Technically, perhaps, any Klan action after the disbandment was "bogus," but individual dens considered themselves genuine and acted, whenever they thought conditions warranted it, in the same way as in former times—except with increasing violence.

The testimony of Cornelius McBride is a good example of what the Democratic minority of the congressional committee dismissed as exaggerated: A native of Ireland, McBride had lived for three years in Cincinnati before moving to Mississippi, where he spent a year each in Chickasaw and Aktibbeha Counties. In the latter he taught a public school for Negroes in Sparta and also a white Sunday school. For six or seven months nothing happened, but during the last week of March 1871, students told him that the Klan was after him. He paid no attention. Then one night a dozen men came, with their faces disguised; they broke the windows of his bedroom and leveled guns at him. The leader shouted, "The God damned Yankee, come out here!" Hoping to escape, he jumped through one of the windows, but he was caught and beaten with pistol butts and sheathed knives. The Klansmen marched him into a nearby field. He refused to take off his night shirt, his only garment; they knocked him down and stripped him naked. His story continues:

Two of them held me down and one of them took a bundle of black-gum switches—a peculiar kind of stick, which stings and raises the flesh where it hits. . . . They said they were going to give me a hundred lashes each. One gave me a hundred; and then another gave me seventy-five. I asked them what I had done to merit such treatment. They said, "God damn you! don't you know that this is a white man's country?" I said the white people were satisfied with my conduct. They have shown it by selecting me to take charge of their Sunday school. They said, "Yes, damn you, that is the worst thing

Ku-Klux Mode of Torture.

These sketches of Klan methods of torture appeared in a pamphlet published in Hartford, Conn., in 1872. The pamphlet related the "Experience of a Northern man among the Ku Klux." *New York Public Library Picture Collection*

about it, having a nigger-teacher to teach the white school on Sunday."
I was fighting them all the time, as well as I could—kicking at them
and doing what I could—for the torture was horrible. I thought they
would kill me any way, when they got through whipping me, and
I begged them to shoot me. One of them came up to me with his
pistol and asked me if I wanted to be shot. I said, "Yes, I can't stand
this." The leader of the party said, "Shooting is too good for this fellow.
We will hang him when we get through whipping him." There was
only one man standing between me and the fence of the plantation.
I observed that and tried to gain his attention, for I was determined
to make an effort to escape. . . . I managed to partly raise myself
on my hand and knee. I then made a spring for this man, and struck
him as hard as I could. I do not know what part of his body I struck,
nor where he went; I know he disappeared, and I leaped the fence.
As I did so they swore terribly, and fired at me, and the shots went
over my head, scattering the leaves all around me. As I went across
the field they kept firing at me, and followed me a short distance.
. . . It was a very cold night, that night was.

McBride got to a friend's house where he spent the night. "The
next day I taught my school as usual." Friends, well armed, stood
by him; but he took the precaution of sleeping out in the woods.
Later he went to the county seat, Houston, and from there to the
governor's office in Jackson, and finally to the United States district
attorney, who took his affidavit and sent a federal marshal to Sparta
in the hope of making arrests. But the guilty men could not be
found.

McBride's stubborn refusal to quit even after being "ku-kluxed"
put him in a special class, a very small and select one. More often,
an initial warning was enough, as was true of four students at
the University of Alabama. The letters they received were saved
by a Professor Whitfield and were produced at the congressional
hearing, together with a dagger the Klan had left sticking into one
of the University doors.

DAVID SMITH: You have received one notice from us, and this shall
be the last. You nor no other damned son of a damned radical traitor
shall stay at our university. Leave here in less than ten days, for in
that time we shall visit the place and it will not be well for you to
be found out there. The State is ours, and so shall our university be.
Written by the secretary by order of the Klan.

SEAVEY: You have received one notice from us to leave. This is the last. We will be out in force in less than ten days, and it will not be good for you to be found out there. We are resolved it shall not be carried on under the present faculty. Some have been wise enough to take our warning. Do the same. The Klan.

CHARLES MUNCEL: You had better get back where you came from. We don't want any damned Yank at our colleges. In less than ten days we will come to see if you obey our warning. If not look out for hell, for, damn you, we will show you that you shall not stay, you nor no one else in that college. This is our first notice; let it be the last. The Klan, by the Secretary.

HORTON: They say you are of good democratic family. If you are, leave the university, and that quick. We don't intend that the concern shall run any longer. This is the second notice that you have received; you will get no other. We *will* have good southern men there or none. By order of the K.K.K.

After these letters were read and made a part of the record, this brief exchange took place:

Q. Did these students leave?
A. They left; they were smart enough for that.

Cornelius McBride, by this measure of smartness, was stupid enough to stay. By the time the last Southern state had regained its sovereignty in 1877, men like McBride had reduced the resistance to educating Negroes and, wherever no public schools had existed earlier, had introduced Southerners to the novelty of paying taxes to educate the young. The Klan had tried, and failed, to prevent the spread of public education, for the better elements in the South began to see that regional inferiority was related to the paucity of schools. But any such reflection, long after the event, is a privilege that was not available to the Northern teachers who did so much, in the aggregate, to promote education in the South.

The dismal record of Klan harassment of these teachers could be documented indefinitely, but two letters written by Alonzo Corliss late in 1869 will round out our picture of what it meant for a teacher to face the wrath of the Klan. The first was written from Company Shops (now Burlington) in Alamance County, North Carolina, on November 30:

Wm. E. Whiting, Esq.
> Dear Bro:
>> We are in trouble. Five men disguised in a Satanic garb, on the night of the 26th inst, dragged me from my bed and bore me roughly in double quick time 1½ miles to a thicket, whipped me unmercifully and left me to die. They demanded of me that I should cease "teaching niggers" and leave in ten days, or be treated worse. I wish to have money enough to come home, or to do what I think best, as the case develops.
>
> Please send me a check forthwith for ($75) seventy-five to use when I need it.
>
> I sent for some books, two months ago; if you have not sent them do not till I write again. I am not able to sit up yet. I shall never recover from all my injuries.
>
>> Truly your Brother
>> Alonzo B. Corliss

The second letter, dated December 13, was from Danville, just across the state line in Virginia. Corliss had tried, without success, to bring his assailants to justice:

Rev. E. P. Smith
> Dear Bro:
>> We are at liberty to choose and look for a place for ourselves for the balance of the year, to be under the control of the Friends of Philad'a.
>
> If there is any place in Va. or Md. which you intend to abandon or which you know to be vacant, please inform me immediately, or in ten days.
>
> We are well enough to teach. We have received the check, but do not think we shall use it but we feel better to have it in our pocket. I understand that you will allow us interest if we do not draw it.
>
> We will inform you when we are settled. When we left Co. Shops the soldiers took down a flag with this inscription. "Blood. Let the guilty beware. Corliss and the Negroes. Death. Don't touch. Hell." Two pistols and a large coffin were drawn upon it. We failed to convict the persons we arrested.
>
>> Truly yours
>> Alonzo B. Corliss

There were heroes in the South in those days, and they were not members of the Ku Klux Klan.

Chapter Seven

GEORGIA SCENES

General John B. Gordon, C.S.A., Grand Dragon of the Ku Klux Klan in Georgia, denied any knowledge of the Klan when he testified in 1871 before the congressional investigating committee. He admitted knowing about an·unnamed organization in his state and made it fairly clear that he had joined it and had even become its leader. But, as he said, "We never called it Ku Klux, and therefore I do not know anything about Ku Klux."

It was a familiar evasion, this use of some other name for the Klan just to enable its members to swear, without committing perjury, that they were not Klan members. Augustus Baldwin Longstreet might have enjoyed it if he hadn't died the year before; it had all the elements of trickery that he had recorded in his famous *Georgia Scenes,* written in 1835 before he began his illustrious career as college president, successively at Emory, Centenary, the University of Mississippi, and the University of North Carolina. But Longstreet had been an ardent advocate of Nullification as well as a frontier humorist, and, in addition, Reconstruction was hardly a time for broad humor of the sort that made him famous.

General Gordon was not trying to be amusing. He did not hesitate to tell the Congressmen why he thought the Klan—by whatever name—had been necessary. "The organization," he said, "was simply a brotherhood of the property-holders, the peaceable, law-abiding citizens of the state, for self-protection. The instinct of self-preservation prompted the organization. . . . We were afraid to have a public organization because we were afraid it would be construed at once, by the government in Washington, as an organization antagonistic to the government of the United States. It was therefore necessary, in order to protect our families from outrage and preserve our own lives, to have something we could regard as a brotherhood—a combination of the best men of the country to act purely in self-defense."

The Georgia Klan first came into public notice in March 1868, shortly after General Bedford Forrest, the Grand Wizard, paid a visit to Atlanta. Klan warnings began to appear in newspapers, and leading Radicals received hostile letters. Since General Gordon was the Democratic candidate for governor, it is hardly astonishing that most of the Klan's activities at this early stage were political.

Georgia had gone the way of other Southern states following the war. The first new legislature, meeting in Milledgeville in December 1865, passed eleven laws that comprised a Black Code to keep the freedmen subservient. Then, in familiar reaction, the federal government dictated a state governmental structure that recognized political equality for Negroes. Some leading whites urged their fellows to boycott elections as a means of protest. But 95,214 whites registered to vote in 1868, as compared with 93,457 Negroes. (In the total population, whites outnumbered Negroes by about five to four.) Less than 10,000 Georgians, incidentally, were disfranchised at that time, too few to have any significant effect on the election, for Gordon lost by a larger margin to his Republican opponent, Rufus B. Bullock. Born in New York, Bullock has sometimes been classed as a carpetbagger, but he had lived in Georgia for much of his life and had served in the Confederate Army, which of course enhanced his voter appeal.

The election also established a new state constitution enough in line with federal wishes to cause Congress to restore Georgia as a state in June 1868. A year later, however, Congress imposed military rule, largely because the new legislature refused to seat the elected Negroes—three in the Senate, twenty-nine in the House. Not even a decision by the state supreme court, in June 1869, that Negroes were eligible for public office could dissolve the resistance; Congress simply lost patience. When the Negro members were finally seated, two or three of them exhibited the kind of statesmanship that only Anglo-Saxons were supposed to be capable of; and this was one more source of irritation for the white supremacists.

The Klan had been quite active in the 1868 election, trying to get Negroes to vote Democratic or not at all; but obviously what had been done was not enough. Thirty-two Negroes elected to the legislature, not only voting on bills but introducing them, were thirty-two good reasons for greater Klan effort. The greater effort prompted greater countereffort by General A. H. Terry, in charge of the military district that included Georgia. This greater countereffort in turn touched off a round of condemnation by newspapers —for in Georgia as elsewhere in the South the press was almost exclusively Democratic. Some of the editorials were so abusive that Congress decided to investigate conditions in the state, especially the reported Klan violence. The editors now had a veritable field day of self-righteous indignation.

The process was an upward spiral, inevitable, predictable, as each side responded to the action of the other. A few editors in Georgia urged their readers to be calm; one of the most conciliatory was Henry W. Grady of the *Rome Southerner and Commercial.* "The eyes of the continent are on us," he wrote. "Remember, brothers, that the strength and power of any secret organization rests in the attribute of mystery and hidden force. . . . Every time you act you weaken your strength; then be quiet."

The congressional investigators set up hearings in Atlanta. They did not send for Grady, but they did insist on grilling the editor of a rival Rome paper, B. F. Sawyer, who had derided the investigation as a rotten concern worse than the Spanish Inquisition. He gave the Congressmen a hard time, remarking at one point that "if your committee was to trouble themselves to shear a pig they would get but little wool." As in the full-dress Klan investigation in Washington, it is a matter of opinion whether much wool was produced: to Klansmen and their defenders the stream of Radicals and Negro witnesses had nothing of importance to say—nothing, at least, that the newspaper editors could not airily dismiss.

One Georgia editor became embroiled in a Klan incident— Charles Wallace of the *Warrenton Clipper,* who was generally supposed to be Grand Cyclops of his local Klan den. He was personally at odds with a certain Dr. G. W. Darden who, he believed, had blackballed him for membership in a Masonic lodge. He published a "card" denouncing Darden in violent language, whereupon Darden loaded his double-barreled shotgun, met Wallace in the street, and shot him dead. Then, calmly, he surrendered himself to the sheriff, C. J. Norris, who locked him in a cell and prudently left town, taking the key with him. About two o'clock the next morning a group of Klansmen took Darden forcibly from the jail, gave him time to write a farewell note to his family, and shot him. A coroner's jury attributed his death to gunshot wounds at the hands of persons unknown to the jury.

Not long afterwards Sheriff Norris returned with a squad of soldiers and with the hope of collecting the reward of five thousand dollars announced by the governor for the arrest and conviction of each Klansman found guilty of taking part in Darden's murder. But the Klan was not without resources; it found a way to make it seem clear that the sheriff accepted a bribe in settlement of the affair. Governor Bullock, for his part, rather overdid his use of the murder to draw Northern attention to Klan violence. His enemies accused him of exaggerating the outrage as a smoke screen to hide the corrpution of his administration. Every Radical governor in the South sooner or later was charged with corruption; it was a favorite Klan device, part of its strategy of shifting as much blame as possible onto its enemies.

Assuming that Wallace *was* the local Grand Cyclops, getting rid of his murderer reflected the impulse of self-preservation that General Gordon considered a valid reason for the Klan's existence. More than half of the acts of violence reported from Georgia, however, were more closely related to the political struggle. Abram Colby's testimony is relevant. "After they had whipped me a long time, they said I had voted for Grant and Bullock. . . . They asked, 'Do you think you will ever vote another damned Radical ticket?' I said, 'I will not tell a lie.' They said, 'No, don't tell a lie.' Then I said, 'If there was an election to-morrow I would vote the Radical ticket.' I thought they would kill me anyway. Then they set in to whipping me again."

The Klan quite obviously supported the Democrats against the Republicans, and Klan action against a Democrat was rare. The Honorable Augustus R. Wright, former judge and member of Congress, was asked this question: "Have you ever known an instance in which the Ku-Klux committed an outrage upon a member of the Democratic party?" He replied, "I know of one instance. They whipped a white man for ku-kluxing without leave from the head man." Moments later he added, "They also whipped a white man who helped a negro in a fight. I think he voted the Democratic ticket."

Judge Wright, elsewhere in his testimony before the congressional investigating committee, described the killing of a Negro as he had heard of it from a young white client of his who had been unlucky enough to be caught and charged with the murder. "This negro," Wright said, "had done nothing wrong. He had just talked about the Ku-Klux—the fight he would make if they came after him." Such "big-mouth" talk being unforgivable in a Negro, several white youths, Klansmen or would-be Klansmen, hunted up the Negro at his home and while pretending to be federal soldiers, "got him to go with them to ku-klux the Ku-Klux, and having got him out, shot or stabbed him, I forget which. So this young man, my client, who was one of them, told me." Wright told the youth—he was only nineteen—that if he ever faced trial he would probably be found guilty, and advised him to leave the region. With money supplied by the boy's family, the judge bought him some clothes and a railroad ticket, and put him on a train.

In Wright's scale of values it is apparent that what most mattered was not the death of a Negro, or the question of bringing his killer to justice, but rather the safety of the young white who had admitted his guilt. But the long-continued violence seems to have engendered a certain callousness among a great many white Southerners. More than one witness from Georgia was quite explicit on the point. G. B. Burnet, who ran for Congress in 1870, said that the whipping and killing of Negroes had become so common in the state in the past two years "that it would take a right sharp case now to attract much attention." He described the Klan whipping of a Negro named Jourdan Ware:

The reason they gave for beating him was that he had made some insulting remarks to a white lady. He remarked "How d'ye do, sis?" or something of that kind, as the young lady passed down the road. Previous to that time he had borne the reputation of being a humble and obedient negro. He had a little farm, and was doing well and was comfortable, though in a neighborhood surrounded by the poorer class of white people, who did not like his residence there. I do not say whether he did or did not make the remark, though from my knowledge of him my opinion is that he did not.

Then Burnet told the story of Joe Kennedy, shot by the Klan for having married "a bright colored woman. The charge they had against Joe was that he had married this mulatto girl, and they did not intend that he should marry so white a woman as she was; and they beat her also for marrying so black a negro as he was." An ironic parallel to this judgment based on relative skin coloration occurred when the legislature refused to seat the elected Negro members: Four were so light-skinned that they were permitted to stay.

Jourdan Ware's relative success in life—he was "doing well and was comfortable"—was in itself a source of irritation to his Klan neighbors. Negroes existed to do the hard work for white men; independence was not something they should seek or achieve. Alfred Richardson was a prosperous Negro grocer in Clarke County. One day he received this message from the Klan, curiously worded in the third person: "They say you are making too much money, and they do not allow a nigger to rise that way; that you control all the colored votes, and they intend to break you up and run you off so they can control the balance." In Tatnall County, another prosperous Negro, Jerry Owens, had actually been driven off his land by the Klan. But this did not satisfy the Klansmen, who sent warnings to three of his Negro tenants:

ADAM STAFFORD: The object of this note is to inform you, that you must vacate Jerry Owens' place. He was run off and his house burnt, and now you are building and improving it. You have been informed once not to do it. Now for the last time, you must vacate that place in one month, or you will be visited and dealt with harshly. When you leave set fire to all the houses and fences. We will come to see you in 30 days if you don't leave.
Tatnall Co., Dec. 13th, 1870.

HENRY FRAZER: We see that you are building on Jerry Owens' place. You must stop at once and vacate in 30 days. When you leave set fire to all the buildings, as it will save us the trouble of doing so. Do it in 30 days; if you don't, when we come we will treat you harshly. So get out in 30 days or you will have to suffer the consequences.
Tatnall Co., Dec. 15th, 1870.

To THOMAS ALLEN (freedman): You are in great danger, you are going heedless with the Radicals and against the white population. . . . You are marked and watched closely by the K.K.K.
By order of the GRAND CYCLOPS.

Warnings such as these were often wondrously illustrated with coffins, skull and crossbones, daggers, nooses, crossed swords, and even sketches of Klansmen in their robes.

In Southern white theory, landownership was a privilege of the master race. Since the right to vote was historically restricted to owners of real estate, commonly fifty acres or more, if Negroes in any numbers were to acquire land they would pose a threat at the ballot box. But cupidity also seems to have been operative. J. R. Halliday of Georgia hinted broadly at this in his testimony: "I noticed that just about the time they (the negroes) got done laying by their crops, the Ku-Klux would be brought in and they would be run off so that they (the owners of the land) could take their crops."

In the words of H. D. Ingersoll of Gloucester, Massachusetts, who had been working since 1865 as general agent of a mining company in Sandsville, Georgia, "They do not generally use any harsher means than will accomplish their purpose." Men like Ingersoll, incidentally, never had any trouble with the Klan, and for this reason they may never have fully appreciated the Southern hostility to most other Northerners—schoolteachers, soldiers, agents of the Freedmen's Bureau. But it is also possible that Ingersoll had developed, after five years, the general callousness regarding violence. A former Georgia governor, after giving the particulars of seven murders by Klansmen, was asked about whippings. "Well," he answered, "I have heard of some, but I paid so little attention to them— that was a matter of no importance—that I do not believe I could undertake to state anything of the sort. Unless a murder was committed it was not considered much at all."

Early and late in the congressional investigation the names of fifty-two men killed by the Klan in Georgia were introduced. Most of the victims were shot or hanged; one was burned to death. Twenty-two other Klan murders were reported, with time and place but without the names of the victims. How many other men and women the Klan killed in Georgia in the five years after the war is impossible to determine. On the record, Georgia, with seventy-four Klan killings cited in the investigation, looked a little better than Alabama, 109.

Despite such figures, and despite such visual evidence as backs crisscrossed with the raw welts left from whippings, General Forrest, when he stood up to testify, reiterated that the Klan's purpose was self-protection. "The first obligation they took, if I recollect it aright, was to abide by and obey the law of the country; to protect the weak; to protect the women and children; obligating themselves to stand by one another in case of insurrection, or anything of that sort." The major flaw in this reasoning is that the Klan had its own measure of what constituted "anything of that sort." To give Forrest his due, however, he had officially declared the dissolution of the Klan in the only general order he ever issued as Grand Wizard; he could always argue, and some people will no doubt always believe, that subsequent violence was not really the work of the Klan, since technically it no longer existed.

But genuine or spurious, the Klan was the instrument for implementing the old Southern adage that black men had no rights which white men were bound to respect. The saga of Perry Jeffers may be taken as illustration. With his wife and seven sons he was living, in 1868, on the Brinkley plantation near Camac in Warren County. They had the effrontery to be prosperous: whites in that part of Georgia complained that the family had too much stock, too much money, and were entirely too independent. They were already well ahead of some of their white neighbors; for one thing, they had excellent credit with merchants in Augusta. Mr. Brinkley, who had owned the family during slavery, treated them well and appreciated their industry, since it meant a steady income for him as landlord. But Mr. Brinkley wasn't one of the neighbors being outdistanced by the Jeffers.

Warned that the Klan was threatening to "visit" their home one night, the family took the precaution of posting a guard. On a Thursday night in November 1868, the son whose turn it was to be awake saw, through a chink in the logs, several white-robed figures. He quickly woke the rest of the family. Under the circumstances it was unwise for the Jeffers sons to panic, but one of them did; he fired toward the ghostly visitors, and had the misfortune to kill one.

Such audacity had never been heard of—Negroes defending their homes, and using guns. When General Gordon and General Forrest and other Klan spokesmen talked about self-defense, they thought of it as one of the sacred privileges of white men. The Klan decreed that all the male members of the Jeffers family must die. On Friday and Saturday nights hooded figures prowled around the house, somewhat warily, taking no chances of a second fatal shot. But Jeffers and his grown sons had fled, fully aware that their lives were forfeit under the Black Code tradition.

By Sunday night the Klansmen had grown bolder; they forced their way into the house and dragged out the youngest son and his mother. The son they shot; the mother they hanged to a tree with a bed cord. Then they piled furniture atop the body of the boy and set it afire; cremation was one way of getting rid of evidence. Mr. Brinkley, hearing the shot, hurried to the scene and cut down the mother before she was dead; he also foiled the Klan by dragging the boy's half-burned body out into the open. Dr. Darden came from near-by Warrenton to conduct an inquest, but the Klan made him desist. "This thing has gone far enough," he was told; "it must be closed up." Four months later Dr. Darden was himself killed by the Klan, as reported earlier.

Jeffers and his older sons had found sanctuary in the home of Sheriff Norris. But with Klan frenzy growing, it seemed prudent for them to be moved across the state line into South Carolina. On November 9 they were put on a train in the special care of the conductor. At Dearing, eighteen miles from Camac, Klan members boarded the train, took the refugees outside, and shot them; the Klansmen didn't even bother to wear disguises. One son managed to escape. Justice, the Klan variety, had been done in elementary Klan arithmetic: a Negro and his five sons in exchange for one white man whom one of those sons had shot and killed in defense of his home.

Another crime meriting Klan punishment was the accidental witnessing of a Klan murder. Joe and Mary Brown of White County were, like the Jeffers family, industrious and thrifty. In the spring of 1869 they found a cabin and forty acres that pleased them, and they were imprudent enough to outbid a white man for the property by twenty dollars. They might have known it would be remembered and held against them. Nothing might have come of it, however, if Mary had not been passing through a field just when two white men with blackened faces waylaid and killed a federal marshal named Cason. She recognized both men despite their disguise, and she was sure that they had recognized her too. She was particularly careful not to whisper a word to anybody about what she had seen, but the Klansmen apparently could not be sure of her. A planter's wife sounded her out, naming the men and asking whether she had told about them. No amount of denying seemed to count. A day or two later word came that she and her family would have to move away. But they stayed.

Several nights later the Klan arrived, routed out the household, stripped both Joe and Mary, and dragged them naked about their yard. Mary asked why and got another question for an answer: who was it she was "going down to Atlanta to swear against?" "Nobody," she answered. They next pulled her up by a trace-chain about her neck, gave her thirty lashes, and told her to name the two men she had seen down by the river that day. She gave the names, but in-

[116]

sisted she had never told anybody. They refused to believe her. They knocked her down with a pistol, beat her again with hickory switches, and choked her with the log-chain until she lost consciousness. Some of the men—there were about thirty in the party—objected to killing her. She was revived by a bucketful of water thrown over her and was permitted to crawl away. Later she said, "I shook like an ague for four days."

Joe's turn came. As his mother told the story:

> They beat him with long sticks and wore out a long fishing pole on him. They had him down, and put a chain on his neck, and dragged him about a good deal. Joe said, "I ain't done anything, gentlemen; what are you abusing me for?" They said, "We will kill you, God damn you. You shall not live here." He said, "I have bought my land, and got my guarantee title for it; why should I be abused in this way?" They said, "We will give you ten days to leave, and then, God damn you, we will burn your house down over you, if you don't go away."

The mother and the rest of the household were next given the Klan treatment. They were not whipped quite so severely as Joe and Mary, but the female members—the old mother, her daughter Rachel, a young girl named Mary Neal, and the even younger daughter of Joe and Mary—were all stripped and systematically raped in the dim light of the approaching summer morning. Thus did the peaceable, law-abiding citizens, the best men of the country, carry out the Klan goal of self-preservation.

To all such stories told to the congressional investigating committee, the Democratic minority had two stock answers: first, that they were grossly exaggerated, if not pure invention, and second, that Klan violence had been precipitated by the steps taken by the Radicals to humiliate the Southern whites and keep the South prostrate, impoverished, and powerless. As one Klan warning stated the case, "We are forced by force to use FORCE." The thirteenth volume of the *Ku-Klux Reports* contains both the majority and the minority conclusions of the committee, as is proper of all such investigations; and readers could choose which of the two to accept. In effect, then, for men and women then living and strongly partisan, the entire investigation was inconclusive, because the opposing conclusions, both bearing the authority of official publication, canceled each other out. Historians, in the decades since, have followed the lead of contemporary readers, selecting whatever details best suited their hypotheses; and it is sadly evident that the eminent historians of the early days of this century sympathized with the South and leaned more on the minority conclusion. A later generation, one less prone to accept the notion that Negroes are congenitally unable to distinguish between truth and invention, and the equally dubious notion that all Northerners in the South during Reconstruction were intent on lining their own pockets while humiliating Southern whites, can read the testimony with something closer to objectivity.

Of numerous other incidents reported from Georgia, one firsthand account may be given, so circumstantial in its detail that it is hard to imagine its being dismissed as invention. The narrator is Henry Lowther of Wilkinson County, who had incurred the hostility of his white neighbors in two ways: leadership of the local Republican Party, and enough astuteness in business to acquire considerable property. The Klan threatened him often, and on several occasions broke into his house. He was finally arrested on a charge of conspiracy and jailed. One cold autumn night the Klan took him from his cell, clad only in a shirt, and mutilated him horribly. Faint with loss of blood and in great pain he staggered back to town.

The first man's house I got to was the jailer's. I called him up and asked him to go to the house and get my clothes. He said he could not; I said, "You *must;* I am naked and nearly frozen to death." That was about three o'clock in the night. He had a light in the house, and there was a party of men standing in the door. I told him I wanted him to come out and give me some attention. He said he would not come. I could hardly walk then. I went on about ten steps further and I met the jailer's son-in-law. I asked him to go and get my clothes; and he said "No," and told me to go and lie down. I went right on and got up to a store; there were a great many men sitting along on the store piazza. I knew some of them, but I did not look at them much. They asked me what I wanted; I said I wanted a doctor. They told me to go on and lie down. I had then to stop and hold on to the side of the house to keep from falling. I staid there a few minutes and then went to the doctor's house, about a quarter of a mile, and called him aloud twice. He did not answer me. The next thing I knew I was lying on the sidewalk in the street—seemed to have just waked up out of sleep. I thought to myself, "Did I lie down and go to sleep?" I wanted some water; I had to go about a quarter of a mile to get some water. I was getting out of breath, but the water helped considerably. I went to a house about fifty yards further; I called to a colored woman to wake my wife up; she was in town. I happened to find my son there, and he went back for the doctor. When he got there, the doctor answered the first time he called him. The reason he did not answer me was that he was off on this raid. I asked the doctor where he was when I was at his house, and he said he was asleep. I said, "I was at your house." The men kept coming in and saying to me that I did not get to the doctor's house, and I said I did. After two or three times I took the hint, and said nothing more about that. But I told my son next morning to go there and see if there was not a large puddle of blood at the gate. They would not let him go. But some colored women came to see me and told me that the blood was all over town—at the doctor's gate and everywhere else. I was running a stream all the time I was trying to find the doctor, and I thought I would bleed to death.

It is probable that the Klansmen also expected him to die and were disconcerted when he made it back to town. The Klan was not always as efficient as it prided itself on being. Dead men could tell no tales, but some of the most horrifying accounts of torture and mutilation were given by men, the lucky few, who were left for dead but did not die.

Former Congressman Wright no doubt spoke for most of his fellow white Georgians when, in the course of his testimony, he told the committee what he thought about giving the vote to the freedmen. "We were very much dissatisfied with that part of the constitution. I wish I could put a hundred thousand negro voters in Massachusetts and let them feel it as we do." What it was he wished the New Englanders could feel he did not say; but what he could probably not have begun to understand was that the people of Massachusetts would have been dismayed by the sudden transplantation of a hundred thousand Georgians of any color. Massachusetts had the oldest public school law in the country, dating back to 1657; Georgia had no public schools at all until December 1864, when General Sherman and Secretary of War Stanton met with Negro leaders in Savannah and decided to set up a federally supported school system. Five hundred pupils were enrolled in that city by the end of the next year. The Reconstruction legislature passed the first public school law in 1870, and schools were begun in the summer of 1871. Then they closed for lack of funds and did not reopen for good until 1873.

Clara Barton, founder of the American Red Cross, went to the South in 1865, commissioned by President Lincoln to search for missing soldiers and to identify graves of unknowns. At Andersonville, Georgia, in 1866 she examined a young Negro girl about eighteen years old. "I found across her back twelve lashes or gashes, partly healed and partly not, some of them cut into the bone. She must have been whipped with a lash half as large as my little finger—it may have been larger; and one of these lashes was from eight to ten inches in length; and the flesh had been cut completely out most of the way. It had been a curling whip; it had curled around her

Thomas Nast in *Harper's Weekly*, October 24, 1874.

arms, cut inside the arm, over the back, and the same on the other side . . . she could not bear her clothing on her at that time, except thrown loosely over her shoulders." She had been gagged by her white employer, thrown on her face, and given the lashing; when her husband found her, she was in "a gore of blood." Her offense was that, in the last months of pregnancy, she had proved unable to do the task of spinning which was given her.

This wanton act of cruelty was not done by the Klan; white Georgians who subscribed to the adage that black men had no rights which white men were bound to respect did not wait for the Klan to do their dirty work. It seems reasonable to suspect that the Klan was blamed for a good many crimes it did not commit, many of them of just such a private nature as the one Clara Barton reported. If the Klan had never been organized, we may conjecture, there might have been just as much violence in the South, given the traditional relationship between the races and the provocations of defeat in war, the freeing of the slaves, and the federal effort of Reconstruction.

From all the evidence, in any event, Klan activity in Georgia was of relatively short duration. By 1871 most of the state's newspapers were following the lead of the Augusta *Constitutionalist* in urging the whites to abandon the Klan and its methods. "In the absence of the voice of protest," the editor wrote, "it has been assumed that these secret organizations possessed the approbation of society. . . . The legislature should speak out, by joint resolutions, condemning in the strongest language secret organizations and midnight mobs, and exhort the people to bring to bear every legal and moral influence for the vindication of the peace, good order and dignity of the state." Not to take such action would put Georgia in a poor position to oppose "the unconstitutional Ku Kluxism of the Congress of the United States."

This editorial campaign and the waning of Klan activity that it promoted did not mean that all Georgians repudiated the Klan or subsequently felt guilty about taking part in its work or supporting it. John C. Reed, in 1905, summarized the Klan's career in Georgia in a book entitled *The Brothers' War*, not with shame but with pride. When in 1867 the freedmen, intoxicated by the novelty of freedom, imperiled decent life, Reed wrote, the Klan organized "in the twinkling of an eye. It mustered, not assassins, thugs, and cut-throats, as has been alleged, but the choicest Southern manhood. Every good woman knew that the order was now the solitary defense of her purity, and she consecrated it with all-availing prayers." Mrs. Perry Jeffers and Mary Brown would hardly have recognized the Klansmen as Reed pictured them.

The election of 1870, Reed continued, was a "decisive deliverance from the most monstrous and horrible misrule recorded among Anglo-Saxons," and he insisted that most of the credit belonged to the Klan. As for himself, he did not hesitate to take some of the credit, personally. "I shall always remember with pride my service in the famous 8th Georgia Volunteers," he concluded. "But I am prouder of my career in the Ku Klux Klan."

Chapter Eight
FRICTION
IN FLORIDA

Northern teachers sent into the South during Reconstruction were shocked by the shabbiness, the poverty, the disorder, and the dirt in the towns where they taught. It was a form of education in regional differences. The aristocratic agrarian economy was simply not conducive to the growth of such neat, attractive towns as in the North and West, where the wealth was not drained off to build plantation mansions outside the towns. Southerners of the same middle class, if they had had occasion to visit the North, might have been equally shocked by the absence of fine country estates. The Northern teachers, social pariahs that they were, were never invited to the Southern mansions and consequently could not describe them in their letters home.

It was partly, of course, a matter of time: Much of the South, once one left the four states—Virginia, North and South Carolina, and Georgia—that comprised the southern end of the original chain of thirteen was of more recent development than any of the Northern states and those to the west as far as the Mississippi. Plantations in what was called the Black Belt, the prime cotton-producing area

[123]

from Georgia across Alabama and Mississippi to Arkansas and Texas, were commonly managed by overseers for absentee owners; and neither the overseers nor the owners felt any great interest in the towns that sprang up as banking and shopping centers, and for the necessary county government.

The Southern state closest to the condition of a frontier in 1865 was Florida. Prince Achille Murat, Napoleon's nephew and the most famous resident in the history of Florida's capital city, in 1827 warned Ralph Waldo Emerson not to go there. Tallahassee was only three years old, and it was a raw and rather dangerous town to visit. Whitelaw Reid, young assistant editor of the New York *Tribune,* inspected the city in 1865, just after the end of the Civil War, and found little good to report. The things that most impressed him were the unpretentious public buildings, the poor and neglected stores and private dwellings, and the wretched sidewalks. Yet Leon County, which Tallahassee served as county seat, was the second most populous in the state, with 15,236 residents in 1870. And Union armies could not be blamed for the town's crude appearance, for this was the one Southern state capital whose capture Union strategists did not consider essential.

Of the thirty-nine Florida counties with any population at all, Leon was one of eight in which Negroes outnumbered the whites. In Tallahassee, there were said to be seven Negroes for every white; and Negro parades through the heart of the city were common events. Perhaps the very numerical advantage of the Negroes prevented conflict; Leon had a much better record than neighboring counties. Fear of racial disturbances prompted the formation of a Young Men's Democratic Club, well-armed and well-known to the freedmen. Its leader, Joe Williams, steadfastly denied that the Club was a branch of the Ku Klux Klan, but its purpose was the same as the Klan's—to keep the freedmen under control. Since Tallahassee was the capital, the Club had a special interest in harassing any Negro who succeeded in being elected to state office.

Historians of Florida, until recently, have followed the regional practice of insisting that Negroes dominated the state government during Reconstruction. In no Southern state was this ever true; it is only part of the carefully elaborated case against the whole Radical program. Fear of just such an eventuality, indeed, was one of the principal motives for Klan activity. If Negroes had continued to enjoy the privilege of voting, the time might well have come, in states where Negroes outnumbered whites, when Negroes would have held all the top offices; but the Klan saw to it that that time never did come.

Klan-like thinking, which includes the sincere belief that Negroes are incapable of any important responsibility, is immune to evidence that any of the few Negroes who did hold high positions were superior men. But certain Negroes who reached places of importance in Florida politics cannot be dismissed by any rational judgment. Far from crippling the state, or retarding its progress, or making the state government a sink of corruption, they must be credited, from objective study of the evidence, with making important contributions, despite whatever the Klan wanted the future to believe.

Two outstanding Negroes may serve as examples. One was the only Negro Florida ever sent to Congress, Josiah Walls; the second was Jonathan Gibbs, who served as Secretary of State under one Reconstruction governor and as superintendent of public instruction under his successor. It might be difficult to find any two white men who have done more for the state.

Gibbs was neither a native nor a freedman; he might be called a "Negro carpetbagger," if such a term were ever used. He was born in Philadelphia about 1827, the son of a Methodist preacher who died when the boy was four years old. Somewhat later, Jonathan was apprenticed to a carpenter, and he followed this trade until he was twenty-one. By then he had become a Presbyterian, and he so impressed everybody who knew him that the Presbyterian Assembly provided him with the money to attend Dartmouth College. He studied the standard curriculum of the period: Latin, Greek, rhetoric, mathematics, morals, and natural philosophy—the makings of a gentleman and of the kind of politician who could, and in those days often did, impress his auditors with Latin and Greek quotations. After graduating from Dartmouth, Gibbs attended the Princeton Theological Seminary for two years. He began active preaching in Troy, New York, moved to his second pastorate in Philadelphia, and, soon after the end of the Civil War, was sent as a Presbyterian missionary to North Carolina, where he not only preached but organized a school for freedmen. In 1867 he was transferred to Florida.

At the constitutional convention that met in January 1868, Gibbs was the outstanding Negro delegate and, some observers thought, superior to most of the whites. The Tallahassee *Sentinel* described him as "active in body and intellect, well educated, and an orator by nature, not a roarer but a convincing, argumentative, pleasant speaker: in this respect the most talented man in the Convention." The Jacksonville *Florida Union* called him a good example of what education could do for his race, adding that he was a man of "pleasing and courteous address." He was of course aligned with the Radicals at the convention, but he showed considerable independence, on occasion openly opposing other delegates of his own party. He stated that his purpose was the creation of a constitution that would protect the rights of both Negroes and property owners.

The strong impression he made at the convention prompted Harrison Reed, the first governor elected under the new constitution, to nominate him for Secretary of State. But Reed had made a slight mistake: He had given Gibbs' first name as John when he sought Senate confirmation and so he decided to withdraw the nomination. George Alden, a white Unionist, was appointed instead. Before the end of 1868, however, Alden resigned to join in an attempt to impeach Reed—the first of three such attempts, all unsuccessful. Reed appointed Gibbs to the vacancy. Gibbs proved an excellent choice; he was able to work harmoniously with other state officials, some of whom were ex-Confederate officers. He also rose above partisanship, sometimes being criticized by his fellow Republicans for his impartiality. The *Weekly Floridian,* issued in Tallahassee and strongly Democratic, bitterly protested a "legal advertisement law" that seemed to subsidize Republican newspapers and to disqualify their Democratic rivals; but the editor commended Gibbs for softening this law's effect. "The harsh operations of the law were 'considerably mollified' by the designation of a number of Democratic journals as 'official papers.' "

But Gibbs was a Negro, a fact that blinded the local Klansmen to all his virtues. On one occasion his brother, Mifflin Gibbs, a lawyer in Little Rock, Arkansas, visited Tallahassee and was astonished to find "considerable of an arsenal" in the attic where Gibbs slept. He slept there not because rooms lower in the house were uncomfortable, but because the attic was the easiest to defend. The Klan harassed all the Radical members of the state cabinet, but Gibbs more than any other. Anybody, white or black, who is on the receiving end of repeated death threats is likely to take certain precautions.

Reed's term as governor ended at the close of 1872. His successor, Ossian B. Hart, named Gibbs as state superintendent of public instruction. Influential Negroes, it has been suggested, threatened to desert the Republican Party if no Negro were given a cabinet post; and Gibbs was easily the most capable and experienced candidate. Once again he justified his appointment. Few men who have held this office have done more than he did to advance education, and none has faced greater opposition. White Floridians shared the general Southern opposition to education of any sort but especially the novelty of schools for Negroes. Being taxed to support such schools was another novelty they resented. Gibbs proved adept in the kind of diplomacy needed to overcome the opposition. During his superintendency, 1872 to 1874, pupil enrollment increased from 18,000 to 32,000, and expenditures rose from $101,000 to $189,000.

Gibbs was also able to make a start toward uniform textbooks in elementary and secondary schools. A harder problem, one nobody could have solved in that period, was finding enough qualified teachers. But his most important contribution was to the state's higher education. As president, ex officio, of the board of trustees for a proposed agricultural college, he developed the procedures for securing funds under the Morrill Land-Grant Act.

On August 14, 1874, Gibbs died, just a few hours after addressing a Republican meeting in Tallahassee. He was forty-seven years old. His brother, in an autobiography written many years later, attributed his death to apoplexy, but at the time there were rumors that he had been poisoned. The newspapers of the state lamented his passing, stressing the loss of one of the finest public servants Florida had ever known—which was no exaggeration. The Klan did not join in the lamentation; for true Klansmen, Gibbs was not so much Public Servant No. 1 as Public Enemy No. 1. The Klan estimate, naturally, has survived.

Congressman Walls was also an outsider, though he was at least Southern-born—in Winchester, Virginia. When the Civil War began, he was forced to surrender his trade as a baker and join a Confederate artillery unit as a servant. In May 1862, he was taken prisoner at Yorktown; but soon after that he was sent to Harrisburg to attend school. Later, as an enlisted man in a Negro regiment, he rose to the rank of sergeant-major and artillery instructor. Mustered out in Florida in 1865, he turned to farming in Alachua County.

Like Gibbs, Walls was a delegate to the state constitutional convention in 1868 and subsequently was elected to the legislature, first to the House and then to the Senate. In the 1870 election he seemed a logical choice for Congress. His Conservative opponent, a white man named Niblack, challenged the count in a court action and eventually won his suit—but only after Walls had served in Washington for more than a year. In 1872 Walls was reelected and served out his term, but after being declared the winner in the 1874 election he was again unseated after serving most of his term. Few other members of Congress have ever equaled his record of being elected three times and unseated twice.

During the period when Walls did sit in the House of Representatives, as Florida's only member, he proved himself one of the greatest boosters of his state—a state with a long and glorious record of boosters. Most of the fifty-one bills he introduced were directly related to benefits for Florida—harbor improvements, deeper channels in navigable rivers, construction of a railroad and of such federal buildings as post offices and custom houses, and for protection of the new citrus industry. On one occasion he moved to transfer a million acres of public land to the trustees of the state agricultural school; but he had to settle for 90,000, a mere 140 square miles.

On only one occasion did Walls speak in Congress about the race question. A member from Georgia had argued against federal aid to education, and Walls remarked that such opposition reflected not so much a defense of states' rights as a typical Southern white resentment over schools for freedmen. While he still had the floor, Walls attacked the notion that Negroes were innately incapable of being educated.

But most of the time Walls acted as if there was no racial division in Florida. He actively helped ex-Confederates remove their political disabilities, and he appointed to West Point the son of an ex-governor who was notoriously opposed to Negro voting and office-holding. What has been called the restoration of local sovereignty to Florida in 1877, but with better logic might be called the restoration of white supremacy, brought an end to Walls's career in Congress—and to the very notion of a Negro being elected to that body. The conspicuous success of his career in Congress, including his aid to former Confederates, lends to the restoration a certain irony of a sort lost on the Klan.

Another kind of irony emanates from a book published in 1888 and widely known, *Carpetbag Rule in Florida.* Attributed to John Wallace, a Negro who served for a time as state senator from Leon County, it was almost certainly written by somebody else, or, if Wallace actually was the author, he wrote what he knew was not altogether true for some kind of consideration. Gibbs or Walls might have written such a book, but Wallace was virtually illiterate—a good example, in fact, of the illiterate Negro legislator so often cited by older historians as the bane of the South. In his preface Wallace wrote that he "had no education while a slave, and never had the benefit of any school before or since he was discharged from the army." (Like Walls, he had served in a Negro regiment.) He went on to say that what knowledge he had of letters was acquired "from constant study at night"; but even this he had to limit because physicians said he was in danger of going blind. But the style, as anyone who has graded student themes for years could instantly judge, betrays an advanced mastery of rhetoric.

The final paragraph of the preface explains why this book has been popular with defenders of the classical Southern interpretation of history, and, though somewhat lengthy, it deserves quotation:

> The design of this work is to correct the settled and erroneous impression that has gone out to the world that the former slaves, when enfranchised, had no conception of good government, and therefore their chief ambition was corruption and plunder; to prove that, al-

though they had been for more than two hundred years deprived of that training calculated to fit a people for citizenship of a great republic like ours, yet their constant contact with a more enlightened race, though in the position of slaves, would have made them better citizens and more honest legislators if they had not been contaminated by strange white men who represented themselves to them as their saviours; that the laws of the State, passed with reference to the colored people in 1865, were not enacted as a whole to be enforced, but to deter the colored people from revenging any real or fancied wrongs that cruel masters may have inflicted while they were slaves; that these laws and the secret leagues, riveted the former slaves to these strangers, who explained them to be tenfold worse than they were; that it was white men, and not colored men, who originated corruption and enriched themselves from the earnings of the people of the State from the year 1868 to 1877; that the loss of the State to the National Republican Party was not due to any unfaithfulness of the colored people to that party, but to the corruption of these strange white leaders termed 'carpet baggers'; that the colored people have done as well as any other people could have done under the same circumstances, if not better. This work is further intended to prove that notwithstanding the blunders of the ex-slaveholder towards the colored people, the deception and betrayal by the carpet baggers of the colored people into the hands of their former masters, yet they, like the thunder-riven oak, have defied the storm which has now spent its terrific force, and like a caravan of determined pioneers cutting out highways in a new country, the Negro is laying the foundation for a civilization that shall be fully equal in every respect to that of any other race or people; and that the ascendancy of the Democratic party to the State government in 1877, has proved a blessing in disguise to the colored people of Florida.

It was masterly strategy, getting an "Uncle Tom" to write such a blanket endorsement of the Democrats as the Negroes' true friends—if Wallace did write it. The inclusion of numerous documents, proclamations, and other official records added impressive support to the thesis that the state, during Reconstruction, was systematically and deliberately mismanaged by "these strange white leaders termed 'carpet baggers.'" The extensive use of figurative language made the book interesting, too. Governor Reed, for example, is reported as commencing a political counterattack "by first using his pruning-hook in his Cabinet. He beheaded Alden and appointed Jonathan Gibbs, colored, as Secretary of State." Then, a page later, "Secret watchers kept on the track of Gleason and Alden until Reed could sharpen his knife for the decapitation of Gleason [the lieutenant-governor, who was conspiring to oust Reed and take his place]."

The volume, with its 444 pages, builds up an elaborate account of the graft in Florida's government during Reconstruction—an account that is still generally accepted as an indictment of the Radicals and as proof of both their deliberate misgovernment and their exploitation of Negroes. Democrats, the reader is invited to believe, would have managed better—always a dubious hypothesis about any party not in control. The Klan had fought to make Florida safe for the Democrats, and this book, published eleven years after the Democrats did regain control, confirms the necessity of maintaining the Democratic Party in power lest a new regime reintroduce the Reconstruction corruption.

An impartial reader would want to know several things, however. He would want to know whether Democratic (meaning all-white) administrations in Florida, before and since Reconstruction, have been in fact less corrupt. He would want to know whether the graft in Florida under the Radical rule was worse than in other states during that period of postwar readjustment. He would bring up references to the Canal Ring in New York, which Governor Tilden broke up, and to such other memorable scandals as the Crédit Mobilier, the Tweed jobbery in New York City, and the exposure of all of Grant's cabinet, except Hamilton Fish, as high-level grafters.

Wallace defends the Negro members of the Florida legislature in a curious way. They stole, he admits, because white men—Radicals, of course, and not Democrats—taught them to. At the time they were elected, they knew nothing about "stealing by legislation," but white men quickly taught them how. By inference, Negroes should never again be exposed to such temptation; white men are too clever, in their innate superiority, and Negroes are only too readily duped by unscrupulous whites. Recent research has revealed, however, that the kind of corruption the Klan insisted it was seeking to reduce or prevent by keeping Negroes from running for office was almost nonexistent in Florida during Reconstruction. The enormity of graft under the Radicals is a gross exaggeration that was used by the local whites to justify their political warfare against the Radicals and also to justify their use of Klan violence to make the state safe for the Democrats. The fiction has been kept alive by state historians betrayed by their own regional conditioning to wish to believe it; and it is now so firmly established that the revisionists face a formidable barrier in their efforts to demolish it.

Klan violence was justified, according to the white conservatives and their historian-defenders, by the extent of the graft. As elsewhere in the South, the violence itself was condemned by many of the "better people," though not by all, but it was held to have been the only means of turning out the Radical rascals and their Negro dupes. What the historians have not thought it necessary to report adequately is that violence was endemic in Florida before a single Radical appeared, and before a single Negro voted or ran for office. The tendency to violence, indeed, may still be noticed in the older parts of the state, long after its frontier condition can be cited as a reason. Negroes and Unionists were systematically repressed before the Civil War. The Klan "habit" was well established in Florida before the Klan was invented. Bodies of "regulators" who had been active before the war served as nuclei for Klan dens afterwards. The most obvious difference, as far as overt behavior is concerned, is that before the war whites and Negroes were about equally victimized, while after Emancipation the Negroes were the special targets of organized hatred.

Slavery, for all its disadvantages, had been a kind of protection; as long as a Negro was somebody's property, his owner had an interest in his remaining alive and in good health. But once a given Negro was his own man, he could not rely on any such economic consideration. Emancipation opened the way for poor whites, who had always hated the Negroes, to assault them on often the flimsiest of provocations, or on none at all. Colonel J. T. Sprague, federal commander of the District of Florida, reported in December 1865, that the state for some time had lacked the power to prevent white violence toward Negroes. Even with federal troops on hand, murders were committed frequently and were not punished, partly because witnesses feared reprisals if they told what they had seen.

Underprivileged whites saw freedmen as rivals for whatever jobs there were, and as early as December 1865 they began to drive the

Negroes away from their work, sometimes with a verbal warning, sometimes adding a whipping to make the warning stick. The first postwar constitution, as elsewhere in the South, restored the ante-bellum restrictions on free Negroes and extended them to all the freedmen. But this constitution was set aside, and the 1868 constitution, formed under close federal supervision, made it obvious that state law could no longer be invoked to keep the Negro subordinate. Quite the reverse: Negroes seemed to be specifically favored over whites, since some whites were still unable to vote bcause of their wartime activities. Everything favored the rapid development of the Klan and of Klan-like groups, whatcvcr thcir namcs, operating outside the law and, in their own view, above the law.

One member of the Young Men's Democratic Club in Leon County, in his testimony before the congressional investigating committee in 1871, exhibited a copy of the Club's constitution. It bore a close similarity to the Klan constitution. This man reported that when he joined the Club hc supposed it *was* the Klan. He insisted, moreover, that the best white men in the county were members; riffraff were not welcome.

Most Klansmen in Florida were not quite so candid, though some of them relaxed in later years. Francis Fleming, governor from 1889 to 1893, somewhat later made a reference to the Klan as having added "a bloody chapter" to the state's history; what he was quite willing to recall as an old man showed just how much Jonathan Gibbs and Congressman Walls had to put up with during Reconstruction.

Fleming, in a typed memoir which is now among the papers of the Florida Historical Society, spoke frankly about the Klan violence. One particularly memorable incident was the Klan's method of avenging the murder of a white man in Ocala. All the Negroes alleged to be guilty were put to death as a matter of course, but the body of one of them was boiled in a sugar boiler to remove the flesh, and his skeleton, wired by an ex-Confederate surgeon, "swung for months from a tall pine at a lonely cross-roads near Ocala as a warning of the fate of other evildoers." The Klansmen who took part in this act of vengeance obviously did not include themselves among the evildoers.

Another member of the Klan in Florida, W. S. Simkins, later became a professor of law at the University of Texas. In 1916, in an article that he published, he boasted of the Klan's success and spoke frankly about his own participation. On one occasion he beat a freedman with a barrel stave and went scot-free simply because people knew that he *was* a Klansman; nobody wanted to invite the wrath of the Klan by reporting the incident.

The Florida Klan waged a virtual open war against the Radicals, both white and Negro, but killed Negro Radicals more often than white. A mere vote for the Republican ticket was often enough to earn a punishment. In Columbia County, which to this day is a stronghold of white supremacy, at least seven Negro Republicans were killed by 1871. The county's state senator, Dr. E. G. Johnson, was eliminated in 1875. Since at the moment Democrats and Republicans were evenly divided, his death gave the Democrats a majority of one in the senate. As one white conservative put it, "Death makes way for liberty."

Editors in some states deplored the killing while arguing that the Klan was necessary. Some Florida editors were less mealymouthed. "Give Way, Carpetbaggers" and "Death to the Scoundrels" were two inflammatory headlines that appeared in the Gainesville *New Era*. The Monticello *Advertiser* suggested editorially, "Let us remove them now, peacefully if we can, forcibly if we must."

The peaceful measures must have proved unsatisfactory, for, in proportion to population, "the tadpole of a state" led the South in the number of Klan killings. In the three years from 1868 to 1871, eight counties yielded an estimated 235 deaths by violence. There may have been more; this was the count of Jonathan Gibbs, known for his official cautiousness. By his count, Lafayette County had four murders, Hamilton nine, Alachua and Columbia sixteen each, Madison twenty, and Jackson 153. This last astonishing figure is the score for what has been called the "Jackson County War." It was not so much a war as a protracted hunting down of Radicals.

Some older historians have averred that the Klan was not actually involved in Jackson County, but contemporary letters that have recently been examined prove that the war was a Klan exercise. Even without this evidence, it would be clear that the local whites were adept at Klan methods. There were the familiar night visits, whippings, warnings, abductions, hangings, and shootings. There was the familiar device of gathering together men from outside the county to do the dirty work while local men were establishing conspicuous alibis. There was the dodge of blaming individual Negroes for Klan killings, and then killing those Negroes, too, as if their guilt were established. If any one thing made the condition so much worse in Jackson County than anywhere else in Florida, it was the fact—at least it was generally assumed to be a fact—that Negro gunfire had wounded a Klan leader and killed his daughter. This added a special provocation to the political motive of reducing Radical influence; the Klan was intent on ridding the county of Negroes.

The Jackson County War began in 1869, but what first caused it is debatable. Two agents of the Freedmen's Bureau, William Purman and Thomas Hamilton, had arrived in 1866. John Wallace described Purman as the diabolical schemer and Hamilton as his instrument— a man of great courage who could not himself have thought up so many ways to harass the local whites. (Hamilton was later a member of Congress.) The two agents, according to Wallace, did everything possible to whip up Negro hatred of the whites, even urging them to burn the cotton gins and other property of the white farmers. Toward the local whites they exhibited "the grossest tyranny," including such things as arresting two white girls for removing flowers from the grave of a Union soldier, and charging fees for supervising labor contracts between freedmen and employers—twenty-five cents for the freedman, half a dollar for the man employing him. Whatever violence happened after such "tyranny and oppression" was clearly the fault of these two monsters, according to Wallace. This was the familiar strategy of Klansmen elsewhere in the South, of transferring the guilt for their violence to their victims.

The chief accusation against Purman and Hamilton was that they incited the Negroes to vote. If all the Negroes in Jackson County voted, and voted Republican, they would of course have unseated all Democratic officeholders and sent Republican legislators to Tallahassee—a horrifying prospect for the local Democrats. Having built up a case against Purman, the whites decided to eliminate him. He was wounded, not very seriously, in an ambush; his companion, Dr. John Finlayson, clerk of the circuit court, was killed.

That was in March. On September 28, for no discernible reason, whites ambushed a group of Negroes on their way to a picnic, killing one man and a two-year-old boy. Three nights later, in the county seat of Marianna, James McClellan was entertaining some friends on his verandah. He was an important local Democrat and, it was thought, the Klan leader. The quiet night was suddenly shattered by a volley of shots. McClellan was wounded and his daughter killed. The assailants were presumed to be Negroes incensed by the senseless ambush killings and incited to violence by Purman—who, incidentally, was in Tallahassee at the time.

The next morning, and for weeks afterwards, the streets of Marianna were crowded with mounted whites from neighboring counties, and from Georgia and Alabama, who left no doubts about their intentions: as reported to the congressional investigating committee, they were bent on killing all true Republicans who would not leave Jackson County. The clerk of the county court, John Q. Dickinson, undertook to send periodic reports of developments to Secretary of State Gibbs. Dickinson was a native of Vermont and a Harvard graduate. Killings occurred at a rate of close to one a day. Some Negroes prudently left town, and so did some of the white Republicans, but enough others remained to make the hunting good.

On October 7, three known Klansmen abducted the entire family of Matt Nickles—husband, wife, and child—killed all three, and threw their bodies into a sinkhole. By the eleventh, Dickinson's tally showed seven Negroes killed and two wounded; not all Klansmen were good marksmen. But just before he mailed his report, Dickinson had to add a postscript. One more man was dead, a white named Fleishman, who had allegedly been selling guns to the Negroes.

By February 1869, Dickinson's dreary list had grown to seventy-five dead. Nine-tenths of the victims were Negroes; the remaining tenth were white Republicans. Dickinson may have hoped that the Republican state administration could think of some way to halt the killings, although it is more likely that he knew how things stood in Tallahassee: Governor Reed barely able to survive politically, and Secretary of State Gibbs in constant danger of assassination. There were no marshals or state police who could be sent to

Jackson County, and the state militia was a joke, for it lacked guns.

Why any Negroes or white Republicans stayed in the county, under the circumstances, is hard to understand. Purman wisely refused to return there. On one occasion somebody asked him whether the Klan whipped people in Marianna, and he replied, "No, sir, they make clean work of it in Jackson County. They believe there in gunpowder entirely."

Dickinson was one of those who grimly hung on, but the day came—in April 1871—when he could no longer send his regular tally to Gibbs. His murder was attributed to a Negro named Bryant; the Klan even invented a motive—Dickinson reportedly had been carrying on a liaison with Bryant's wife. By now the war was petering out. One local woman, some years later, could reminisce, naively, that the county had had "no serious trouble" with the Negroes for some time. One Klansman, less naively, boasted late in life that the killings had totaled more than 170. Secretary Gibbs's estimate of 153 seems more reliable, but in any event it was one of the cleanest sweeps the Reconstruction Klan ever made.

Just why this one county should be the setting for such a massacre may never be known. Its location is a possible clue: it is in an angle along the northern boundary of Florida, and it has lengthy common borders with both Georgia on the east and Alabama on the north. Klansmen from both states could easily cross the line to participate in eliminating the hated enemies.

The county's anti-Negro bias has apparently changed in the ninety years since, for more than half the eligible Negro voters were registered in 1960, as compared with a mere handful in Gadsden County just to the east, and with none at all in Liberty County nearby.

Most of the killings elsewhere in the state were also politically inspired; they were the extreme form of the Klan effort to keep Negroes from voting. It is hard to overestimate the courage of the Negroes. Despite the Klan violence they turned out on election day in sufficient numbers to keep the Republicans in power until 1876. Today, where white supremacists still insist that Negroes must not be allowed to vote, usually the worst that can happen to a stubborn Negro voter is the loss of his job. Bad as that may seem, it is mild compared with the situation in the 1870's, when even the rumor of his having voted could condemn a Negro to death, or perhaps just a whipping.

White Republicans also needed courage. L. G. Dennis, from Massachusetts, was both federal revenue collector and state senator for Alachua County. A dozen Klansmen held a mock trial in a Gainesville street and condemned him to death. The charge: being a Radical. It was pretty obvious that he was one; it was also considered reason enough for him to die. The Klan did not, however, execute the sentence. Dennis was sent a warning, in poetic form:

K.K.K.

No man e'er felt the halter draw
With good opinion of the law.

K.K.K.

Twice the secret report was heard
When again you hear his voice
Your doom is sealed.

K.K.K.

Dead men tell no tales.

K.K.K.

Dead! dead! under the roses.

K.K.K.

Our motto is death to Radicals—Beware!

K.K.K.

State Senator E. G. Johnson of Lake City also received a warning, in October 1871. There were four thousand Klan members in Florida, he was informed; and "all the Ku Klux laws, all the courts, all the soldiers, all the devils in hell can not stop the resolves of the brotherhood. The destroyers of our rights—that is, unprincipled leaders such as you—if they persist, will fall one by one; it is sworn to by brave men, who are obliged to act in secrecy from the force of circumstance." Johnson published the letter in the Lake City *Herald* and for some years heard nothing further from the Klan. This would follow logically, for if the Klan did carry out its threat after the warning was published, everybody would know it was the Klan's work. But in 1875 Johnson *was* killed, which somewhat offsets this logic.

Not all the Klan violence in Florida was politically motivated, though most of it seems to have been. In 1868 an entire Negro family in Jefferson County—husband, wife, and four children— were whipped for a simple reason: They apparently had not learned that whites did not allow "damned niggers to live on land of their own." Property was a privilege of the superior race. In Clay County a Negro couple, Sam and Hanna Tutson, were stripped and whipped because they refused to give up their land even after a warning. One of the Klansmen, a deputy sheriff, threatened to kill Mrs. Tutson if she would not have sexual relations with him. Later, when she reported this to the sheriff, he put her in jail for a day for lying. But it is refreshing to learn that he dismissed the lecherous deputy.

Some whites were punished, too. R. W. Cone of Baker County earned his stripes by serving on a jury that listened to Negro testimony against a white man. In 1871 a Jewish merchant in Columbia County was killed because he had built up an extensive trade with Negroes. In May 1874, near Brooksville, a white man who had been living with a Negro woman was hanged. In July 1875, two men accused of rape—one white, the other Negro—were forcibly taken from the jail in Milton and hanged from a tree. It is quite clear that the Klan in Florida, though it may have been preoccupied with politics, came up to the standards of Klansmen everywhere in preserving public morality.

Governor Reed asked for federal troops on at least three occasions: In July 1868, in October 1870, and in 1871. But no troops were furnished. For unknown reasons the men in Washington would not even send arms for the militia that Reed organized. Reed finally ordered a supply of guns from New York, but they never arrived. Somewhere along the main line between Jacksonville and Tallahassee they disappeared from the train. A Klansman boasted many years later that most of the telegraph operators and the train crew were members of the Klan; it was a simple matter to pick up a Klan squad at one station and let them off at the next without asking their business. The guns were found scattered and broken along the right of way, though a few turned up later after a Klan raid.

The Florida Klan was active during the entire Reconstruction period, but after the three-year reign of terror from 1868 to 1871 there was a relative lull until the election of 1876. Florida was one of the last states to be fully restored to local white control, and there was a good deal of impatience, together with a "now or never" feeling. If Republicans were allowed to win *this* election, it might mean that Negroes would be able to vote for years to come, and this was unthinkable. The Klan this time avoided the grosser varieties of violence, but its milder methods were effective enough. Negroes who may have thought the Klan was dead were taken from their cabins at night and threatened with hanging if they did not promise to vote for the Democratic candidates. Later it was learned that they also had to swear that they would never report being coerced in this way.

Republican rallies were surrounded by large numbers of Klansmen on horseback. The word was passed along that Democrats intended to go to the polls armed and would not hesitate to shoot down any Negro they found trying to vote. One of the most astonishing actions was a threat, delivered in person to the incumbent governor, Stearns, that he would be put to death if a single white man was killed on election day. Then on that day armed platoons of Klansmen patrolled the roads to keep Negroes away from the voting places. Both parties won in Florida. In the disputed presidential election Rutherford Hayes was finally declared winner of the Florida electoral vote, but the new governor was a Democrat, George F. Drew. Republicans from that time forward could have no hopes of electing state officers ever again (though in recent years they have been successful in a few populous downstate counties). The real losers in 1876 were the Negroes; after enjoying some of the rights of American citizens, they were forced back to the second-class status decreed for them by white supremacists. It might have been better for them had they never sampled the sweets of voting and holding office; losing these was hard. Some advances they clung to, such as schools for their children and the right to own land, though few of them ever did. What stung the most was their clear knowledge that white men, in self-claimed superiority, had deprived them of their civil rights by force—by the violence of the Ku Klux Klan.

Chapter Nine

THE FREEDMEN'S BUREAU

Historians sympathetic toward the South and authors of pro-Klan novels have created an enduring adverse image of the Freedmen's Bureau. Pernicious, vindictive, and corrupt it never was, except in Southern myth. It was created by Congress to help the former slaves through the difficult transition to the freedom and equality the nation had decided they should have; but since this very purpose was a threat to white supremacy, it was inevitable that Southern whites would do everything possible to discredit it. Instances of actual oppression were seized upon to illustrate the alleged wickedness of the entire Bureau; and the corrupt practice of certain agents, especially in cotton deals, was magnified so that it appeared to be the deliberately encouraged practice of all the agents. The Bureau was a symbol of what most Southern whites feared, hated, and resisted. In its actuality, as an operating agency, it was a prime target of Klan violence. But it is not incumbent on us to prefer the image to the facts.

Southern white insistence, before the Civil War, that slaves were content with their lot is a good example of wishful thinking. Some undoubtedly were, particularly the favored house slaves, an elite that looked down on the lowly field hands. But the underground railroad is evidence of a widespread discontent, and so is the lesser known effort of many slaves to find refuge in federal forts.

The war multiplied these fugitives. Owners abandoning their plantations could take with them only their house slaves; the more numerous field hands either stayed and lived off the land, became homeless vagrants, or headed for the nearest Union army, which they supposed had come south with the intention of giving them their freedom. As the war progressed, the number of refugee Negroes became a serious problem. Some Union generals simply turned them away or tried to enforce the Fugitive Slave Act by returning them to their owners. Other generals, less sympathetic toward the South, put them to work and turned away the owners instead. One Abolition-minded general expressed the view that the refugees were "people whom Providence has entrusted to our care."

Ben Butler, commanding Fortress Monroe in Louisiana, hit upon a compromise that was reasonably satisfactory to both the owners and the Abolitionists. By calling the refugees "contrabands," he did not challenge their status as property, but he did insist that the rules of war permitted him to keep them under his surveillance as long as their owners were in rebellion against the Union. His superiors in Washington approved, and his invention became standard practice. Congress, which early in 1861 declared that the war's purpose was not to free the slaves, shifted in its thinking along with the bulk of Northerners, and by July of that year declared that soldiers' duties did not include the capture of slaves and their return to their owners. This nullified the Fugitive Slave Act as far as the army was concerned, but it did not solve the problem of what to do with the fugitives.

Work that could be found for contrabands in forts and camps was of real value in freeing soldiers for military duty, but it could not be expanded indefinitely. A good many plantations had come under army control, and it seemed logical and profitable to put the refugees to work in the fields. Cotton was the chief interest, for its price was steadily rising in the New York market. Where profits are visible, however, entrepreneurs gather; and many of these, not content with the 5 or 6 per cent that the army allowed them as contractors, found means of increasing their share. Southern whites who were not getting the proceeds of this cotton blamed the government for encouraging profiteers.

Secretary of the Treasury Salmon P. Chase, in December 1861, sent Edward L. Pierce to Port Royal Island off the South Carolina coast to see what could be done for the Negroes there. Pierce's report, dated February 3, 1862, was published in the New York *Tribune*. Lincoln and other high officials were so favorably impressed that they decided to appoint salaried superintendents in order to eliminate the contractors. Unfortunately, no money was advanced to support the plan. An appeal for private donations, spearheaded by Secretary Chase and Senator Charles Sumner, stimulated the formation of freedmen's aid societies, and within a month forty-one men and twelve women were sent aboard the S.S. *Atlantic* to Port Royal, many of them as teachers. Pierce hailed them as "some of the choicest young men of New England, fresh from Harvard, Yale, and Brown and from the divinity schools of Andover and Cambridge."

Not all the *Atlantic* passengers were choice young men, however; a few were more mindful of profits than of benevolence. Two members of the military establishment at Port Royal, Colonel Nobles and Lieutenant Colonel Reynolds, sided with the profit-seekers; both had been there before Pierce, and both have been described as resembling old-line plantation overseers. The resulting clash of interests made Port Royal a microcosm of the entire South. A new commanding general, David Hunter, was strongly Abolitionist: he went so far as to seek permission, which was given, to organize Negro regiments. But not even Hunter could eliminate the contractors, and the conflict continued for the rest of the war.

As Abolitionist sentiment grew in the North, Congress passed act after act to improve the welfare of the slaves. Lincoln, mindful of opinion in the neutral border states, moved cautiously, but as early as September 1862 he completely reversed his campaign pledge not to interfere with slavery. During that month he showed his cabinet a preliminary draft of a proclamation freeing the slaves in all areas at war with the Union. After making alterations suggested by various cabinet members, he issued the proclamation on January 1, 1863.

The Emancipation Proclamation stirred up a great debate. One group of citizens advocated a program of colonization, and about 450 former slaves were actually shipped to Haiti—but with such poor results that most of them soon returned. A better device was enlisting Negroes into the army; by the war's end there were 186,000 colored troops. A third solution, one that led to the formation of the Freedmen's Bureau, is attributed to General Grant. Confronted with large numbers of fugitive slaves, he ordered a chaplain named John Eaton to establish "contraband camps." Eaton, formerly superintendent of schools in Toledo, accepted the assignment with little enthusiasm. But he did a competent job. The camps he organized were financed by donations and by a percentage of the proceeds from cotton grown at the camps and sold in the North.

An American Freedmen's Inquiry Commission composed of Samuel Howe, Robert Dale Owen, and James McKaye, and representing thirty freedmen's aid societies, put pressure on Lincoln in a letter dated December 14, 1863: "Has the government any moral right," they asked, "to free the slave without seeing to it that, with every chain it breaks, the best within its power is done to keep the freedman from hankering after his master and his bondage, from feeling that his liberty is a burden, his life a curse?" The logic of this appeal could hardly be ignored, and Congress responded, in the following March, with a bill to establish a Freedmen's Bureau. Wrangling over which federal department would house it delayed final passage until March 3, 1865, when a "Bureau of Refugees, Freedmen, and Abandoned Lands" was authorized and assigned to the War Department.

President Johnson named as commissioner General Oliver O. Howard, a Bowdoin graduate and a man of total integrity, so pious and so strait-laced that during the war he had often irritated his fellow generals. Neither a Radical nor an Abolitionist when he assumed the post, he gradually developed a sympathy for the Abolitionists, although he scrupulously avoided any action or statement that could be construed as partisan. He steadfastly refused to let the Bureau become, as its detractors have insisted it was, a political arm of the Radical Republicans. It is a matter of record, indeed, that Bureau officials were often under attack because they refused to be parties to the political activities of the Radicals.

Congress had appropriated no funds for the Bureau, and Howard soon learned how dependent he was on the army and the private aid societies. The army, for example, supplied most of the rations the Bureau distributed (in 1867–68, a total of 2,802,478 rations to 16,804 separate individuals). The societies provided most of the teachers and most of the money to pay them (at a rate never more than $500 a year). Friction was inevitable, but Howard was a master of tact and was able to secure good co-operation, on the whole, from the several Northern groups, official and private, that sponsored the work in the South. His only serious trouble came from President Johnson, who in 1866 not only vetoed a bill to extend the Bureau's life but restored so many of the confiscated plantations, along with pardons to their owners, that the Bureau could not fulfill the promise of "forty acres and a mule" for every freedman. After Congress overrode the veto, moreover, Johnson gave the Bureau the most grudging kind of support and was petty enough to deny an army promotion to General Howard's brother.

Howard expected opposition from the Southern whites, but he also hoped they would listen to reason. He was overly sanguine about the willingness of local courts to break with tradition and give Negro defendants equal treatment with whites. Throughout the South, Negroes had never been tried by juries, their testimony had never been accepted against whites, and they had always drawn harsher punishment than whites for the same offenses. Howard quickly learned that Southern whites had no intention of listening to his kind of reasoning. Modification of court practices would have been tantamount to admitting racial equality—something that adherents of white supremacy were determined not to do. The only way to secure equity for Negroes was to set up special Bureau courts. These embittered the South, but Howard's job, as he saw it, was to help the freedmen, not to preserve Southern tradition.

In actual practice, the courts that Howard established had varying success. In Virginia each Bureau court had three judges: a planters' representative, a Bureau agent, and a delegate chosen by the Negroes. In most other parts of the South, a single judge, chosen by the Bureau, was the rule. The single-judge court was criticized, with some validity, for giving the functions of judge, sheriff, and clerk of court to a single individual. Where there were three, the planters' representative commonly refused to serve if the Negroes chose a fellow Negro; and when this happened the planters could accuse the two remaining judges of partiality, even though many of the decisions—the majority of them in Virginia—favored the whites. One serious handicap was the total lack of appropriated support; fines and fees were the only source of court income—in other words, the only means of paying the judges, who as a consequence were tempted to set larger fines and fees than if their incomes were independently provided. Southern opinion opposed these courts as abominations, but it seems probable that what Southern whites most resented was being fined for treating Negroes as the inferiors they honestly supposed them to be.

The Freedmen's Bureau is heroically portrayed in *Harper's Weekly*, July 25, 1868.

Another widespread source of resentment was the labor contract system which the Bureau developed and supervised. Planters considered it their privilege to determine what they should pay for labor that under slavery had cost them nothing except food, clothing, and shelter. What they proposed to pay, indeed, in the first days of emancipation, would have provided no more, and probably less. The Bureau contracts called for somewhat better wages but, in return, the Bureau was able to force the Negroes to work and to stay on the job, to the great benefit of the planters. The chief instrument of this coercion was the threat of transporting Negroes to places far from home, to work for strangers, and the even worse threat of exposing them to state vagrancy laws if they would not work. Far from pampering its wards, the Bureau kept them strictly in line and treated them sternly when they showed signs of laziness or insubordination. The Bureau was the only agency able to keep the Negroes working; this fact of life forced the planters to accept the terms of the Bureau contracts, which only added to the planters' resentment. The charge that the Bureau actively encouraged Negro idleness is one of the most absurd facets of the Southern myth of Reconstruction.

General Howard held his employees to a very high standard of conduct, while the military system of record-keeping—required of the Bureau as a branch of the War Department—left little time for leisure. One result was a rapid turnover in assistant commissioners, meaning the men in charge of Bureau operations for individual states. In the seven years of the Bureau's existence, Alabama, Florida, Maryland, and Texas each had five different assistant commissioners; North Carolina had six; and Louisiana had no less than seven. Most of them resigned because the work was too exacting; a few were dismissed for inefficiency or for vindictive treatment of local whites.

The worst single act of oppression was committed by General Edward A. Wild, assistant commissioner for Georgia. Learning that the family of one John Chenault was in possession of gold stolen from a train, he led a contingent of forty soldiers to the Chenault farm, ransacked the house, and strung up the two Chenault men by the thumbs to make them talk. On the second day an assistant inspector-general arrived and ordered Wild to desist. The incident gave the Bureau a bad name, not only among Southern whites but with the regular army as well; even one such action was certain to yield an adverse image. But it is flagrant distortion to conclude that all the assistant commissioners were equally wicked.

Howard could dismiss such men as Wild, but he could not keep all his minor officials from engaging in corrupt behavior. A few of them, in partnership with Northern investors, undertook to employ Negroes to grow cotton and pocketed a share of the profit, or accepted commissions for hiring Negroes out when crops were ready to harvest. The agents were poorly paid, and temptation was hard to resist. There were, moreover, never enough agents to do all that the Bureau was instructed to do; even at its peak, in December 1865, the Bureau had only 799 employees, and by the end of 1868 the number was down to 158. A single agent might find himself the only federal man in two entire counties; one agent complained that he was responsible for two thousand square miles. What is remarkable is not that some Bureau officials were cruel and others corrupt, but that the great majority were conscientious and hardworking, humane, and tactful. That they were condemned by contemporary Southern whites is understandable, but that historians should have echoed the condemnation is one of the sad ironies of supposedly reputable scholarship.

The most effective work of the Bureau was no doubt in education, largely because it complemented work already begun and solidly supported by Northern churches and philanthropic societies, but also because the freedmen were eager to learn and willing to pay their modest share of the cost. In 1868 the Bureau could report 4,026 schools of all sorts, with 2,295 teachers and 241,819 pupils—one-seventh of all Southern Negroes of school age. Since no Southern Negroes had ever been educated at public expense under slavery, white opposition was very strong, although, once the schools were established, the *idea* of educating Negroes began to find acceptance among the better white elements. An enduring monument to the Bureau and the private groups is the impressive list of institutions they founded that are still serving the South, among them Hampton Institute in Virginia, Atlanta University, Fisk University in Nashville, Lincoln University in Missouri's capital city of Jefferson City, and Howard University in Washington, which immortalizes General Howard. The obstructionist tactics of the Klan were most effective in rural areas and villages; urban experiments were much less vulnerable.

We have become accustomed in this century to programs of federal assistance to many groups of individual citizens, as an implementation of the welfare clause of the Constitution. Whatever opposition exists is a residue of the long-dominant political philosophy that the government should help business enterprises, as Alexander Hamilton stoutly maintained, while individuals should help themselves. In a land of unlimited resources, poverty was prima facie evidence of depravity, according to the Puritan ethic. The Freedmen's Bureau, first of all federal efforts to aid a particular segment of the population, was viewed with considerable apprehension; even General Howard, convinced as he was that the freedmen needed help, viewed the Bureau as a temporary expedient, to be abandoned just as soon as the Southern states were sufficiently restored to take care of their own.

Federal welfare programs have always caused uneasiness, moreover, because they mean federal intrusion into local affairs and threaten to alter familiar and beloved social patterns. When social alteration was as great as Southern whites feared, as a result of extending to Negroes the privileges traditionally limited to whites, resistance was certain to be great. The more conscientious the Bureau agent might be in performing his duty, the greater the hostility he could expect, and the more intense the local and regional campaign to discredit what he was doing. Since the big lie carries more conviction than isolated arguments, Southern spokesmen sweepingly condemned the Bureau as unauthorized by the Constitution and its agents as vindictive and corrupt. Historians, not quite so violent in their opposition, spoke rather of the majority of Bureau agents as being vindictive and corrupt. The net result has been that when a given Bureau official or agent is found to have been honest and generous, he is labeled an exception. This is one more example of the amazing success of pro-Southern propaganda.

General Howard took every possible precaution to avoid offending Southern whites, and he removed employees who did offend them. He welcomed complaints, insisting only that they be specific. If he was guilty of wavering from absolute objectivity, it was in his discounting of reported Klan atrocities. Sitting in his Washington office he must have found it hard to believe the more lurid tales in letters from his scattered agents. Even so, he came to realize that the acts of violence could not be charged against the irresponsible lower-class whites acting alone; such people had to have the acquiescence of the controlling majority who considered the Negro inherently inferior. In an undated speech he recognized the existence of groups

> who combine openly & secretly to keep the negro in practical slavery, pay him reluctantly, do not treat him as a man entitled to a man's privileges, break their labor contracts to deprive the laborer of his hire, attempt to govern with the pistol and the whip, hinder education, destroy schoolhouses, and in several of the States they killed freedmen's agents and maimed others for life; they murder and mutilate the freedmen and nothing can reach them but the vigorous, united arm of the Government, prepared to vindicate its laws and defend *all* its citizens.

In his 1868 report, which is embodied in the *Report of the Secretary of War*, Howard nowhere mentioned the Klan by name, but he cited copious examples of its obstructionist tactics along with the general Southern resistance to Bureau activities. In a region that had never previously accepted the principle of tax-supported education, he observed, opposition to the schools created by the Bureau and the Northern aid groups was widespread. Civil authorities, instead of co-operating to punish the miscreants, winked at school-burnings and at all other outrages. Maryland, somewhat ahead of other Southern states in having schools for Negroes, limited their support to the taxes the Negroes paid; but even so there was considerable white opposition to the schools. White attitudes in Virginia, Howard thought, were improving, but he had to report some instances of violence by "illegal groups" (his polite equivocation for the Klan); a favorite device was putting a noose around a Negro's neck to deter him from voting. In Florida, Negroes were comparatively well off; there was so much land in the public domain that many Negroes had already been settled on places of their own, with from ten to forty acres. In Georgia, opposition was virtually everywhere, and civil authorities were unable or unwilling to punish the guilty. The worse crime in the past year that had come to Howard's attention was at Louisville, a Georgia town not far from Augusta: A Negro was burnt alive for the alleged rape of a white woman.

All these things Howard reported with his usual objectivity. But he included also some statements from Bureau officials and other federal men in various parts of the South who didn't hesitate to name the Klan. Louisiana's Governor Warmoth, writing from New Orleans on August 1, 1868, described the terrible conditions in that city and state. Not the Ku Klux Klan, but the Knights of the White Camellia, sought to drive out all Union men and to terrify Negroes into voting "right." The organization, according to the Governor, was "founded for the purpose of placing and keeping the colored people in a condition of inferiority. . . . Many prominent citizens of the State are leaders in it." The members drilled openly in the streets of New Orleans. The presence of federal troops alone prevented the K.W.C. from disrupting the legislature. Unless the government could find the means of breaking up the order, Warmoth thought a bloody revolution was probable.

As a kind of footnote to this statement, the Assistant Adjutant-General cited the Constitution, Article IV, Section IV, which guarantees a republican government in every state, and an Act of Congress approved February 28, 1795, authorizing the imposition of military government in any state judged to be in a condition of insurrection. The annual report then proceeds to describe situations in other states comparable to what Governor Warmoth reported for Louisiana, with urgent appeals for military support. It is amply clear that the War Department did not jump at every chance to send troops into troubled areas to offset the Klan and similar terroristic groups, but rather that it rejected most of the pleas for troops. It would have been a practical impossibility to furnish all the troops requested, for the army had been reduced in strength to 48,000 men, and was being further reduced at just that time—

the goal for January 1869, was 43,000. Only a portion of this number could be assigned to the South. The Klan, at the same period, numbered well over half a million.

The annual War Department report contains a very interesting report on conditions in Tennessee, written by a three-man legislative committee. There was no question, the investigators concluded, that the Klan existed. They estimated its strength in Tennessee at 40,000, the figure given by General Bedford Forrest. "As to the objects and purposes of this organization they can only be known by their acts and sayings while in their masks and ghostly uniforms." They killed by hanging, shooting, or whipping to death, and justified their actions by claiming that the current Tennessee government was illegal and its overthrow desirable. Public opinion supported the Klan so firmly that civil authorities were powerless to move against it even if they wished to. Many ex-Confederates disapproved of the Klan, but "most, if not all, persons engaged in these violations of the law, and who belong to the 'Klan,' so far as known, were enemies of the government of the United States during the late civil war. . . . As they go in masks and disguises, it is not known who is and who is not in the order." Federal troops might not be able to identify and punish the members, but they could protect the voters and ensure a fair election. The Klan had threatened "that no more elections shall be held in Tennessee in counties where they have the power to prevent it."

Corroborating this committee report was a letter from Major General George H. Thomas, of the Department of the Cumberland, who wrote that "the State of Tennessee was disturbed by the strange operations of a mysterious organization known as the Ku Klux Klan." This, it should be remembered, was little more than a year after the famous organizational meeting at the Maxwell House in Nashville. There was also the account of a police raid in Memphis, in April 1868, which netted several Klansmen and papers containing detailed plans to assassinate all persons who interfered with their activities. A further report described a clash at Murfreesboro, where a hundred Klansmen had tried to take four Negroes from the jail. Captain Joseph Gelray, a Freedmen's Bureau inspector, said that Negroes had stopped reporting Klan outrages because the Klan had threatened to shoot any Negro seen entering a Bureau agent's office. Gelray concluded, "In my opinion, if something is not done to give the friends of our country protection, and to punish the Ku-Klux Klan in the greater part of Tennessee, another war will result, as practically the negroes are still slaves and the confederacy a triumphant success."

In the face of such reports from different parts of the South, General Howard seems to have been altogether too optimistic about the immediate future. For example, he dissolved the Bureau courts at the end of 1868 in the belief that local courts would henceforth treat Negroes fairly. He apparently had too much faith in the Radical legislatures and in their ability to bring county officials into line; he underestimated the grass-roots opposition to state governments that were Radical only because Congress had virtually dictated the state constitutions and the methods of election. His own integrity and his reliance on reason may have blinded him to the probability of minimal reason and maximum emotionalism in the affairs of the South. And his habit of discounting atrocity reports no doubt led him to discount also the violence the Klan would continue to resort to as the means of preserving white supremacy. In his optimism he acquiesced a little too readily in the dissolution of the Bureau and may deserve some of the blame for the Klan's eventual success.

The Freedmen's Bureau existed for slightly more than seven years; Congress voted its termination on June 10, 1872. Viewed in historical perspective, it is not easy to see why the Klan considered the Bureau its deadly enemy. At no time was the Bureau directly concerned about the Klan; the most authoritative history of the Bureau, George R. Bentley's *A History of the Freedmen's Bureau* (1955), doesn't even mention the Klan. Perhaps the most reasonable explanation of the Klan's virulent attitude is that the Bureau, as the one official agency specifically charged with helping the former slaves, symbolized in Southern white thinking the government's commitment to eliminate the racial differential that the South, and the Klan as its active agent, were determined to preserve. The sober facts reveal very few instances of vindictiveness among Bureau agents, and very little corruption. If a Freedmen's

[154]

Bureau had to exist—and it is hard to see how the government, after freeing the slaves, could have failed to create one—no commissioner could have been more scrupulously fair to the South or more insistent that his employees share that fairness. The Klan's case against the Bureau had the thinnest kind of support, and yet the Klan's case has found its way into the history books that have conditioned the thinking of millions of Americans.

Chapter Ten
THE BATTLE
OF THE
BOOKS

Most historians of the Reconstruction period, until very recently, have leaned toward the "classical" Southern position, which they themselves did so much to create. Whether because they were Southern by birth or education, or because they shared the general American trait of sympathy for the underdog, they built up an impressive body of interpretation that today's "revisionists" are hard put to replace. This is the present battle of the books. But an older battle, in fiction, was no less interesting. In actuality it was rather one-sided, for only the first of the novels about the Klan, Albion Tourgée's *A Fool's Errand,* is Northern in its viewpoint.

This novel sold more than 200,000 copies, a figure so large that we may wonder why other writers in the next few decades did not try to repeat its success with other books casting Klansmen as villains. The very absence of anti-Klan novels after the first gave the fictional victory to the pro-Klan forces by default and created the impression that nobody thought the Klan was evil in any important way. Perhaps that *was* the prevailing opinion in the latter part of the nineteenth century and well into the twentieth; and perhaps the pro-Klan novelists merely confirmed the general attitude, which saw more glamor than viciousness in the Klan.

By definition Tourgée was a "carpetbagger," a term applied to any Northerner who went South during Reconstruction for other than commercial purposes. After the Southern states had all regained their sovereignty in 1877 the adverse connotation of the term spread to all parts of the country, and it has since become fixed in general thinking. All carpetbaggers were evil; that was the sum of it. The stereotype is so firmy set that Tourgée's latest biographer, Theodore L. Gross, describes him as an exception: in actual practice, Gross writes, Tourgée "was, unlike so many other Republican judges, neither corrupt nor venal."

The corruption and venality of carpetbag judges were largely figments of partisan imagination, and parts of one of the most successful propaganda campaigns ever known in this country. Conservative Southerners had good reason to hate all Northerners, especially those who moved South and became public officials. Judges were particularly hated because they disregarded the regional tradition that discounted Negro testimony in any legal action involving the two races. Since these Northern judges threatened to establish a color-blind sort of justice, they were of course enemies to be discredited by any and every device, including reiterated accusations of corruption and venality. That some of them were corrupt and self-seeking is probable; some judges are corrupt and venal in every society, in every period. The success of the campaign of vilification may be measured by the stubborn endurance of the belief that carpetbaggers were commonly wicked and that an honest one was a conspicuous exception.

Gross does, however, explain what it was that made Tourgée an exception: "Of all those authors who fictionalized the Reconstruction era, Tourgée was the only one who lived in the South throughout the entire period, and the only one who offered a first-hand account of Reconstruction in terms of the political, social, and economic conflicts between Southerners and Radical Republicans." And "nowhere else in the history of American letters are the experiences of a carpetbagger reported so comprehensively."

Born in Ohio in 1838 and educated at the University of Rochester,

Tourgée had two separate careers in the Union Army. He enlisted as a private in the New York regiment but before the end of 1861 was invalided out of service as the result of a spinal wound. After a period of convalescing, he secured a commission as lieutenant in an Ohio regiment and served until 1864. In October 1865, he moved to North Carolina and stayed there for fourteen years, most of the time in Greensboro. The old spinal wound gave him trouble all his life, but he was never a man to brood over injuries either physical or verbal.

As much as any other Northerner who obeyed the impulse to move South after the war, Tourgée was passionately devoted to Negro freedom and equality. He was even critical of the Radical governor of North Carolina, William Holden, for what he considered political expediency and temporizing. As second to Holden in the state's Union League, he could not openly oppose him, since such a split would have been fatal to the Republican cause. But he survived Holden politically. He was elected in 1868 for a six-year term as judge of the Superior Court, Seventh Judicial District. Tourgée could not be removed from office when the Democrats swept the state in 1870 and made Holden their chief victim by successfully impeaching him. While serving as judge, Tourgée, with two colleagues, made a valuable contribution to jurisprudence by drafting *The Code of Civil Procedure to Special Pleading*. During his final three years in the state he served in an appointive post in Raleigh, handling claims for federal pensions. In the fall of 1879 he returned to the North and within two months brought out, anonymously, *A Fool's Errand by One of the Fools*.

Friends and foes alike saw a parallel with *Uncle Tom's Cabin*, especially the next year when a reissue included *The Invisible Empire*, a grouping of documents supporting various episodes of the novel and comparable to *A Key to Uncle Tom's Cabin*. One significant difference between these two supplements is that Mrs. Stowe collected her evidence *after* writing her novel, while Tourgée had available his own court records involving the Klan and copious other primary source material. What gave *A Fool's Errand* its unique and lasting distinction, however, was its assignment of the villain's role to the Klansman. The Klan novels that followed reversed this casting, making the Klansman the hero and the carpet-bagger the villain.

In such books as Thomas Nelson Page's *Red Rock,* Thomas Dixon's *The Clansman,* and Joel Chandler Harris's *Gabriel Tolliver,* the hero is a sterling champion of Southern tradition and the villain is the stereotyped carpetbagger, unscrupulously intent on stirring up racial strife, humiliating the proud Southern gentlemen, and, in the process, amassing a personal fortune. The uncanny resemblance of this formula to the classical Southern myth nurtured by eminent historians about the turn of the century is probably no accident, for both drew upon the widely circulated defense of the Ku Klux Klan. Just how much the novels influenced the historians would, however, be impossible to estimate.

Gilbert Hotchkiss in *Gabriel Tolliver* (1902) is a good example of the villain as presented by the pro-Klan writers. At one point in this novel Harris pauses to editorialize, as follows:

> You find the type everywhere. . . . The Hotchkisses swarm wherever there is an opening for them, and they always present the same general aspect. . . . They live and die in the belief that they are promoting the progress of the world; but if their success is to be measured by their operations in the South during the reconstruction period, the world would be much better off without them. They succeeded in dedicating millions of human beings to misery and injustice, and warped the minds of the whites to such an extent that they thought it necessary to bring about peace and good order by means of various acute forms of injustice and lawlessness.

It is significant, as Gross points out, that the authors of most of the pro-Klan novels were writing a generation after the event. They had not been active participants in those events, as Tourgée had; Page was seventeen years old in 1870, and Dixon was sixteen. More importantly, their work falls into a recognizable genre that sought to glamorize the Old South, memorializing a way of life whose loss was to be regretted. The genre was a curious eddy in the stream of American fiction, going counter to the main current of emerging realism in the works of Eggleston and Howells, Crane and Norris. It was not the only romantic eddy; there were also the entremely popular rags-to-riches stories by Horatio Alger and, in the 1890's, the Graustark series and the imitations of *Trilby*. But the fiction nostalgically re-creating the Old South, and especially the pro-Klan novels, has had an enduring effect that the other forms of romanticism have not, for it has conditioned several generations of Americans to tolerate the old Klan as an agency striving to preserve a beautiful civilization in its unequal conflict with the materialistic North.

Sometimes merely seeing one of the numerous stage productions of *Uncle Tom's Cabin* roused Southern novelists to offer the opposing view; this is said to have been true of Dixon, for one. But Tourgée's book was also familiar to most of the pro-Klan writers, for they openly or subtly attacked him in their texts. He made a good target, personally, as an active carpetbagger, but his novel was vulnerable too, for it had its share of glamorizing. The hero (who in obvious ways is based on Tourgée himself) has virtually no faults, and the Union League is unvaryingly pictured as the innocent victim of Klan aggression.

Tourgée named his hero Comfort Servosse and made him the son of a lumber tycoon in Michigan. After earning his A.B. and a law degree at the University of Michigan, Comfort marries and starts a law practice. The Union defeat at Bull Run galvanizes him into enlisting. He becomes captain of Company B, the "Peru Invincibles," in an infantry regiment, and by the war's end is a colonel. All this takes only three short chapters to tell; as the fourth chapter opens the war is over and Servosse is home again. But life in a small Michigan town seems dull, and he announces to his wife that he wants to go south to live. She is willing. As in all the Klan novels, the Southern state where they settle, and which becomes the setting of the action, is not specified.

Servosse buys the "old Warrington place," with its six hundred acres, for $5,000. Almost at once his wife finds herself ostracized for entertaining Northern schoolteachers. An item in the local paper reports that Mrs. Servosse "has chosen to slander our first ladies by comparing them with the nigger schoolmarms who have come down here to teach social equality by example." The Servosses learn that "N.T." is a euphemism for *nigger teacher*.

At a meeting that Servosse attends, the Thirteenth Amendment is discussed and denounced. Forced to speak, he points out that Negro voting and testifying, like the worthlessness of Confederate money, are facts that cannot be wished away. He suggests voluntary enfranchisement of Negroes who own property—a hundred dollars in real estate, perhaps. Having thus openly taken a stand so alien to local thinking, he is henceforth a marked man. The first show of opposition occurs on his way home, when enemies try to kill him. But it is one of the plotters, instead, a man named Savage, whose horse trips on the taut wire across the road. Savage drops out of view, and it is supposed that he is dead.

Three Negroes are arrested for his murder. At their hearing, Servosse asks if they haven't a right to a defense; the question causes "a look of blank amazement, not unmixed with righteous indignation." Servosse then calmly announces that Savage is alive and recovering at his own house; he had taken him there after the accident. The Negroes are released, and Savage, by the time he is completely recovered, becomes Servosse's staunchest friend.

One morning Servosse finds on his door a warning to leave, signed "The Capting of the Regulators." He publishes the note in the Verdenton *Gazette*, and in time receives a letter from a stranger in a distant part of the state citing an exactly parallel circumstance. Other letters arrive. In one is this statement: "The *fact* of slavery is destroyed; the *right to enslave* is yet as devoutly held as ever. The right of a white man to certain political privileges is admitted; the right of a colored man to such, it will take generations to encourage." Servosse's encouragement to Negroes to buy and hold land and to ride their own horses runs counter to what Southern white men considered rights peculiarly their own.

As the book progresses, action dwindles and commentary increases. At one point Tourgée compares attitudes North and South, before and after the war, in parallel columns; though lengthy, the device deserves quotation:

ANTE BELLUM

Northern Idea of Slavery

Slavery is wrong morally, politically, and economically. It is tolerated only for the sake of peace and quiet. The negro is a man, and has equal inherent rights with the white race.

Southern Idea of Slavery

The negro is fit only for slavery. It is sanctioned by the Bible, and it must be right, or, if not exactly right, is unavoidable, now that the race is among us. We can not live with them in any other way.

Northern Idea of the Southern Idea

Those Southern fellows know that slavery is wrong, and incompatible with the theory of our government; but it is a good thing for them. They grow fat and rich, and have a good time, on account of it; and no one can blame them for not wanting to give it up.

Southern Idea of the Northern Idea

Those Yankees are jealous because we make slavery profitable, raising cotton and tobacco, and want to deprive us of our slaves from envy. They don't believe a word of what they say about its being wrong, except a few fanatics. The rest are all hypocrites.

POST BELLUM

The Northern Idea of the Situation

The negroes are free now, and must have a fair chance to make themselves something. What is claimed about their inferiority may be true. It is not likely to approve itself; but, true or false, they have a right to equality before the law. That is what the war meant, and this must be secured to them. The rest they must get as they can, or do without, as they choose.

The Southern Idea of the Situation

We have lost our slaves, our bank stock, every thing, by the war. We have been beaten, and have honestly surrendered: slavery is gone, of course. The slave is now free, but he is not white. We have no ill will towards the colored man as such and in his place; but he is not our equal, can not be made our equal, and we will not be ruled by him, or admit him as co-ordinate with the white race in

[162]

power. We have no objection to his voting, so long as he votes as his old master, or the man for whom he labors, advises him; but, when he chooses to vote differently, he must take the consequences.

The Northern Idea of the Southern Idea

Now that the negro is a voter, the Southern people will have to treat him well, because they will need his vote. The negro will remain true to the government and party which gave him liberty, and in order to secure its preservation. Enough of the Southern whites will go with them, for the sake of office and power, to enable them to retain permanent control of those States for an indefinite period. The negroes will go to work, and things will gradually adjust themselves. The South has no right to complain. They would have the negroes as slaves, kept the country in constant turmoil for the sake of them, brought on the war because we would not catch their runaways, killed a million of men; and now they can not complain if the very weapon by which they held power is turned against them, and is made the means of righting the wrongs which they have themselves created. It may be hard; but they will learn to do better hereafter.

The Southern Idea of the Northern Idea

The negro is made a voter simply to degrade and disgrace the white people of the South. The North cares nothing about the Negro as a man, but only enfranchises him in order to humiliate and enfeeble us. Of course, it makes no difference to the people of the North whether he is a voter or not. There are so few colored men there, that there is no fear of one of them being elected to office, going to the Legislature, or sitting on the bench. The whole purpose of the measure is to insult and degrade. But only wait until the States are restored and the "Blue Coats" are out of the way, and we will show them their mistake.

[163]

None of the Southern novelists went to such trouble as Tourgée to be objective in presenting the opposing regional views. Men on both sides would presumably have nodded in agreement over some of his comments—as when he wrote, "The spirit of the dead Confederacy was stronger than the mandate of the nation to which it had succumbed in battle." And it was hardly controversial to say that Southern Unionists, who opposed secession and put loyalty to nation above loyalty to state or region, nevertheless shared the general Southern opinion about the races: "The inferiority, inherent and fore-ordained, of the colored man was as much an article of faith with them as any portion of the Sacred Word." Somewhat less agreement might be evoked by his criticism of newspapers as vehicles of invective, and his even stronger criticism of Northern newspapers which, "almost without exception, echoed the clamor and invective of the Southern journals" and showered the same contempt on Northern men who went South, even accepting the pejorative label for them of "carpet-baggers." Northern editors should have known better, if they recalled the difference in meaning of the term "abolitionist," as Tourgée detected it:

AT THE NORTH

Abolitionist.—One who favors the emancipation of slaves.

AT THE SOUTH

Abolitionist—One who favors emancipation + infidel + murderer + thief + ravisher + incendiary + all hell's accumulated horrors, "not other wise appropriated." [The terms *at the North* and *at the South,* though they sound odd today, were standard regional usage in the nineteenth century.]

When Northern editors borrowed the term "carpet-bagger," they did not seem to realize that it too had different connotations North and South—again as Tourgée compared them:

AT THE NORTH

Carpet-bagger—A man without means, character, or occupation, an adventurer, a camp-follower, "a bummer."

[164]

The Battle of the Books

Carpetbagger—A man of Northern birth + an abolitionist (according to the Southern definition) + an incarnation of Northern hate, envy, spleen, greed, hypocrisy, and all uncleanness.

"So the South cursed 'carpet-baggers' because they were of the North; and the North cursed them because the South set the example."

When Tourgée introduces the Ku Klux Klan he remarks that the first Northern reaction was infinite amusement over its antics in frightening the Negroes. "So the Northern patriot sat back in his safe and quiet home, and laughed himself into tears and spasms at the grotesque delineations of ghostly K.K.K.'s and terrified darkies, for months before any idea of there being any impropriety therein dawned on his mind or in the minds of the wise men who controlled the affairs of the nation." (It might be remarked here that Tourgée often distinguished between the wise men who stayed safely away from the Reconstruction and the fools like himself who felt impelled to journey to the South—hence the title *A Fool's Errand*.) But if men far from the scene were amused, Servosse was not; he was deeply aware that the Klan was up to much more than grotesque antics. Reports of Klan violence came, in letters, from other counties; here are two that Servosse—or Tourgée—received:

It seems as if things were getting too bad to think of with us. Two white and three colored men were terribly beaten in this county on Wednesday night. On Friday night two colored men were hanged. They were accused of arson; but there was not a particle of evidence of their guilt; indeed, quite the contrary; and they were men of good character, industrious, and respectful.

James Leroy was hanged by the Ku-Klux on Tuesday night, his tongue being first cut out, and put in his pocket. He was *accused* of having slandered a white woman. The truth is, he was an independent colored man (though nearly as white as you or I), who could read and write, and was consequently troublesome on election-day, by preventing fraud upon his fellows.

The most significant Klan action in *A Fool's Errand* closely parallels the murder of John Walter Stephens, state senator from Caswell County, North Carolina, in the spring of 1870—the central incident leading to the "Kirk-Holden War" and, because Governor Holden could not prove Klan involvement, the basis for his impeachment. Tourgée changes the victim's name to John Walters, the thinnest kind of disguise. He introduces an affidavit that 'follows almost verbatim one that had been given him by a servant who accidentally overheard a Klan leader describing the Stephens murder. It was the kind of document that could not have been introduced as evidence in a Southern court for two reasons: it had no corroboration, and Negro testimony was commonly dismissed as inadmissible. Tourgée would have been astonished, had he lived until 1935, by the deposition written by one of the Klan killers of Stephens and made public that year; as was pointed out, the deposition completely corroborated the statement of the Negro servant and in effect made Tourgée's use of the incident history instead of fiction.

The Invisible Empire, which Tourgée added to *A Fool's Errand* in the 1880 edition, was intended, he said, "to present in a more concrete and specific form some *authenticated record of events.*" Besides giving the factual basis for incidents in his novel, it gives his considered opinion of the Klan and its background. The North-South differences, Tourgée thought, were permanent and irreconcilable. He called the Klan "the organic representative of the ideas, the sentiments, the determination of 'the South,'" and he expressed the opinion that only the education of all could "change the spirit that moved these horrors." He insisted that the Klan was organized and kept alive by the better citizens of the South, for the poor whites were too powerless and disorganized to achieve the discipline that the Klan exhibited. Two-thirds of all Klan actions, he estimated, were politically motivated; the crime most commonly punished by the Klan was voting for Republican candidates or urging others to do so. He dismissed the "self-Protection" that the Klan gave as one of its major reasons for existing; or rather, he viewed "self-Protection" as protection not from any Negro violence but from the punishment the Klan's own violence would, under ordinary circumstances, have earned. After scrutinizing the Klan through other sources, one cannot read *The Invisible Empire* without feeling profound respect for Tourgée's perspicuity and objectivity, remarkable for one so close to the events and so much embroiled in the Radical-Conservative struggle.

The success of *A Fool's Errand* prompted an answer in the form of *Thorns in the Flesh*, which appeared in 1884. The entire title page is reproduced on the following page because it so well reveals the author's motive and attitude.

In *A Fool's Errand* a Klan plot to kill Servosse is foiled when his daughter rides through the night to warn him—a stock device reminiscent of melodramatic thrillers. Also the daughter finally marries a leading enemy, an ex-Confederate general. But Tourgée's lapses from realism are mild compared with Floyd's. *Thorns in the Flesh* is replete with devices of romantic fiction. The hero, Charles A. Stewart, has left his father's plantation in Virginia and has developed a plantation of his own in northern Alabama near Huntsville. He is very handsome and remarkably articulate in defending the South against Dr. Hansel, proprietor of the boarding school which the heroine, Florence Seymour, is attending. Stewart (called "Mr. Stewart" throughout the book) has as his closest companions an almost-white brother and sister, children of an octoroon mother from New Orleans, who had been wrongfully deprived of their inheritance and even sold back into slavery. A wealthy Parisian of the same family finally restores their wealth to them. Fox, the brother, quotes Latin at the drop of a hat and is ostentatiously learned in a variety of subjects.

But the complex plot is almost buried in lengthy disquisitions about contemporary history. Dialogue in the opening chapter sounds like regional arguments on parade. One man, after exalting American civilization, goes on to observe:

> . . . there is danger that, in the heat of passion, which is already very great at the North, and which must necessarily be greatly intensified by future conflict, the promptings of a high civilization may be disregarded. There is much more danger of this at the North than at the South, for, besides the different qualities of the two civilizations, resulting chiefly from Puritan religionism having been substituted for Christianity,—these people are, of course, destined to be grievously

THORNS IN THE FLESH.

[A ROMANCE OF THE WAR AND KU-KLUX PERIODS.]

A VOICE OF VINDICATION FROM THE SOUTH

IN ANSWER TO

"A FOOL'S ERRAND" AND OTHER SLANDERS.

•

SYLLABUS:

SLAVERY—A THORN, grown into the very flesh and blood
of the country and of society.

ABOLITIONISM—A THORN in the side of Southern love for
the Union.

THE "HIGHER LAW" DOCTRINE—A THORN in the heart of
the Southern hope for peace and fair play.

WAR—A CROWN OF THORNS, which conferred upon the brow
of the South a regal majesty—a fathomless woe.

RECONSTRUCTION—A PATH OF THORNS over which Carpetbaggers—unfitted for such authority—led the
captive South.

PARTISAN ANIMOSITY—THE HIDDEN THORNS that crippled
the South in her march toward sôcial peace,
political harmony, and material restoration.

MISREPRESENTATIONS—THE LITTLE THORNS that exasper-
ated those who honestly desired peace and unity.

*"A masterly showing of historical faĉts threaded upon a romance of
closer adherence to reality and yet of greater and more thrilling power than
'Uncle Tom's Cabin' or 'A Fool's Errand.' "—*THE STATE *(Richmond, Va.).*

BY N. J. FLOYD.

MANY GRAPHIC ILLUSTRATIONS.

HUBBARD BROS., PUBLISHERS:
PHILADELPHIA, CINCINNATI, CHICAGO, NEW YORK, BOSTON,
KANSAS CITY.

1884.

disappointed in their present silly expectations of a cheap and easy victory; and under the humiliating sting of that disappointment there is danger that factions, communities and parties, up there, may surrender themselves to the wild and reckless leadership of such miserable fanatics as Wendell Phillips, 'the infernal machine set to music,' Thad. Stevens, the evil spuke with a monk's visage, and thousands of other and similar sons of the Evil One, who wear the cloak and mask of Christianity and philanthropy, and hate us,—for the conceited bigot's best reason—because we laugh at their sanctimonious hypocrisy. . . .

On the train bearing him homeward, Stewart meets an invalid lady who seems to know something of great importance concerning Fox and his sister; but instead of ferreting out the mysterious truth he launches into a debate with her about the merits of slavery. The train is derailed; Stewart saves the invalid's life; and while they are waiting for the cars to be righted he resumes:

And yet the condition of the most degraded slave in the South is infinitely preferable to that of his brother in Africa; for in addition to his greater enjoyment of physical comforts, he has the blessed hopes vouchsafed by the Christian religion. Both these, I earnestly believe, he enjoys more unreservedly and in a higher degree than the poor peasantry of any country on the globe. He knows, no matter what may befall, that, so far as his physical comforts are concerned, he will never suffer the pangs of hunger nor the pinchings of cold; nor for the want of a roof to shelter his family, however numerous and helpless; and that when the decrepitude of age shall overtake him he will be nursed and provided for in his second childhood as he was in his first.

In her school, meanwhile, Florence proves herself a worthy mate for Mr. Stewart in her spirited arguments with Dr. Hansel. At one point, "with an amused smile," she tells him "that in all New England only fifty-three negro slaves were emancipated by law; the others being sold before the time for the law to go into effect." This has always been a major point in the classical Southern theory, used again and again to bolster the charge that the North was grossly hypocritical in urging Abolition. Its utter absurdity is quickly apparent from even a casual glance at the official census figures from 1790 to 1860. Some Northern states, notably New York, New

Jersey, Connecticut, and Pennsylvania, did have substantial numbers of slaves, even after 1800; but other states had so few that hypocrisy had no chance to operate. Massachusetts, notorious as the breeding ground of Abolitionism, in her entire history as a state had only one slave, who was reported in the census of 1830. In that same census Massachusetts reported more than seven thousand free Negroes. By 1860, the last census reporting any slaves anywhere, Massachusetts had 9,602 free Negroes; Indiana had 11,428; Ohio had 36,673; New York had 49,005, and Pennsylvania had the most, 56,949.

The number of slaves freed in the North, moreover, was far less, census by census, than the increase in the total slave population of the nation; and the substantial number of free Negroes in the Northern population in the years before the Civil War is clear proof that most of the slaves were not sold south in anticipation of state action abolishing slavery. Florence Seymour in *Thorns in the Flesh* represents a common human willingness to accept and repeat as true whatever fanciful notions there may be to support what one wishes to believe. Fifty-three indeed! It was bad enough that contemporary defenders of slavery swallowed such fanciful absurdities; the greater tragedy is that people *still* accept them, along with the rest of the elaborate inventions supporting the Southern interpretation of American history.

A little later in the book Mr. Stewart explains to Dr. Hansel how the South could charge the North with violating the Constitution:

It should be self-evident, doctor, to one who understands the theory and history of the old government. Our colonies, which were first leagued together under Articles of Confederation, when they deemed it desirable to form a more perfect Union, appointed a convention to form the compact or agreement known as the Constitution. This Constitution, as you well know, was a compromise between greatly conflicting sentiments and interests. One by one the states, which were beyond doubt then sovereign, seceded from the old Confederation and joined the new Union, by voting to adopt the new Constitution; some of them, notably New York, Virginia, and New Jersey, intimating or directly declaring their right to secede again, if such action should ever seem to be demanded by the best interests of their people. Massachusetts has threatened more than once to secede, you know, and several other New England states pretended to think seriously of it; but, as there was no objection raised, they took counsel of thrift, and did not break the heart of the Union. The Constitution adopted delegated no authority to the central government to meddle with the internal affairs of the states in any manner or for any purpose. It follows, then, that the abolitionists at the North who clamored for the abolition of slavery in the South, and flooded Congress with petitions looking to that end, proposed to act without the sanction of law, and were therefore a lawless party.

Stewart also remarked to Dr. Hansel that in Massachusetts "only the worst men there, as a rule, have come to the front in politics." The almost-white Fox devises a scheme to rid the county of two notorious Radicals. "The Spirits of the Lost Clan of Cocletz," he tells Stewart, "must swoop down upon them there and then [at the old Cocletz gin-house] and bear them off into infinite space, before the eyes of the negroes. . . . You recollect the Knights of the Golden Circle!"

"Kuklos!" exclaimed Mr. Stewart.
"A union of the practical in the Golden Circle, with the mysterious in the Lost Clan, will make an excellent and interesting secret organization." Then, after the plot succeeds and the two Radicals are banished, Fox tells the story of the Co-Clotz Indians. Dr. Hansel dismisses it as superstition and is offended when Mr. Stewart suggests a parallel between Klan actions and the Salem persecution of witches in the 1690's. That was two centuries ago, Hansel protests, but Mr. Stewart quietly observes, "The communities, which, in the past, put supposed witches to death by hanging and burning, are not supposed or considered to have been a particularly degraded people." And Stewart further defends the Klan activity by mentioning some of the bad behavior of Union troops during the Civil War.

The reader is now well past the 400-page point and has been lectured about the Union Leagues, the Negro schools and their teachers, and the iniquities of the Freedmen's Bureau, all of which justified, for the author, the resort to Klan-like behavior, whatever the name. Like certain other pro-Southern writers, Floyd draws a sharp line between the better element that comprised the honorable societies and the ignoble elements in spurious groups. But let him speak:

It should not be denied that outrages, or rather, acts of violence that were not fully justified by the crimes committed, were perpetrated here and there, by mobs of persons styled "Ku-Klux Klans," acting under sudden impulses of outraged feeling; nor can it be denied by the *well informed,* that these, when they greatly exceeded the bounds of a proper punishment for the crime committed, were called to account by the "Knights of the Golden Circle," the "Knights of the White Camellia," the "Angels of Avenging Justice," the "Spirits of the Lost Clan," or the "Centaurs of Caucasian Civilization." The reader can have his choice of names. Nor can it be successfully denied that "The Order" did more to prevent horrible crimes and to tide civilization of the negroes over the fearful period of anarchy referred to, than could have been done by the Freedman's Bureau and all the troops,—or twice the number,—stationed in the South, even had all the officials been wise men and true Christians and patriots, which was very, very far from being the case, as all Fools who did errands have testified and can testify.

The writer has now nothing more to say concerning the so-called "Ku-Klux Klans," but he claims that the mere fact that the country,—particularly the cotton and sugar belts—from the Chesapeake to the Rio Grande, was not drenched in the blood of riots and assassinations, during the period of reconstruction and rehabilitation, proves the Southern white people to be possessed of a civilization having certain qualities of excellence which, no matter what may be the brilliant destiny of the leading human race in the future, can never be surpassed while men shall continue to be frail and fallible. And he here records the prediction that the time will come when the candid and unprejudiced historian, who has thoroughly informed himself respecting the period extending from 1859 to 1884, as he glances sadly back at the wrongs and outrages of the past, . . . will gently whisper to the invisible guardian spirit at his side: "Ah, noble people! As political brethren, they were generous, magnanimous and forgiving; as military foes, they were chivalrous and brilliant; but under the numberless wrongs and persecutions which succeeded their downfall they were sublime!"

But Floyd does have something more to say about the Klan and its provocation. On page 583, after the various pairs of lovers have been married, Horace Greeley shows up. He is a cousin of the girl who has become Mrs. Stewart. He listens, with the patience of a prominent Democrat, as Mr. Stewart sums up the Southern position:

> I think the so-called Ku-Klux take but little account of such physically inoffensive things as negroes' votes. They care but little who may be President or members of Congress, so long as they know they have only themselves to depend on to meet the present emergency, and to keep under control the tide of anarchy and barbarism, which threatens to overwhelm us, before the negro shall be permitted to indicate in what direction his natural instinct will lead him. In order to ensure the mastery for the Republican party over the negro, it is necessary to fire his heart against the Southern white people. This being done, he is not satisfied with political vengeance,—to his mind, a milk-sop sentiment,— but yearns to taste of vengeance in its full flavor, and through the medium of his physical senses. His teachings having thus inspired him with a desire to injure, deface, destroy, or appropriate our property, and to commit lawless acts against our persons, and crimes against the peace of society, nature's first law demands that some power shall step forward and check his mad career. I think the acts of the so-called Ku-Klux are designed only to punish such acts of villainy, and to intimidate the vicious.

Thorns in the Flesh was published in Philadelphia; the next Klan novel, Thomas Jefferson Jerome's *Ku-Klux Klan No. 40,* was published in Raleigh, North Carolina, eleven years later, in 1895. In his preface Jerome says the Klan was dead, and adds, "I would to God that the very recollection of the existence of such an organization could be lost, and that all record of its deeds could be effaced." But he quickly launches into a long catalogue of the crimes of Congress during Reconstruction and asks who could possibly wonder that white men formed the Klan?

In Jerome's book, Den No. 40 meets in Glen Echo to discuss suitable punishments for the most notorious enemies of Southern chivalry and tradition. Peter Tinklepaugh is a Connecticut teacher who has married a local Negro woman; but he evades punishment, or rather defers it, by insisting that his father was a free Negro. He later joins forces with a carpetbag lawyer named Weston in issuing a Radical newspaper in which they play up every local

Klan outrage in a bid for Northern sympathy and, more specifically, for federal support, which arrives in the form of troops. They kill an old man and blame his murder on the Klan. The federal troops arrest the leading Klansman, John Latham, and string him up in an effort to extort a confession; but they overdo it, and he dies. Judge Farwell, from Massachusetts, at first opposes the Klan at every step, and in his conduct on the bench shows his antipathy— for example, sustaining the challenge to a juryman for obvious prejudice against Negroes.

As the lurid events reach their climax, the parallel to the Kirk-Holden War becomes apparent; at one point the chief justice of the state declares the power of the judiciary has been exhausted; this had been a crucial point in the struggle between Governor Holden and the Klan in 1871. But if Judge Farwell is modeled after Tourgée, the parallel breaks down at the end, for Farwell loses all patience with the federal officers, especially the local military commander "Cross-eyed Telf," and switches from the Republican to the Democratic standard. The election produces a sweeping Democratic victory, and the offending Republicans lose their hold. All the good people—the Southern Democrats—are rewarded, and all the bad people are punished.

Ku-Klux Klan No. 40 is a minor classic that probably deserves to be better known. Unlike *Thorns in the Flesh*, it avoids the lengthy exposition of Southern views in the dialogue, but it does manage to work in virtually every facet of the regional thinking. For example, one character reports having overheard General Sherman give orders to burn every building on a certain plantation except the main house, which he had commandeered for himself and his staff. But apart from a measurable improvement in the techniques of fiction, this novel, like its predecessor, is only apprentice work to the three books best known in this genre: *Red Rock, Gabriel Tolliver,* and *The Clansman,* all written at just the period when eminent historians were beginning to consolidate the Southern interpretation of our history.

Thomas Nelson Page (1853–1922) is the most famous of the American writers who glamorized the South and created the nostalgic myth of magnolias and moonlight, aristocrats and loyal, lovable slaves, and all the other appurtenances of this romantic local color. From his first short story in 1884 until 1913, when Page became our ambassador to Italy, his career was that of staunch defender—or creator—of legend. Because he was a much better writer than Floyd or Jerome, his Klan novel *Red Rock* (1898) is a notable advance over *Thorns in the Flesh* and *Ku-Klux Klan No. 40*. But it uses some of the same devices and consistently reflects the same regional viewpoints about Reconstruction.

The Freedmen's Bureau agent, Jonadab Leech, is a totally vicious villain without a single saving grace. At the end of the book he is revealed as a scoundrel who has abandoned his wife and child; the wife had come south to teach in a Negro school. The regular Army officers share the local loathing for Leech, which is monumental. His very name is obviously symbolic.

Leech enrolls the Negroes with promises of land and is not above inciting them to arson—the familiar story of hinting that matches cost only five cents a box. By ruthless and unfair taxes and fines, Leech manages to get title to the fine old houses of the neighborhood: "Red Rock," the ancestral home of the Grays, and "Birdwood," the Cary plantation. Jacquelin Gray comes home to find Red Rock in the hands of his father's former overseer, Still, who is now one of Leech's henchmen and beneficiaries. But like the other Southern aristocrats—General Legare, Dr. Cary, and Steve Allen (leader of the local Klan)—Jacquelin is extremely noble in the face of adversity. Negroes who had been children when he left home are now "playing at the game of freedmen," and, at Leech's prompting, are daily more insolent. The only effective counteraction, in the form of Klan visitations, is possible because the Negroes—as Page pictures them—are easily influenced.

Just when things look most ominous for the local whites, with their leaders jailed and facing certain conviction on Leech's trumped-up charges, a letter from Dr. Cary to an old college chum, Senator Rockfield, effects their release. In a climactic courtroom scene, Still is exposed as a cheat in his acquisition of Red Rock, and Jacquelin regains the old family place. Dr. Cary's letter is reminiscent of the message sent by John Leland of South Carolina in 1872 when he and some five hundred other white leaders were arrested, herded to Columbia, and denied the right of habeas corpus. This is only the most obvious parallel to actual events that the author puts to good fictional use. But unlike his forerunners in the genre, Page is too good a craftsman to turn dialogue into partisan harangues. *Red Rock* is a very readable novel and the best of its type.

Almost as good a novel is *Gabriel Tolliver: A Story of Reconstruction* (1902), by Joel Chandler Harris. Best known for his long series of *Uncle Remus* stories, Harris wrote enough local color fiction about Georgia aristocrats, poor whites, and ex-slaves to merit some attention even if he had never tried his hand at Negro folk literature. The rare good humor of Uncle Remus is notably lacking in *Gabriel Tolliver*, however, for this is a bitter novel indeed.

The news of Lee's surrender comes as a great shock to the people of Halcyondale and other places in the rural South, who have not been at all prepared to consider the possibility of defeat. Negroes are suddenly no longer cheerful; many of them join "the restless, migratory throng" with no place to call home. Gabriel tries to find out what the Union Leagues are up to—"the Union Leagues established in the South under the political department of the Freedmen's Bureau." Hiding in a closet, he hears a speech delivered by a typical carpetbagger, Gilbert Hotchkiss, in the course of which there is a strong hint about the low cost of matches.

Harris uses some of the unartistic devices of Floyd and Jerome, including lengthy expositions about Radical misrule. In Chapter 18, "The Knights of the White Camellia," he refers to "the awful fact that the prime movers in the reconstruction scheme (if not the men who acted as their instruments and tools) were intent on stirring up a new revolution in the hope that the negroes might be prevailed upon to sack cities and towns, and destroy the white population." This is the only inference, Harris insisted, that could be drawn from the congressional debates of 1867–68.

Harris then opens fire on the new state conventions that superseded the first postwar efforts to draft new constitutions. They were, he asserts, "well named the mongrel convention . . . made up of political adventurers from Maine, Vermont, and other Northern states, and boasted of a majority composed of ignorant negroes and criminals," while local white leaders were disfranchised. It was, in his view, a deliberate scheme of the Radicals for "placing the governments of the Southern States in the hands of ignorant negroes controlled by men who had no interest whatsoever in the welfare of the people."

Gabriel, concealed in a tree, watches as thirteen white-clad Klansmen ride three times around a church in which a local Union League is meeting; friends tell him these are not Ku Klux but Knights of the White Camellia. He also learns that orderly groups such as this sometimes are imitated by less responsible men: "Violent men will get in the saddle, and outrages will be committed, and injustice done." A Klan warning, printed on handbills and posted all over town, has a sobering effect; the freedmen show a sudden willingness to return to work.

Hotchkiss is portrayed as the worst Radical type, with the strong implication that all Radicals are just as bad. Harris says that Hotchkiss "was one of the men who urged John Brown to stir up an insurrection in which innocent women and children had been the chief sufferers." In a lengthy paragraph, Harris pictures the Abolitionist type: narrow-minded bigots, intensely in earnest, "who believe that philanthropy, and reform, and progress generally are worthless unless it be accompanied by strife, and hate, and, if possible, by bloodshed. You find the type everywhere; it clings like a leech to the skirts of every great movement. The Hotchkisses . . . are as productive of isms as a fly is of maggots."

If Radical incitement of Negroes to commit arson is one convention of these Klan novels, another is the sympathetic officer in the regular army. Captain Falconer, locally hated and ostracized in the early action of the story, turns out to be the son of an esteemed old friend of a local leading citizen. Concerning the captain, Harris writes, "It would be hard, if not impossible, to find a man in [the entire United States army] who does not shrink from the dirty work of the politicians."

Gabriel, arrested for a murder he did not commit, is taken to a prison in Savannah, where he suffers torture in the form of sweatbox and wrist-rack. But in the most readable chapter of the book, he is rescued by a complicated ruse; and, when civil government is restored shortly afterward, he is united with his beloved in a suitably happy ending.

The last and most influential of this series of pro-Klan novels was Thomas Dixon's *The Clansman: An Historical Romance of the Ku Klux Klan,* which appeared in 1906. In a preliminary address "To the Reader," Dixon pays tribute to the Klan, "which over-turned the Reconstruction regime," and explains its hierarchy: the Grand Wizard, ruling the entire Klan, a Grand Dragon over each state, a Grand Titan over each congressional district, a Grand Giant over each county, and a Grand Cyclops over each local Den.

"In the darkest hour of the life of the South," Dixon wrote, "when her wounded people lay helpless amid rags and ashes under the beak and talon of the Vulture, suddenly" appeared the Klan, "reincarnated souls of the Clansmen of Old Scotland." This sets the tone for the book, which makes use of all the devices older authors had used and adds new ones. Venerable Senators in Washington, and their lovely daughters in love with dashing federal officers, and unscrupulous political tricksters, and Negro dupes of Radical leaders, and the clash of hooded Klan members with Union Leaguers and Freedmen's Bureau agents—everything is here, with much more lurid detail than in any of the earlier books. Southern whites and their Northern sympathizers are the good people; the wicked people are the self-serving, vindictive Radicals and their agents. The plot is the struggle between them; the denouement is the victory of the good people over the bad. Worst of all the villains is Thaddeus Stevens, described as trying to "Africanize" ten sovereign states of the Union. But despite his control of the Senate, even he fails; the Klan is more than a match for him.

The Clansman, the climactic novel in the series that began with *Thorns in the Flesh,* appeared at the perfect psychological moment, when muckraking journalists were creating vast suspicion of government corruption and when eminent historians were well along in grinding out formidable accounts of the Civil War and Reconstruction that were heavily weighted on the side of the South.

The Clansman did not stand alone among Dixon's works; it was actually a sequel to *The Leopard's Spots,* and was followed by *The Traitor;* but when D. W. Griffith decided to make a Klan moving picture, it was *The Clansman* that he asked Dixon to recast as a script. The result—*The Birth of a Nation*—made moving picture history, with a very long initial run and frequent revivals, all of which helped confirm the Southern interpretation in the mind of the common man, as the historians were confirming it in the minds of serious readers. Meanwhile, from *Thorns in the Flesh* through *The Birth of a Nation,* the other side, which Tourgée had treated in *A Fool's Errand,* produced no new champion and virtually died out of American thinking. Nor has it been found in fiction in the years since, although *Gone With the Wind,* in 1936, proved that the Reconstruction theme still had great public appeal. As a "battle of the books," the literary record shows one broadside fired by Tourgée and answered over the years at fairly regular intervals; it is a very one-sided battle, if battle it can be called at all.

The "Shot Analysis" of *The Birth of a Nation,* prepared by Theodore Huff and issued by the Museum of Modern Art in 1961, has a particular value in showing how far the film went in presenting the traditional Southern interpretation. In those days before sound, dialogue was dubbed in; and along with it, editorial announcements and opinions. The title after Scene 83, for instance, is as follows: "The gathering storm. The power of the sovereign states established when Lord Cornwallis surrendered to the individual colonies in 1781, is threatened by the new administration." Scene 114 is followed by this comment: "Abraham Lincoln uses the Presidential office for the first time in history to call for volunteers to enforce the rule of the coming nation over the individual states."

At the beginning, Negro slaves are shown as happy and contented; but the war brings a great change. Negro soldiers pillage and burn, while Confederate families suffer in every way—loss of their sons in battle and economic pressure so great that it forces them to sell their most cherished heirlooms and furniture to aid the cause. An intermission follows the sixth reel. Then comes: "Second Part—Reconstruction. The agony which the South endured that a nation might be born." Woodrow Wilson is brought in to support the thesis; one quotation from his writing refers to the birth of the Klan: "The white men were roused by a mere instinct of self-preservation." It is not so much the Negroes that threaten their extinction, however, as the Radicals in control of Congress. Scene 552 is followed by this title: "Starting the ferment. The black party celebration. Inducing the negroes to quit work," and after Scene 560, "The Freedman's Bureau. The negroes getting free supplies. The charity of a generous North misused to delude the ignorant."

A crowning scene, and one that could hardly have been omitted, shows the "arrogant, insolent, illiterate, bad-behaved Negro majority in the South Carolina House of Representatives"—the scene used over and over, with telling effect, in countless history books. But hope was not totally lost as long as the brave Southern whites could organize. Following Scene 755 is this conclusive statement: "The Ku Klux Klan, the organization that saved the South from the anarchy of black rule, but not without the shedding of more blood than at Gettysburg, according to Judge Tourgée of the carpetbaggers."

It is curious that the literary treatment of the Civil War and Reconstruction was so one-sided. One reason may be the general revulsion toward government caused by the corruption under President Grant, when public faith was so grossly betrayed. Many of the leading figures in the federal program for reconstructing the South were, by 1876, exposed as grafters, and even those who were not dishonest suffered through a kind of guilt by association. Another reason may be the latent romanticism of the American people, producing a sympathy for the defeated Confederacy that was a strange bedfellow for the rising interest in native realism. Mark Twain came close to deflating the Southern myth in *Huckleberry Finn;* if in that book he had included a satirical portrait of a Klansman, Tourgée might not stand alone as spokesman for the "Northern" viewpoint.

But whatever the reasons for the dearth of novels sympathetic to the Northern cause, it is surely reasonable to link the revived Klan to the film that capped the long series of fictional support for the Southern viewpoint. *The Birth of a Nation* opened in 1915, and in that same year the modern Klan was organized. Recent historians belabor the point that the two Klans, the old and the new, have virtually nothing in common. But this one-sided battle of the books clearly shows a continuity. This continuity helps explain why men hostile to federal pressures and uneasy about the growing power of various minority groups would be inspired by *The Birth of a Nation* to re-create an organization that was so obviously successful during Reconstruction in preserving the special advantage of white Protestants long in the land. Without the novels glorifying the Klan, and without the film that one of them became, it may well be doubted whether the modern Klan would have been born. Nowhere better than in this continuity of fiction can the link be seen between the "old" and the "new" Klans.

Fear of Negro rule in North Carolina was still evident in 1900, when the Raleigh *News and Observer* published this cartoon by Norman E. Jennette.

Chapter Eleven
THE
KLAN
REVIVED

The twentieth-century Klan began as the dream-child of a lanky Alabamian named William Joseph Simmons. At different times in his life—he was born in 1882—he had been a probationary Methodist preacher and a traveling salesman; and he may have taught American history, briefly, at Lanier University, a small college in Atlanta that the Klan later owned. The one enduring passion of his life was fraternalism. "I believe in fraternal orders," he once asserted, "and fraternal associations among men." He proved it by joining a dozen or more Masonic orders and the Woodmen of the World. His nights were filled with lodge meetings. As leader of the Woodmen's drill team he picked up the title of "Colonel."

In 1911, while convalescing in a hospital after a serious automobile accident, Simmons had plenty of time to review his life. As he later reminisced, it was then that his fondest boyhood dream—reviving the old Ku Klux Klan—returned with compelling urgency. His father had been a Klansman; and his Negro "mammy" had often regaled him with exciting Klan stories. A new Klan would raise American fraternalism to heights never achieved before.

Unfortunately for his reputation for veracity, one man in a position to know deflated the colonel's romantic story—Edgar I. Fuller, a former Klan official who resigned and told all in *The Visible of the Invisible Empire, or The Maelstrom* (1925). According to Fuller, a onetime head of the Woodmen of the World, Jonathan Frost by name, saw in a passing reference to the Reconstruction Klan the chance to found a new fraternal order. He presented the idea at a Woodmen convention, and Simmons stole it outright. "All the story told by Simmons," Fuller insisted, "of visions of his youth taking form, is a myth. . . . If he dreamed at all, it was the fitful stirring of delirium in a diseased mind," for his most obvious traits were "physical laziness, mental inertia, and moral insensibility from his boyhood." Simmons' claims of having briefly attended the University of Alabama and of studying medicine were typical of his world of fantasy; his schooling, indeed, had been very limited. His relation to the Methodist Church was hardly as he recalled it: On trial as an itinerant preacher, he was soon dropped for inefficiency and unreliability. Even in the selling of ladies' garters, he wore out the company's patience by his slovenly habits. He did prove adept, however, at selling burial insurance to his fellow Woodmen of the World.

Fuller's testimony, that of a hostile witness, should no doubt be somewhat discounted; but whatever the source of Simmons' great idea, it is known that after dark on Thanksgiving Day of 1915 he led fifteen followers to the top of Stone Mountain, east of Atlanta, for the first initiation ceremony of what he called the "reincarnated Klan." It was not greatly different from the ritual devised at Pulaski, Tennessee, back in 1866. On an altar—a projecting bit of rock— were placed an American flag, an open Bible, an unsheathed sword, and a canteen of water. (Later on, "initiation water," scooped from the Chattahoochee River near Atlanta and sold for ten dollars a quart, was one of several lucrative sources of income for Simmons and his successors as Grand Wizard.) The one striking innovation on Stone Mountain was the erection and burning of a cross, the only source of light—and warmth—for the shivering original Knights of the modern Klan.

A week later Simmons incorporated the organization in Fulton

County (Atlanta), which has remained to this day a hub of Klan activity. The old Klan had never sought the legal recognition that incorporation represents; its leaders, who put all their reliance on total secrecy, would have been aghast at the very idea. But from the outset Simmons conceived of an organization well protected by legal status, as widely publicized as possible, and amply productive of income—for himself.

A tall, slender man whose pince-nez glasses provided a certain air of distinction, Simmons was an effective public speaker; but, though crowds enjoyed his spellbinding elocution, he enlisted new members at a very disappointing rate. The war in Europe was a formidable rival for interest. By the time the United States entered the war in 1917, the Klan had fewer than two thousand members, mostly in Georgia and Alabama, enough to issue a public denunciation of a shipyard strike in Mobile and to march in a reunion parade of Confederate veterans, but not nearly enough to attract more than local attention. To make matters worse, an assistant absconded with what there was in the treasury, and Simmons had to mortgage his home to keep the Klan alive. Those were lean days, but Simmons had unquenchable faith in his dream-child.

A residue of idealism kept Simmons from accepting offers made by men solely interested in profit and woefully indifferent to the spirit of true fraternalism. But in 1920, after four years and more of discouragement, he finally gave in; the promise of $100 a week for life was too attractive to resist. The day he signed the contract, June 7, 1920, marks the real beginning of the Klan as it flourished and became a national byword.

The offer that Simmons could not resist was made by Edward Young Clarke, a onetime newspaperman who, during the war, had gained a certain proficiency in directing patriotic fund-raising campaigns. In the course of organizing a Harvest Festival in Atlanta, Clarke had met an engaging widow, Mrs. Elizabeth Tyler, who not only shared his opinion that the public existed to be fleeced but who also had some money of her own—quite a lot of it, in fact. The two formed a Southern Publicity Association and raised money for such groups as the YMCA, the YWCA, and the Salvation Army. Hungry for bigger things, they saw an untapped potential in the Klan. Colonel Simmons had all the qualities of an ideal front man; he had only to consent to let them manage the Klan's entire operation.

Everybody had some knowledge of the Reconstruction Klan, however hazy, if only from *The Birth of a Nation*, first shown in 1915 and one of the great successes of moving picture history. One writer intimates that seeing it gave Simmons the idea of reviving the Klan. If any film has ever been a stimulus to intolerance, this one certainly was. Its effect on the mass audience was to provide a kind of sanction for hate feelings and to glamorize secret societies devoted to preserving race distinctions and to resisting central government. Once the Klan was available, it would seem likely that men would hasten to join it—the kind of men, at least, who wanted some release for their frustrations.

But Simmons was a little too prone to stress the fraternal side of his Klan and to underplay the appeal to intolerance. Furthermore, racial antagonism was, at the moment, too slight to be a good lever for recruitment. Once Clarke and Mrs. Tyler took over, they studied the situation with the critical eyes of professional publicists and decided that the growing popular concern over postwar morals was the thing to manipulate. They devised a propaganda campaign to create an image of the Klan as a guardian of public morality. Using Colonel Simmons as mouthpiece, they made a great show of endorsing and supporting worthy causes of every kind. Early in the life of the old Klan certain devices had proved very effective, such as asking an illiterate Negro to "hold my head for awhile," and handing him a gourd that resembled a head. The comparable effective gimmick of the new Klan was a column of Klansmen in full regalia marching down a church aisle during a service, depositing a donation on the communion table, and marching out— all in perfect silence. Who could oppose an organization so obviously devoted to good clean living and to encouraging all that was best in American life?

Meanwhile it was important to identify the enemies of true Americanism. It was absurdly easy to point them out: all the recent immigrants from odd corners of Europe who exhibited no fondness for Anglo-Saxon tradition and resisted quick assimilation, even choosing to stay in congested city slums and, by their very presence, to make the big cities more sinful and un-American than ever. (Our historic agrarianism played a part here; in Klan thinking, village and farm people were the best variety of Americans.) And then there were the readily identifiable minorities, especially the Jews and the Catholics, the former allegedly incapable of assimilation and intent only on getting rich fast, and the latter notorious for their allegiance to the Pope and for deliberately working to Romanize America. One very effective Klan device was the wide distribution of a "Knights of Columbus oath," not the real oath but a forgery that outlined a plot to subordinate the nation to the Papacy.

The ten questions put to all would-be Klansmen illustrate the concept of true Americanism that the modern Klan sought to establish:

1. Is the motive prompting your ambition to be a Klansman serious and unselfish?
2. Are you a native-born white, Gentile, American citizen?
3. Are you absolutely opposed to and free of any allegiance of any nature to any cause, government, people, sect or ruler that is foreign to the U.S.A.?
4. Do you believe in the tenets of the Christian religion?
5. Do you esteem the U.S.A. and its institutions above any other government, civil, political, or ecclesiastical in the whole world?
6. Will you, without mental reservation, take a solemn oath to defend, preserve, and enforce same?
7. Do you believe in clanishness [*sic*] and will you faithfully practice same toward Klansmen?
8. Do you believe in and will you faithfully strive for the eternal maintenance of white supremacy?
9. Will you faithfully obey our constitution and laws, and conform willingly to all our usages, requirements, and regulations?
10. Can you always be depended on?

The years 1921 through 1926 produced a remarkable number of books and pamphlets attacking and defending the Klan. In the pro-Klan books can be found a systematic analysis of the points made in these initiation questions, sometimes even chapter by chapter. *What Is Ku Kluxism?* (1923) (with no publisher named on the title page, but submitted to the Library of Congress by J. S. Fleming of Goodwater, Alabama) is one continuous essay of eighty-seven pages. The subtitle is "Let Americans Answer. Aliens Only Muddy the Waters," but it covers the entire range of Klan antipathy: public and private immorality, Catholics, Jews, Negroes, as well as aliens. Its major emphasis, in fact, is on the Catholic "conspiracy." Colonel Winfield Jones's *Story of the Ku Klux Klan* (1921) and a later abridged version called *Knights of the Ku Klux Klan* (1941) took up the test questions one by one. The *Story*, appearing so soon after Clarke and Mrs. Tyler assumed control of the Klan, was timely in the extreme. Jones said he was not a Klansman, and that Colonel Simmons had given him access to the Klan records only "with great reluctance," but this may have been a dodge to make the book look like the objective appraisal of an outsider. The revision, twenty years later, was published by the Tocsin Press, owned by an arch Klansman named E. N. Sanctuary, composer of Klan songs.

Jones closed the *Story* with an optimistic prediction:

> The Anglo-Saxon is the typeman of history. To him must yield the self-centered Hebrew, the cultured Greek, the virile Roman, the mystic Oriental. The Psalmist must have had him in mind when he struck his soundless harp and sang: "O Lord; thou hast made him a little lower than the angels, and hast crowned him with glory and honor. Thou hast made him to have dominion over the works of thy hands; thou hast put all things under his feet." The Ku Klux Klan desires that its ruling members shall be of this all-conquering blood. . . . The Ku Klux Klan was planned for the white American.
>
> In brief, the Ku Klux Klan desires to be, hopes to be, plans to be, and will be a great, influential, helpful, patriotic, American fraternal order, taking its allotted place with similar secret brotherhoods, and with them working out our Christian civilization, adding to the gifts and graces, the prosperity and happiness of mankind, and standing for the noble, the true and the good, for the majesty of law, for the advancement of the human race.

The Klan Revived

The Ku Klux Klan Under the Searchlight by Leroy A. Curry, and *K.K.K. Friend or Foe: Which?* by Blaine Mast, both appeared in 1924, a banner Klan year. Curry deemed the Klan essential for reviving true Americanism and its Christian base, and praised it for fighting all forces that threatened to undermine the solid old American principles. His favorite phrase was "this great American Organization." Blaine Mast described Jews as shrewd rich lechers, luring Gentile girls into joyrides and then into hotel rooms; but he added that Jews weren't the only sinners in America. One of his most interesting passages refers to the Catholic conspiracy, but could be taken in quite another sense by an unsympathetic reader: "A nation's greatest enemy is never without—*It is always within!* The worse political enemy is he who stirs up civil strife, as witness our Civil War in 1861–1865." A religious war, he added, would make the Civil War seem mild; "intolerant, lop-sided, radical leaders are never safe to follow."

The Klan, by inference, offered leadership that was safe. This line of argument has a familiar ring in the 1960's when the radical right wing offers what it considers a safer guidance than that provided by our recent Presidents.

Except for the eighth test question on the preservation of white supremacy, the new Klan sounds less like the "reincarnation" of the old Klan that Colonel Simmons liked to talk about than a re-crudescence of the nativism that has been a virtual constant in American history. Each great wave of fresh immigration has been followed by a reaction, most notably the Know-Nothing movement just before the Civil War and the A.P.A.—the American Protective Association—at the end of the nineteenth century. Both of these were particularly opposed to Catholics. The Know-Nothings, alarmed by the propensity of Irish Catholics to enter politics, sought deliberately to bar all foreigners, especially Catholics, from running for office. Among the older Protestants there was a general revulsion from such innovations as the Continental Sabbath, imported by German migrants, which meant attending church early on Sunday morning and spending the rest of the day in relaxation and pleasure—a pattern far removed from the strict sabbatarianism practiced by New England Protestants and pietistic sectarians else-.

Thousands of Klansmen parade down Pennsylvania Avenue in a show of strength in Washington in 1925. *Wide World Photo*

where along the Atlantic seaboard. Milwaukee, St. Louis, and Cincinnati, centers of German settlement, seemed, to the scions of Cotton Mather, to be cities of perdition. In New England, trains didn't run on the Sabbath, and housewives didn't cook—the beans and brown bread eaten hot on Saturday night could be eaten cold on Sunday in the intervals between prolonged church services. There was no question, surely, that new immigrant groups were profoundly challenging the good old American customs.

The A.P.A. was more recent in memory. It began in the further Midwest—Iowa, Kansas, Nebraska—and it was deliberately encouraged by forgeries of Catholic documents. In whole counties Protestant families kept their guns loaded and barricaded their houses. The A.P.A. evolved into a political pressure group, but what most of its scattered rural members remembered was the threat of overt violence—specifically the alleged Catholic plot to massacre all Protestants. Many of these Protestants were of recent migration, people whose own experience in the Old Country had included actual religious persecution. Americans longer in the land were less susceptible; they had a greater sense of security and of belonging. Where the bulk of the population had been long in the land, the

Klan capitalized on the fear of subverted customs; where everybody was of recent migration, the Klan concentrated on threats to their acceptance. In much the same way, a little later, the Klan could be Republican in Ohio and Democratic in Mississippi in its effort to gain political power.

In both the old Klan and the new, wide discrepancies can readily be detected between stated purposes and actual practice. The rank-and-file members could only judge by what the leaders handed out; and since the copy was skillfully prepared, it sounded fine. Ed Clarke and Bessie Tyler kept a sharp eye on the current news, waiting for events they could turn to their own purposes. Foul murders by white Protestants could be ignored; a foul murder by a member of an un-American minority could be seized upon to rouse public indignation and to draw new members to the Klan, which never stopped declaring its endorsement of law and order.

The Leo Frank story antedates the modern Klan, but provides a model of how indignation can be aroused and converted into mob action. On April 27, 1913, a fourteen-year-old girl, Mary Phagan, was found dead in an Atlanta factory where she had been employed; she had been brutally assaulted. A Negro workman was one suspect, but the man tried and condemned to die for the crime was the Jewish plant superintendent, Leo Frank. Tom Watson, demagogic editor of *The Jeffersonian* (and later one of Georgia's United States Senators), played up the lurid details. When Governor Slaton commuted the sentence to life imprisonment the day before he retired from office, Watson outdid himself in vituperation; the predictable response was a mob of five thousand men storming Slaton's house. On August 12, 1915, Watson editorialized: "The next Leo Frank case in Georgia will never reach the courthouse. THE NEXT JEW WHO DOES WHAT FRANK DID IS GOING TO GET EXACTLY THE SAME THING THAT WE GIVE TO NEGRO RAPISTS." Four days later, twenty-five men, only two of them masked, took Frank forcibly from the Georgia state prison and hanged him in Marietta, north of Atlanta, where Mary Phagan had lived.

The Klan, it is clear, has made capital out of linking Jews and Negroes. A broadside in current circulation announces in heavy type: "NIGGER! YOU TOO CAN BE A JEW." And other hate literature identifies Jews with nonwhites in the population.

It was not a sordid crime, however, that gave the Klan its first big publicity, but rather a series of sensational articles in the New York *World* in September 1921. Papers in eighteen other cities picked the series up, and for a while it was prime headline news. What the editors could not realize was that newspaper exposure and even ridicule accelerated membership in the Klan. Members of Congress, Jewish or Catholic themselves or representing districts with heavy Jewish, Catholic, or Negro population, clamored for an investigation. Representative William D. Upshaw of Georgia, one of the first Klan candidates to be elected to Congress, tried to divert attention by calling for investigations of *all* secret societies; Klansmen often complained that theirs was the only secret organization to be the object of opposition.

In the Congressional hearings the first to testify was Roland Thomas, the member of the *World* editorial staff who had conducted the investigation. He had given three months to it, he reported, but he had to admit that much in the series was based on hearsay; journalists had no power of search or subpoena. The star witness was C. Anderson Wright, an ex-Klansman, who gave damaging evidence about the Klan's financial dealings. Most of the ten-dollar Klecktoken (initiation fee) went to the local, state, and national organizers (called Kleagles); as former state Kleagle for New York, Wright knew what he was talking about. He was supported by a postal inspector who could report that the Clarke-Tyler combination had received more than $850,000 in the period from June 1, 1920, to September 24, 1921. In rebuttal the Klan's attorney, Paul Etheridge, and Representative Upshaw defended the purpose of the Klan and paid glowing tribute to Colonel Simmons. Then Simmons himself took the stand for several sessions and proved a perfect witness, unruffled, urbane, and charming. He charged that the *World* had been motivated only by a desire to increase its circulation. Winfield Jones, who was present, subsequently asserted that the Klan "greatly profited by the newspaper attacks on it and the congressional investigation."

The Klan series in the *World* and the investigation by Congress can be viewed as launching the public debate in print that followed. Jones got his book out before the year was over. For a man who had been reluctant to show the Klan records to Jones, Simmons was very free with statements, for Jones quoted him extensively, as in this passage:

> We antagonize no man's religion. I have heard of only one case where a Kleagle circulated anti-Catholic propaganda, and he was instantly discharged.
> We are not anti-Jewish; any Jew who can subscribe to the tenets of the Christian Religion can get in.
> We are not anti-negro. Scores of other fraternal organizations do not admit negroes. We are not anti-foreign born, we merely require that members be native born Americans.

The foregoing only paraphrases another statement that Simmons once made, though this one is positive instead of negative:

> The Knights of the Ku Klux Klan is a purely patriotic fraternal organization designed to memorialize the Klan of the Reconstruction period and to perpetuate the principles for which it stood. . . . It stands for the preservation of American ideals and institutions, the protection of the home, the chastity of womanhood, the maintenance of the blood-bought rights and liberties of the Anglo-Saxon race. . . . The Ku Klux Klan stands unreservedly and unashamedly for white supremacy in America.

Jones described the Colonel as "a wise and thoughtful man . . . hatred and passion never disturb his thoughts . . . a real Christian." Clarke and Mrs. Tyler had been luckier than they knew, for Simmons projected an amazingly good image; his behavior under questioning by Congressmen made him seem to deserve all of Jones's extravagant encomiums. He might be only a figurehead, but the Klan could not have had a better one. With the money rolling in, Clarke increased the Wizard's salary to $1,000 a month, gave him a lump sum of $25,000 to compensate for the five lean years, and installed him in a fine mansion on Peachtree Street, "Klan Krest," which cost $33,000. In addition, Simmons received a dollar and half of each Klecktoken, and royalties for the regalia he had supposedly invented. One critic has estimated his total profit from the Klan as $300,000, but it was probably more.

Ed Clarke, the man who had figured out all the angles, was doing somewhat better. He received three dollars from each new member, twice as much as Simmons, and he was a major owner of the Gate City Manufacturing Company, which made all the regalia. One estimate of his income, at its peak, was $40,000 a month, but some of this, of course, had to go to Bessie Tyler, and there were such expenses as buying out hostile periodicals and subsidizing friendly ones. It was not *all* gravy, as some Klan detractors have intimated.

Nor could Clarke sit back and enjoy life, like Simmons, or develop the taste for good liquor that in time was the Colonel's downfall. The national organization required a good deal of attention, for a good Kleagle was hard to find and harder to keep satisfied. The Cyclops of the individual den, or Klavern, received fifty cents of each Klecktoken, while the local Kleagle, who did the active recruiting, received four dollars, and the state Kleagle, sometimes called Imperial Representative, ordinarily got one dollar. Clarke honored himself with the title of Imperial Kleagle—he was, after all, the acme of the recruiting pyramid. When things were going well, everybody made money. But more than once a state Kleagle made so much money that he tried to keep it all; and then Clarke had to dispatch one of his legal staff to enforce remittance. Even more troublesome was the occasional power struggle that split one of the Realms, as in Pennsylvania.

In that state, as elsewhere, the press denunciations of 1921 proved a stimulus to recruitment. F. W. Atkins of Philadelphia was granted the eastern part of the state, and Sam Rich of Pittsburgh the western part; the Susquehanna River was the dividing line. Rich hired A. L. Cotton as a local Kleagle and sent him to Erie, where he promptly got himself arrested; he was thus a martyr, and the publicity stimulated Klan growth there. Atkins got into serious trouble when he joined a conspiracy with other nearby Klan leaders to break away from Atlanta; with a little better planning they might have succeeded, but they bungled the job and Atkins was fired. Rich, by remaining loyal to Atlanta, was rewarded by being given the entire state. Atkins had to make do with a pittance, something between $25,000 and $35,000, his collections being at a low point when the plot failed.

Atkins at least had the decency, before he absconded, to destroy his records, which if made public could have done great harm to the national Klan. But without the records, it took a good deal of time and patience to rebuild the Klan in the eastern part of Pennsylvania. Rich appointed Morris E. Freeman to manage the old Atkins territory, but this was a mistake, for Freeman was no man for finance and made a mess of his job. Rich then sent Cotton, the Erie martyr, to take over, and thus regained total control. They had poor luck with only one group, the Pennsylvania Dutch, who liked the anti-Catholic efforts but stubbornly withheld the blind obedience that the Klan demanded. By the late summer of 1923 Klan strength in Pennsylvania was about 260,000, about 10 per cent of the adult males in the state.

D. C. Stephenson, Imperial Representative for Indiana and Ohio, was one of the most successful organizers. His quarterly report, for the period from March 17 to July 15, 1923, included a payment of $641,475. He was sent a personal check in appreciation, made out for $5,000; but he sent it back. After all, he was collecting a capitation fee of $1.25 from each member. Whether Indiana was particularly fertile ground for the Klan, or whether his talents made it powerful there, might be hard to determine. But Indiana certainly was one of the Klan strongholds, and Ohio was not far behind.

The Klan records show deposits in many different banks, sometimes in checking and savings accounts, sometimes in safe deposit boxes, and sometimes, although it violated the law governing the use and control of trust funds, in the personal accounts of individuals. It has been estimated that by 1925 six million Americans had joined and paid the ten-dollar Klecktoken. Counting the sales of regalia and "initiation water," something like $75,000,000 was paid into the Order by the members. The Klan was big business. Its litigation alone approached the $10 million mark. It should not be astonishing, incidentally, that Ed Clarke, always canny, forced the

Klan attorneys to split with him the fees they charged to defend Klansmen who got into trouble with the law.

It was acutely embarrassing to Simmons when, in 1922, one of his oldest Klan friends, Imperial Kligrapp (Secretary) Wade, charged in a lawsuit that Simmons was more often drunk than sober and that Clarke was the real leader of the Klan. This may have prompted Simmons to ask Clarke to find him a personal assistant. The man Clarke chose was a Dallas dentist, Hiram Wesley Evans, who had made quite a name for himself in Texas Klan circles. He was given the title of Grand Dragon. Then Simmons made the mistake of taking a six-month leave of absence, and, while he was absent, Evans maneuvered himself into power.

When Simmons returned, he summoned a Klonvokation on November 27, 1922. He assumed he would be re-elected Grand Wizard, and proposed for Evans the new title of Emperor. But he was no match for the sharp-minded men around him. At four o'clock one morning he was awakened by Grand Dragon Stephenson, of Indiana, and Fred Savage, head of the Klan's fifty-man secret police force. They warned him that if he let his name be offered for re-election, his character would be violently attacked on the floor, something the Klan could not afford to let happen. Stephenson and Savage apparently represented a group of Klan officials, mostly Grand Dragons, who were sick and tired of control by Simmons, Clarke, and Bessie Tyler. They badgered Simmons into naming Evans as his successor, and he did just that at the Klonvokation. All he could salvage for himself was the title of Emperor which he had suggested for Evans.

From the Klan point of view, Evans was an improvement over both Clarke and Simmons. A Vanderbilt graduate, he had been reasonably successful as a dentist, and he had none of the conspicuous vices of Simmons. He dressed well and was a good public speaker. He had a much better sense of the groups in America with interests parallel to those of the Klan, especially large corporations. And he recognized that Clarke was no Klansman at heart. He at least shared with Simmons the dedication to fraternalism.

In the fall of 1919, before they had even conceived of approaching Simmons, Clarke and Mrs. Tyler had been arrested by Atlanta police in a house that Mrs. Tyler owned. Both were drunk, and neither was fully dressed; they must have made a public nuisance of themselves. They were fined nominally for disorderly conduct. Simmons in his bland good nature overlooked the peccadillo, if he ever knew about it. But Evans was made of sterner stuff. Even though the pair had given false names, Evans was able to ferret out the sordid details, and, although he never made them public, he decided that Ed Clarke and Bessie Tyler had to go. It was more openly known that Clarke had deserted his wife, who had sued him for divorce. And it was a flagrant disregard of Klan principle when, in 1922, Clarke met with the great Negro visionary, Marcus Garvey, to discuss Garvey's plan to resettle American Negroes in foreign countries.

Mrs. Tyler remarried in 1923 and died in 1924. Clarke was arrested in Houston in the fall of 1923 for transporting whiskey, and in 1924 was fined $500 for violating the White Slave Act. Oblivion overtook him after an abortive attempt to found his own Klan-like order. But whatever can be said and proved against Clarke and Mrs. Tyler, they had been the making of the modern Klan in the two years that they controlled it. The Klan had simply reached a stage at which they were clearly expendable, doing more harm than good. Simmons could not be gotten rid of; he still held his Klan copyrights, he could still be useful in many ways, and people still remembered his excellent performance at the congressional hearing. Beyond all these considerations, of course, was the well-publicized fact that he had founded the Klan. Like the six founders of the original Klan at Pulaski in 1865, Simmons basked in the immortality that Americans commonly give to founding fathers of famous institutions.

Evans made numerous changes. In respect to organization, the most significant change was putting all officials on salary. But of greater importance was his stepped-up campaign to give Klansmen their money's worth by making the Klan a force in politics. He apparently hoped to elect enough Klansmen to control Congress and even the White House. As groundwork for these ambitious plans he sought to win favor with the nation's Protestant clergy-men and to develop a nation-wide pattern of sympathetic journal-ism.

Money was no problem. It was a simple matter to send a $50,000 check to support a pro-Klan candidate in some election, or even to take $25,000 in bills along with him on a trip, for personal dis-tribution, if this seemed expedient. Money was lavished on peri-odicals. *Dawn,* published in Chicago, *The Fellowship Forum* in Washington, *The Searchlight* in Georgia, *The Fiery Cross,* and *The One Hundred Percent American* were among the best-known of the Klan periodicals, though some of them took pains to conceal the Klan support. E. N. Sanctuary's Tocsin Press in New York, meanwhile, was virtually a Klan publishing house.

Champion of Protestantism that it claimed to be, it was essential for the Klan to seek the support of Protestant clergy, or at least to minimize clerical criticism. Simply by not protesting when robed Klansmen marched into churches with donations, clergymen tacitly gave approval; it might have been difficult to order the column to leave. Besides, money is money, whatever its source.

Some Protestant leaders did speak out, however, against the Klan. Three at least, and no doubt others, were so strong in their denun-ciation that the Klan took countermeasures in the hope of dis-crediting them. Dr. C. B. Wilmer, of the Protestant Episcopal Church in Atlanta, was investigated in two states by police officers in an effort to ruin his career. Dr. Plato Durham, a Methodist minister and a professor at Emory University outside Atlanta, was branded a Negrophile by the Klan. Ashby Jones, Baptist, was pub-licly slandered for his opposition to the Klan's anti-Negro measures; that he happened to be the son of J. William Jones, Robert E. Lee's chaplain and eventual biographer, did not make him immune from Klan attack.

The method used against these clerical critics was relatively sim-ple: a request for information was sent to a trusted ally in the community where the clergyman lived or had once lived. In the case of Dr. Wilmer, the investigation came to nothing, as the fol-lowing communications reveal:

The Klan Revived

Atlanta, Ga., March 23, 1921.

G. L. Williams,
910 East Main Street,
Richmond, Va.

Am desirous of securing at once information as to character and standing in Lynchburg of Reverend C. B. Wilmer, now Episcopal rector in Atlanta, who formerly lived in Lynchburg. Am informed he taught a Negro school while living in Lynchburg, and that his standing in Lynchburg was not of the best kind, socially. Get this information for me at once, personally, at our expense, and give me a full and complete history of Wilmer in Lynchburg, if possible. This is a chance for you to perform real service. Wilmer is leading attack on this organization at this time and is head, in Atlanta, of Inter-Racial Committee, which is branch of Negro association in New York. Wire me first possible moment what you find and send full report by special delivery. Acknowledge receipt of this telegram.

E. Y. CLARKE.

Confidential

Greensboro, N.C.
April 7, 1921.

Mr. C. L. Rogers, Patrolman,
Lynchburg, Va.
Dear Sir:

The Rev. C. B. Wilmer, white, of Atlanta, supposed to have been a teacher in a Negro school for two years at Lynchburg, and is alleged to have mistreated and neglected his sister while in Lynchburg, finally having to leave Lynchburg.

I wish you would make a quiet investigation regarding this man and let me have full particulars of what you are able to develop.

Yours truly,
J. F. WILLIAMSON
Captain of Police

The Klan Revived

SOUTHERN RAILWAY COMPANY

Lynchburg, Va.
April 9, 1921.

Mr. J. F. Williamson,
Captain of Police,
Greensboro, N.C.
Dear Sir:

With reference to your file attached with regard to Rev. C. B. Wilmer, white, of Atlanta, Ga., supposed to have been a teacher in a Negro school for two years at Lynchburg, Va., and alleged to have had difficulty with his sister while in Lynchburg, Va., finally having left here.

I beg to advise that I have investigated your request as you desired, handling the case with Mr. E. E. Glass, confidentially, who has been superintendent of schools in this city for forty-three years. Mr. Glass advises that he knew Rev. C. B. Wilmer very well and that he never did teach school in Lynchburg, Va., but he was an Episcopal minister and was interested in a Negro school about twenty-five years ago on outskirts of city, where now I.O.O.F. orphanage stands, and that the station named Wilmer, on Southern railway, just south of Durmid, Va., was named in his favor. Mr. Glass states that he knew of Rev. Wilmer having difficulty with his sister, and when he left Lynchburg that there positively could not have been anything against him, as he was a gentleman beyond reproach. Mr. Glass referred me to Col. William King, one of our very best citizens.

Col. King advises that he knew Rev. Wilmer very well and cited about the same as Mr. Glass, in regard to his life while in Lynchburg, Va. He states that Rev. Wilmer's sister married a reformed Jew, named Yeager, who was associated with Rev. Wilmer in the work at this Negro school, and that they did have some difficulty which was at least twenty-five years ago.

Yours truly
G. L. ROGERS
Patrolman

The same patrolman, G. L. Rogers, interviewed Plato Durham, who turned out to be no rabid "nigger-lover." Negroes, he said, were inferior beings, and their progress was certain to be very gradual. He offered the opinion that Negroes themselves, by and large, preferred separation of the races. But he reiterated his charge that the Klan was an evil force, as a small group trying to enforce laws secretly by illegal methods. Since Evans already knew of

Durham's opposition, this interview was no more satisfactory than the investigation of Dr. Wilmer.

One project that the Klan hierarchy seriously considered was the unification of Protestant denominations. Catholics and Jews were both unitary; the multiplicity of Protestant churches was a formidable handicap. True, it was possible and profitable, sometimes, to exploit their rivalries; but there was always the risk of alienating Klansmen from each other. It is ironical that movements to unite Protestants are today commonly condemned by "hundred-percent Americans" who suspect a Communist plot and who, in their efforts to discredit churchmen working for unification, use the same methods the Klan used in the 1920's to discredit opponents of unity.

One other project that was discussed as a possibility was the creation of a Klan church. If Protestant churches were unwilling to unite, a new church, based on Klan principles, might enlist millions of citizens who put true Americanism and true religion above any denominational commitments.

The Klan shared its Protestant restrictiveness with the Masons, and more than once sought to capitalize on the parallel. Kleagles commonly remarked to prospects, in an offhand manner, that "the Klan is, in fact, a Masonic movement." Many leading Klansmen, in both the old Klan and the new, were Masons; Evans himself had gained the 32nd Degree. But Masonic leaders objected to this maneuver even more than the clergy. Typical of numerous statements publicly repudiating the Klan bids for brotherly approval is this passage, taken from an article by Justice Arthur S. Tompkins, Grand Master of the Masonic Order of New York:

> Our Democracy cannot permanently endure unless all classes, creeds and races are allowed to live and worship freely and peaceably under the equal protection of the law. Any movement that is calculated to fan and intensify the fires of religious bigotry or class antagonisms or race prejudices will be deprecated and deplored by men who love their country, and who want to keep it noble and make its future greater. There are peaceful and lawful agencies for the punishment of crime, the protection of individual and property rights, the redress of wrong, the vindication of the right and the preservation of our institutions and all the things that we Masons hold dear.

The Klan Revived

The Grand Master of the Masons in Texas, Andrew L. Randall, was no less emphatic, declaring that the Klan, by undertaking to "set aside and supersede the legal agencies of the state," and to become "a secret and irresponsible criminal court and a night-riding executioner of its own decrees, is opposed to and subversive of the American system, under which every man has a constitutional right to a fair trial by jury." Herold J. Richardson, senior grand warden and potentate of Media Temple in Rochester, New York, doubted that many Masons were Klansmen; but if some were, "there should be no hesitation in exposure of the man who not only betrays his fraternity, but also his pledge to the flag." Even stronger is a statement made by Richard H. Hanna, deputy to the supreme council of Ancient and Accepted Scottish Rite Freemasonry, on October 25, 1921: "True Masonry insists on just laws rigorously enforced and is ready at all times to assist the constituted authorities in that enforcement, but never to *violate the laws in the enforcement process.* This Ku Klux Klan is to be avoided as one would a pestilence."

Such language must have puzzled a good many Klansmen who sincerely believed that they loved their country with a special fervor and that what the Klan did was for the country's advancement. It is tempting to suppose that the average intelligence of Klan members was low; what else could explain their willingness to contribute good money to an organization that gave them nothing in return (except a chance to hate)? Wizard Evans virtually admitted in an article that his followers were relatively simple, motivated more by emotion than by reason; the passage illustrates a recurring popular suspicion of intellectuals, though in those days he didn't have the term "egg-head" at his disposal:

We are a movement of the plain people, very weak in the matter of culture, intellectual support, and trained leadership. We are demanding, and we expect to win, a return of power into the hands of the everyday, not highly cultured, not overly intellectualized, but unspoiled and not de-Americanized, average citizen of the old stock. Our members and leaders are all of this class—the opposition of the intellectuals and liberals who hold the leadership and from whom we expect to wrest control, is almost automatic.

This is undoubtedly a weakness. It lays us open to the charge of being "hicks" and "rubes" and "drivers of second-hand Fords." We admit it. Far worse, it makes it hard for us to state our case and advocate our crusade in the most effective way, for most of us lack skill in language. . . .

Every popular movement has suffered from just this handicap. . . .

The Klan does not believe that the fact that it is emotional and instinctive, rather than coldly intellectual, is a weakness. All action comes from emotion, rather than from ratiocination. Our emotions and the instincts on which they are based have been bred into us for thousands of years; far longer than reason has had a place in the human brain. . . . They are the foundations of our American civilization, even more than our great historic documents; they can be trusted where the fine-haired reasoning of the denatured intellectuals cannot.

The article containing these candid statements appeared in *The North American Review* in the spring of 1926, a time when the Klan had begun to lose its momentum.

The high-water mark of the Klan under Evans was undoubtedly 1924, when his campaign to gain political power was at its most violent. He had naturally turned first to Texas, where he had many friends with influence and where the political picture was familiar to him. A letter, two memoranda, and an executive order show something of the methods he developed:

IMPERIAL PALACE
INVISIBLE EMPIRE
KNIGHTS OF THE KU KLUX KLAN

Atlanta, Ga.
June 10, 1922

Brown Harwood, Grand Dragon,
Realm of Texas,
Fort Worth, Texas.
Faithful Klansman:

Referring to Executive Order No. 391, regarding special fund for educational campaign in Texas, it is extremely important that we have every Klansman in Texas understand the vital importance to the organization of the election of Klansman Earle B. Mayfield to the United States senate. The offer to divide the Klan vote by not centering on one man must be prevented, and if the funds accumulated under authority of the above executive order are not sufficient, we can arrange to supply you with additional funds as needed.

You will, from this time forward, keep me constantly posted on the situation; and if you think my presence at any time in Texas is necessary, do not hesitate to notify me.

Yours in the Sacred Unfailing Bond,

(Signed) H. W. Evans,
Imperial Dragon

Atlanta, Ga.
June 20, 1922

MEMORANDUM:

To N. M. Furney, Cashier.
From Imperial Dragon.

Attached herewith is expense bill from the Grand Dragon of the Realm of Texas. It may seem excessive, but conditions in Texas warrant these expenditures at this time.

(Signed) H. W. Evans

HWE-LM

A K L V

Atlanta, Ga.
April 21, 1922

MEMORANDUM:

To N. M. Furney.
From Imperial Dragon.

I have agreed with the Grand Dragon of the Realm of Texas to put up not in excess of ten men as lecturers and special investigators at work in Texas at this time, and he will, from time to time, notify you of their names and you will put them on payroll when requested by him so to do, and at such salary and expense as he may direct. These men will report direct to him and to me through him, but their expense accounts will come direct for the men to save delay, and are to be paid by you without being referred to finance committee, unless they seem to you to be excessive.

The above action is made necessary on account of the turbulent political conditions in Texas at this time and to hold the Klan vote solid in the coming senatorial election in that Realm. The above expenditure to be charged to field work general account.

(Signed) H. W. Evans

HWE

No. 391

EXECUTIVE ORDER

To The Grand Dragon, Realm of Texas, and His Hydras, Great Titans,
Furies, and to be respected by all Cyclops and Citizens of the
Invisible Empire in the Realm of Texas.

From The Imperial Dragon.

Greetings:

The Grand Dragon is hereby authorized to create a special fund for
educational purposes in the present political campaign in Texas, and
in the creating of same he is authorized to withhold for the next quarter all funds due the Imperial Palace, including the Palace pro rata
of Klecktokens and the Imperial Tax, and also all funds now due the
Palace from Klans in arrears to the Imperial Palace. The funds thus
created to be distributed by the Grand Dragon, in his discretion, as
the emergency of the case may warrant. The funds thus withheld with
the amount computed will be charged off properly at the Imperial
Palace and no indebtedness stand against the Realm of Texas or any
Klan on account of this special fund. It is estimated by Accounting
Department that this should give the special fund around $50,000 or
$60,000, but if this is not sufficient, provision will be made for other
funds when required.

Done at the Imperial Palace in the Imperial City of Atlanta on this
Dismal Day of the Wailing Week of the Mournful Month of the Klan
LV and the year of our Lord, 1922.

(Signed) H. W. Evans,
Imperial Dragon

From recent events, Texans had ample reason to know about the
Klan. On May 7, 1922, Den No. 7 in Beaumont tarred and feath-
ered Dr. J. S. Paul and R. S. Scott for alleged immoral behavior
and later sent to the newspapers its own version of the incident:
The action had been deemed necessary because the law was too
slow. Then in Austin on December 16 Peeler Clayton was shot
dead on the corner of Sixth and Brazos Streets; his offense had
been accidentally blundering into a Klan meeting. And in Teneha
a Mrs. Beulah Johnson was stripped and beaten, her hair cut off,
and a coat of tar and feathers applied. The charge was bigamy,
though no complaint had ever been entered against her in the
courts.

Colonel Simmons always insisted that the Klan never stooped to such violence, but Klansmen, sworn to defend morality and convinced that the law moved too slowly, had slight sense of shame for the Texas violence; and it is a moot question whether the incidents hurt or helped the Klan's incursion into Texas politics—its first big bid for national power. One opponent of the Klan, John J. Gordon, in a booklet titled *Unmasked* (1924), insisted that Senator Mayfield was not only a Klan mouthpiece but the stooge of William A. Hanger of Fort Worth—the man who had supposedly manipulated the elevation of Evans to the post of Imperial Dragon. Hanger represented several big corporations—oil companies, packing houses, interurban trolley companies—all interested in reducing wages of their employees. Gordon charged that a $2,500 contribution to Mayfield's campaign fund went unreported; but what he most wished to point out was that the Klan was being used in this election as a tool of big business. It seems more likely that the Klan saw eye to eye with big business, although the Klan's opposition to organized labor may represent more than mere coincidence.

Perhaps the most exciting political struggle was in Oklahoma, where Governor Walton conducted a virtual war against the Ku Klux Klan. Born in Indiana in 1882, Walton had moved with his family to Nebraska and then to Arkansas before he found a railroad job in eastern Oklahoma. He took up engineering and in 1917 was elected commissioner of public works in Oklahoma City. He had opposed a plan to build a reservoir and was denounced by all the local newspapers except one. Organized labor supported him; once during a strike he had sided with the unions, with the result that he was given an honorary membership in the Stage Hands and Theatrical Workers' Union. When elected mayor over a Klan candidate, Walton had brought suit against one of the papers that had opposed him; he seemed to like controversy and thrived on it. He attacked the Klan openly. He notified the police department that no Klansman would henceforth be permitted on the city payroll. The Chamber of Commerce fought him bitterly; its members included packing-house owners who were fighting unionization of their employees.

After he was elected governor of Oklahoma, Klansmen in Okmulgee County flogged some girls and young men whom they caught

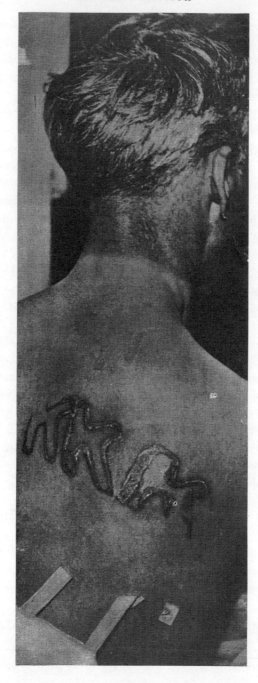

In 1924, the Reverend Oren Van Loon of Berkley, Mich., a Detroit suburb, preached a sermon condemning Klan cross burning in the area. He disappeared. Eleven days later, he returned, bearing the brand of the Ku Klux Klan.   *New York Public Library Picture Collection*

riding together in automobiles; Walton put the entire county under martial law. Then in Tulsa the Klan whipped a Jew named Nathan Hantaman, who later told the governor, "I had rather they would have killed me than to beat me the way they did. I was strung up by my hands to a tree and each man took his turn in whipping me. I started to fight them but it was useless. I often was near fainting when it seems that I was aroused by a blow on the head. When they got tired beating me they dumped me out of a car onto the Sand Springs road." After hearing this story, Walton put Tulsa under martial law. He also got the first conviction of Klansmen in the entire nation.

Next came the village of Broken Arrow. Four Klansmen were arrested for flogging a woman, Myrtle Spain; all four pleaded guilty. A former constable confessed to being a member of a Klan group of ten who had flogged a man named Goolsby and his wife, whom the city marshal had arrested and turned over to the Klan.

At this point Governor Walton decided it was time to order the Klan to unmask. N. C. Jewett, the Oklahoma Grand Dragon, defied the order; but local officers upheld the Governor by stopping parades of Klansmen in masks. Various Chambers of Commerce attacked Walton, but when he was given the opportunity to present factual evidence, as in Tulsa, local leaders admitted the need for martial law. A military court collected impressive evidence: seventy-six flogging incidents were reported, many of them for mere suspicion of guilty behavior. The Klan encouraged the state legislators to impeach Walton, but he refused to call a special session of the legislature for the purpose; instead, he summoned the legislature to meet for the express purpose of enacting anti-Klan legislation.

Aldrich Blake, Walton's one-time executive counselor and, in 1924, president of the Visible Government League, an amalgamation of all the anti-Klan forces in Oklahoma, described the situation in *The Ku Klux Kraze*. Klansmen, in his opinion, were to be pitied as dupes of the Order, lost in a thick haze of propaganda and unconscious of wrongdoing. Their persecution of bootleggers and scarlet women had the ironic effect of driving those in Tulsa to Oklahoma City, and those in Oklahoma City to Tulsa. What most hurt the Klan was the courage of some of its victims. J. L. Barnes of Coalgate, flogged by twelve Klansmen in full regalia, left the state as ordered but, after martial law was declared, returned and named six of his assailants. Two weeks later he died as a result of the flogging. Much the same story concerns E. R. Merriman, whose testimony before the military court is explicit:

> On March 7, 1922, while I was eating, supper in the car barn restaurant at Fourth Street and Olie, two unmasked men came in representing themselves to be the law and stated that they had a warrant for my arrest for carrying concealed weapons. I never gave it any thought but requested that they give me time to finish my supper and they said no; for me to come on with them. They handcuffed me and carried me on the outside. . . .

His head covered, Merriman was asked about his conduct with a certain girl. He denied everything, but with no effect; he was stripped to the waist and given twenty-seven lashes. He was ordered to leave the city, and he did. Then, when he returned and filed charges, naming eighteen men, the police did nothing. His boss asked him to withdraw the charges on the threat of dismissal.

The *Oklahoma Leader* editorialized, "The Klan is the 'beatinest' thing that ever came down the pike. It's a fraternal order for the promotion of strife; an empire for the promotion of democracy, a criminal conspiracy for upholding the law; a peace crusade by violence, and a new sort of Christianity that would flog Christ for being a Jew and a foreigner." That same year of 1924, Blaine Mast published *K.K.K. Friend or Foe: Which?* In it he insisted that the Klan stood foursquare on the deity of Christ and concluded: "The ethics of the Ku Klux Klan is the 'Sermon on the Mount.'" And a Klan pamphlet was issued with the startling title "Christ and Other Klansmen," which averred among other things that "Christ and Klansmen are builders," and that "God is the author of Klanism."

Leroy A. Curry entered the Klan-Walton battle in 1924 with *The Ku Klux Klan Under the Searchlight*. His wife Beulah wrote the preface; she described her husband as a man of no bad habits and said he was self-made despite three college degrees. Curry divided all Americans into three classes: the ignorant and illiterate, the cosmopolitans who refuse to adapt to Anglo-Saxon ideals, and the true

Americans. He strongly opposed the teaching of evolution in public schools, arguing for Bible study instead. Like other Klan apologists, he seemed to think that big cities were un-American; the *real* Americans, he argued, were small-town and rural folk, and the *most* American of all were the farmers. Walton's supporters, he thought, were men who put political affiliation ahead of American ideals. He appealed to all mothers to oppose Walton, chiefly because Walton opposed Prohibition. The Klan and Prohibition were virtually synonymous in Curry's vocabulary; the enemies of Prohibition were the deadliest enemies of America.

In preparing for its bid for national power in the summer of 1922, the Klan organized a special group called the Imperial Klan. On the local level the strategy called for the election of sheriffs who were Klansmen themselves or friendly to the Klan. But the big effort was to overthrow anti-Klan governors like Walton in Oklahoma and to elect Klansmen to Congress. Oregon's governor, Ben W. Olcott, also openly opposed the Klan; he was defeated in his bid for re-election. So was Governor Hardwick of Georgia, who had publicly attacked the Klan. Clifford Walker was elected instead, and thereafter the Klan had easier days in the state. Congressman W. D. Upshaw, a close friend of Mrs. Tyler, was one of the country's most outspoken Klan champions. In Indiana, Ed Jackson was nominated for governor on the Republican ticket; he ran openly as the Klan candidate against Indianapolis mayor Lew Shank, a critic of the Klan, and won handily. In Missouri, native son James A. Reed lost out to William Gibbs McAdoo in the Presidential primary. Of all the candidates, McAdoo seemed to the Klan the most amenable to its principles. Grand Wizard Hiram Evans is said to have conferred with him at French Lick Springs in May 1923. Alabama's Underwood attributed his defeat by McAdoo to Klan strategy. Active in many of these high-level doings was the sculptor Gutzon Borglum, who on one occasion introduced Evans to President Harding; the most immediate result was the establishing of a major Klan office in Washington.

In Colorado, the election of 1924 was as heated as in Oklahoma. The Klan had not been taken seriously in the state when it first appeared there in 1921, but its tried-and-true methods—especially its appeal to "right" religion and 100% Americanism—quickly built up membership and influence. Judge Ben Lindsey, famed for his advocacy of juvenile courts, was an open enemy of the Klan, which did everything possible to discredit him. At one point he remarked, concerning the rank-and-file Klan members, "They paid ten dollars to hate somebody, and they were determined to get their money's worth." The most popular Klan method was heckling speakers at political rallies. At one huge meeting at the Denver city auditorium, Klan forces insulted Colonel Philip Van Hise, the district attorney, and kept up a barrage of hisses and catcalls while policemen stood idly by. By 1924 the majority of the state legislature were Klansmen, and non-Klansmen were being dismissed from state jobs wherever it proved possible. Grand Dragon John G. Locke picked an active Klansman, William J. Candlish, for Denver's police chief and had the Klan mayor appoint him. This prompted an investigation of Locke, which yielded the interesting information that he had paid no federal income tax since 1913. A judge ordered Locke to produce his records, but they had disappeared. Locke drew a fine of $1500 and ten days in jail. Governor Morley, presumably out of friendship, had a salary voucher for $1,599 made out to Locke and appointed him his aide-de-camp, a colonel in the state medical corps, and director of recruiting and publicity for the Colorado national guard. But none of these posts materialized. A news item in the *Rocky Mountain News* (Denver) for March 7, 1925, reported Governor Morley's dining in Washington's Congressional Club with Hiram Evans, Locke, H. C. McCall, and other high Klan officials.

What finally ruined the Klan in Colorado was that the men with most to gain by its power in the state began to fight among themselves and split into factions. One faction withdrew, adopted the name of Minute Men, and seized the Klan real estate; men loyal to Evans fought to regain it. With a firmer internal discipline, in Colorado and elsewhere, the Klan might well have secured permanent control of state politics and, possibly, control of the national government that Evans dreamed of—a dream far beyond anything that ever went through the mind of Colonel Simmons.

The splintering had happened before and would happen again. In Indiana, D. C. Stephenson, the man who had once sent to the Atlanta headquarters a quarterly collection of more than $600,000, was at odds with Evans as early as the fall of 1923, as this telegram shows:

TELEGRAM

67CZ
G 552
F A Columbus, Ohio.
1117 A October 12, 1923.
Dr. H. W. Evans,
Room 1528, Washington Hotel,
Indianapolis, Indiana.

I have been very much grieved to learn that you were in Indianapolis, engaged in a campaign to assassinate my character, and to know that this was your process of disposing of anyone who stood in the way of your cohorts, Comer and Christy. Comer recently circulated reports in Illinois that I had been kicked out of the organization. Christy told this all over Texas, and there were some men here to verify the statement that I had been ruthlessly removed from my connections. I learned in Indianapolis last night that you were operating in the character campaign, endeavoring to destroy the confidence of my strongest friends in me. I am, indeed, sorry that you have brought about a condition in which it is apt to be necessary for me to resort to the first law of the land, self-defense. If you insist on going further with your attack upon my personal integrity, I shall be compelled to write a page in the history of these days which will be a final answer to the vulgar cowardly lies which are now being directed at me and which all honorable men will resent with a decision which will rock the foul cesspools of hate and jealousy which now flood the dollar-grabbers in Atlanta. I am constrained to the opinion that a lot of us would muster a great deal more respect for your opinion if you would keep your promise to refund to me all that I have advanced to support your foul doctrines. Anyway, I want you at once to see that I am given back the funds that I have expended out of my personal account, or issue a statement that you do not intend to do so. Also, I wish you would cease to show my telegrams and cease to show your answers which you report were sent to me, but which, in fact, never were sent to me nor even were intended to be sent, but were designed by such double-dealers as your cohorts, Comer and other such double-crossing artists. If you intend to make an issue with my friends in Indiana, why do you not play the part of a man and invite me to sit in conference when you are making your allegations? I challenge you or any of your cohorts to meet me before any organization in the state of Indiana and sustain the foul lies which Comer and Christy and others have circulated in Indianapolis during the past twenty-four hours. I assume you know I control papers in both Indiana and Ohio, and I am just a little inclined to the opinion that you are not unaware of my courage to use two papers to vindicate myself. All the honorable men in the nation demand that you answer these things and pull off your character vultures or present some reason why they should proceed with direct assassination of the reputation of men who are morally, intellectually, and financially their superiors. To this telegram I demand that you wire Dr. McDowell your instructions.

(Signed) D. C. Stephenson
12:40 P.M.

The Klan did not, however, destroy itself by internal dissension. The relative dearth of open condemnation by people of stature and influence suggests there was a general hope that it might simply collapse if it were ignored. But it took courage in many parts of the country, in 1924, to condemn the Klan; of the candidates for office who did speak out, or repudiate its support, a distressingly large percentage were defeated.

One of the losing gubernatorial candidates that year was William Allen White, distinguished editor of the Emporia *Gazette*. He ran with no real hope of winning; as an independent, he was bucking both the major parties. What prompted him to enter the race for governor was the fact that the Klan endorsed both the Republican candidate, Ben Paulen, and the Democratic incumbent, Jonathan Davis. Neither disclaimed the Klan association. Paulen, as a member of the Republican resolutions committee, engineered the deletion of an anti-Klan statement, and at the party convention he prevented a debate on the Klan. Asked if he was a Klansman, he answered that he was not "at this moment." White, in announcing his own candidacy, made it clear that he was not so much running for governor as for principle, "to laugh the Klan out of Kansas." He toured the state by automobile, spoke 104 times to an estimated 100,000 people, and in the election got 150,000 votes, about a quarter of the total cast.

As he admits in his very candid autobiography, White in his early years was a smug apostle of the status quo, as intolerant as any Klansman. He became a liberal and a crusader by gradual evolution. By 1920 he was aware of the Klan, and in 1921 he began his anti-Klan editorials—well before the series began in the New York *World*. Emporia elected as mayor a professed Klansman; neither White nor his reporters could get any news items from the police, though one police magistrate did give him information about cases after they reached court. Several of the *Gazette* reporters were sent threats, which alone would be enough to alert White to the Klan menace.

White's first Klan editorial appeared on July 28, 1921; it reported a Klan organizer in town and his poor success: "It is to the everlasting credit of Emporia that the organizer found no suckers with $10 each to squander here." American courts, legislators, and executive officers, he insisted, were strong enough to keep the peace. "For a self-constituted body of moral idiots who would substitute the findings of the Ku Klux Klan for the processes of law, to better conditions, would be a most un-American outrage which every good citizen should resent."

A week later he had to admit his mistake; the organizers *had* found some suckers. White called the Klan "an organization of cowards and traitors" and "a menace to peace and decent neighborly living." He hoped to learn who the local Cyclops was: "He is a joke, you may be sure. But a poor joke at that."

Herbert Bayard Swope, editor of the New York *World*, asked White to wire his judgment of the Klan, and he did so on September 17. He reviewed the local situation and concluded: "The picayunish cowardice of a man who would substitute Klan rule and mob law for what our American fathers have died to establish and maintain should prove what a cheap screw outfit the Klan is." About a quarter of the people in Kansas were Jews, Catholics, and Negroes—not enough collectively to fight the Klan but enough to make good targets for its attacks. To White's delight, the Emporia Ministerial Association denounced the Klan's campaign against these three minorities. In an editorial on May 22, 1922, he cited the denunciation as proof that "Emporia has no time and no room for the oily-tongued organizer who is selling memberships at so much per." He ridiculed the Klan attempt to bribe a preacher by "pompously marching up the aisle of his church in their silly nightgowns and giving him $25—a little less than 20 cents apiece for each clansman." Instead of throwing the money back, as some Kansas City preachers had done, White thought it should be accepted and given to a colored church or to the Knights of Columbus. "That would show the Klan what honest people thought of its cowardly program."

White's language reached its colorful peak during the campaign. In the announcement of his candidacy, issued September 20, 1924, he said:

> I want to offer Kansans afraid of the Klan and ashamed of that disgrace, a candidate who shares their fear and shame.
>
> The issue in Kansas this year is the Ku Klux Klan above everything else. It is found in nearly every county. It represents a small minority of the citizenship and it is organized for purposes of terror, directed at honest law-abiding citizens: Negroes, Jews and Catholics. These groups . . . menace no one. Yet, because of their skin, their race, or their creed, the Ku Klux Klan is subjecting them to economic boycott, to social ostracism, to every form of harassment, annoyance and every terror that a bigoted minority can use. . . .
>
> I am proud of my state. And the thought that Kansas should have a government beholden to this hooded gang of masked fanatics, ignorant and tyrannical in their ruthless oppression, is what calls me out of the pleasant ways of my life into this disgraceful but necessary task. . . . It is a national menace, this Klan. It knows no party. It knows no country. It knows only bigotry, malice and terror. . . . This Klan is preaching and practising terror and force. Its prototype is the Soviet of Russia.

At one point in the campaign, White had this to say, in the Kansas City *Times*, about his Republican opponent:

> The gag rule first came into the Republican Party last May. A flock of Dragons, Kleagles, Cyclops and Furies came up to Wichita from Oklahoma and called a meeting with some Kansas Terrors, Genii and Whangdoodles. . . . A few weeks later, the Cyclops, Kleagles, Wizards, and Willopses-wallopuses began parading in the Kansas cow pastures, passing the word down to the shirt-tail rangers they were to go into the Kansas primaries and nominate Ben Paulen.

[214]

White's campaign attracted national attention. Some editors were critical: the *Christian Science Monitor* thought he could have found a more important issue than the Klan, and the New York *Evening Post* thought the Klan was already moribund in Kansas; we may wonder how the editor knew such a thing. But editors in all parts of the nation encouraged and praised White for breaking through the veil of silence that had favored the Klan's growth. One Catholic editor remarked that White had chased the Klan from the cow pasture to the polls; and it is at least possible that his ridicule so angered Klansmen that all of them voted.

It was White's only venture into active politics. He found it exhilarating and believed, when the election was over, that he had indeed laughed the Klan out of Kansas. In a brief "Personal Word" he said the seed had been sown, and the fight would go on. In 1926, when the next political campaign was under way, he expressed exuberant satisfaction:

> The Ku Klux Klan in Kansas is a busted community. It went into the recent Kansas primary full of fight. It tried to control the Supreme Court. Instead the Klan was overwhelmingly defeated by the voters . . . two candidates who openly denounced the Klan were nominated by good pluralities.
> Two years earlier, the Klan . . . was sitting on the moon with its toes in the stars. Now its endorsement is a liability, and its friendship is a reflection upon a Kansas politician's patriotism and good sense. That much has been done in a two years' fight in Kansas. It can be done in any state where the decent elements exhibit courage and hard work.

To bolster the Kansas Klan's sagging fortunes, Hiram Evans visited the state in the spring of 1926; White's greeting was inspired:

> Doctor Hiram Evans, the Imperial Wizard of the Kluxers, is bringing his consecrated shirt tail to Kansas this spring, and from gloomy klaverns will make five Kansas speeches. We welcome him. Enter the wizard—sound the bull roarers, and the hewgags. Beat the tom-toms.
> He will see what was once a thriving and profitable hate factory and bigotorium now laughed into a busted community, where the cock-eyed he-dragon wails for its first-born, and the nightshirts of a

once salubrious pageantry sag in the spring breezes and bag at the wabbly knees.

The Kluxers in Kansas are as dejected and sad as a last year's bird's nest, afflicted with general debility, dizziness on going upstairs, and general aversion to female society.

In 1928, White found himself on a blacklist of the Daughters of the American Revolution. He retorted that the D.A.R. membership roll had become a sucker list for super-patriotic organizations and observed that its blacklist was weighted with the names of Jews, Catholics, and Negroes, and individuals who defended these groups. "My guess is that when the list was made up, a kluxer sat in." And he added: "The D.A.R. has yanked the Klan out of the cow pasture and set it down in the breakfast room of respectability. . . . The president is a lovely lady but in her enthusiasm she has allowed several lengths of Ku Klux nightie to show under her red, white and blue."

It is an old trick of satirists, from Jonathan Swift to Benjamin Franklin, to announce the death of a hated rival and thereafter blandly ignore his protests that he is still alive. William Allen White was no doubt too sanguine; the monster he had pricked with his poison pen refused to die. To be effective, satire needs an audience with a modicum of reasonableness, something generally deficient in the kind of men who joined the Klan. Yet White must be credited, as one of his biographers has suggested, with spearheading the fight against the Klan and lifting the veil of secrecy that made it seem deadlier than it really was. No other enemy of the Klan, either in Reconstruction days or in the twentieth century, chose ridicule as a weapon. It was a stroke of genius, giving heart to the vast silent majority who could now laugh about the Klan instead of merely shuddering at what it threatened. When to this we add his courage in running for governor, a step no other liberal ever took, we must give him credit as the most effective opponent the Klan has ever had.

Chapter Twelve

A KLAN FOR ALL SEASONS

Leaders of the original Klan, alarmed by the mounting violence they could see no way of controlling, took the desperate step in 1869 of disbanding the organization. The order announcing the disbandment was the only general order ever issued by the Grand Wizard, Bedford Forrest. Seventy-five years later, in 1944, the modern Klan was also disbanded, as the only alternative to paying a bill for back taxes. On neither occasion, however, did the Klan die; it continued to operate without national unity, sometimes in smaller regroupings, sometimes on a guerrilla basis.

Any alarm felt by the modern Klan's leaders has been caused not by reported violence but rather by the drop in their personal incomes as a result of declining membership. This commercialism in the modern leaders may mark the chief difference between the old Klan and the new. But cynical exploitation of the membership is only one of the vices that have been attributed to the men leading the Klan in this century; the records show a rather high incidence of personal immorality.

Since a reputation for immoral conduct would be hard to square with the high-sounding phrases devised to win recruits, it was the course of prudence to keep private vices a secret. Concealment hasn't always been possible, however. Hiram Evans could quietly dismiss Ed Clarke and Bessie Tyler, for personal misconduct that he considered a potential liability to the Klan, but neither he nor anybody else could suppress the scandal that in 1925 enveloped the very successful Grand Dragon of Indiana, D. C. Stephenson, the man who in 1923 sent Evans the arrogant telegram quoted earlier. It was no ordinary scandal, but one well suited to the man, and it accelerated the decline in membership that had begun the year before.

Stephenson—known to his cronies as Steve—was a supersalesman in an era of high-pressure salesmanship; but instead of Fords or fashions or Florida real estate, he sold a chance to hate. Like Hiram Evans, he had spent his formative years in Texas, but not until he moved to Indianapolis, after serving in the First World War, did he really find himself. He was not content with ruling the Klan in Indiana; he used his role as Grand Dragon to work his way into state politics. Nor was he the kind of man to lay aside his profits for a rainy day; instead, he entertained lavishly at his mansion in an Indianapolis suburb. He also owned a $75,000 yacht, the *Reo Mar*, but fire destroyed her at Toledo in June, 1924.

Steve was quite a lady's man, and it was widely rumored that a good many women were intimately acquainted with the geography of his mansion. A certain young lady named Madge Oberholzer, employed in the State Department of Education, caught Steve's lecherous eye; but though she was willing to go with him to parties, she drew the line at any greater intimacy. The more she rebuffed him, the more he wanted her. It became virtually an obsession.

On the evening of March 15, 1925, after some heady drinking, Steve summoned Madge to the mansion and informed her that she was to accompany him to Chicago on the next train. She declined the invitation; but she was no match for the two bodyguards who helped Steve drag her to the depot. As the train sped through the night, Madge, according to her subsequent account of the experience, was brutally attacked by Steve.

At Hammond, just short of the state line, the three men took

Madge from the train. Accounts differ as to just what happened in Hammond; Madge took or was given poison, and Steve either searched in vain for a hospital that would admit her, or refused to let her seek medical aid. Next day they drove back to Indianapolis. On April 4 a grand jury indicted Steve and his cronies on a long list of charges including assault and battery, rape, mayhem, and kidnaping. Then on April 14 Madge died after being unconscious for two weeks, and the headline story on the 18th was "Klan's Ex-Dragon Held for Murder." So many unsavory details were printed that the public ignored Steve's protest that he had been framed. Whether Madge died of the assault or of the poison, she was dead; and Steve was clearly implicated.

The nation-wide revulsion caused by the newspaper accounts of this sordid crime would alone have done considerable damage to the Klan. But there was more to come. Grand Wizard Evans, who owed his position partly to Steve, hastened to repudiate him as a Klan official; and the Indiana political clique also denounced him. Embittered, Steve threatened to tell all he knew; he tried to use this threat as a lever to secure his release. But it didn't work. He was tried and found guilty of second-degree murder. Then, fearing he would talk, officials kept him strictly incommunicado.

Steve may have suspected just such an outcome, for while he was awaiting trial he carefully put all his records in order and packed them in several black boxes. Reporters used every device they could think of to break through the barrier of official silence, and eventually one of them got the word from Steve as to where the black boxes were. Once the newspapers began printing extracts, it was no longer possible to keep Steve's tongue tied. He poured out facts about the entire Klan operation in Indiana and enough about its links with politics to convict a member of Congress, the mayor of Indianapolis, the sheriff of Marion County, and several lesser figures. The governor, Ed Jackson, was indicted for forgery but escaped trial by invoking the statute of limitations. Steve himself was sentenced to life imprisonment.

William Allen White had been effective against the Klan in Kansas even though he never did learn the name of the state's Grand Dragon. Indiana Klansmen, in contrast, were treated day after day, in their papers, to exact details of how *their* Grand Dragon had been operating—names, dates, terms of agreements made, and sums of money involved. Given minimal intelligence, they could hardly have failed to see the wide gulf between the Klan as they had supposed it to be and the Klan of actuality. By coincidence a Senate committee in Washington was just then investigating the sources of contributions to political campaigns, and one byproduct was a revelation of the very large sums the Klan had been spending to swing elections.

Members dropped out by the thousands. By 1926 the Klan had shrunk from its peak of five million to less than two million, and by 1927 to about a third of a million. The few who remained were a hard core who didn't care *what* crimes their leaders committed; who wanted to get their full money's worth; who needed the Klan as an outlet for their hate, or had become too fond of Klan fraternalism to give it up. Since 1927, in any event, the Klan has appealed mostly to men on the bottom rung of the socio-economic ladder, the kind least welcome in other fraternal orders. Men of any education and social respectability found Klan membership a handicap. Today former members are very careful to conceal this part of their personal history, with the fantastic result that entire cities boast of never having had any Klan members at all. Known Klan affiliation, no matter how brief or how remote in the past, has become a definite political liability, although expressing Klan principles is a positive help in some communities, if not a necessity, for men seeking election to public office.

Meanwhile, the declining membership posed a serious problem for Hiram Evans. In the 1928 Presidential campaign he was able to work up a fairly strong opposition to Al Smith, who was offensive to the Klan on four counts: as a Catholic, as a wet, as a liberal, and as the product of a big city. In 1934, Evans launched a full-scale Klan attack on the New Deal for its friendliness to organized labor. But when such issues as these did come along, it proved easier to whip up voter emotions than to entice new members into the Klan. Perhaps the time had come to follow Bedford Forrest's example and dissolve the Klan; increasingly hostile pressure from federal agencies gave this idea a certain attractiveness. But Evans was too shrewd a man to abandon the tangible assets that, by the terms of the original charter, were his to do with as he chose.

The Klan had become so unprofitable that managing it took second place in Evans' attention. He had organized a firm in Washington that sold asphalt and other road and street materials; and he was doing very well. He decided that the Imperial Palace in Atlanta, standing virtually idle, was more of a liability than an asset, and he sold it. (He did not sell it to the Catholic Church for conversion into a rectory, as some Klansmen later indignantly charged; it was the buyer, a business firm, that resold it to the Church. But Evans did accept an invitation to attend the consecration, on January 11, 1939, of the cathedral that was erected next door. One reporter with a flair for colorful detail noted that during the ceremony a shaft of sunlight fell on the former Dallas dentist.)

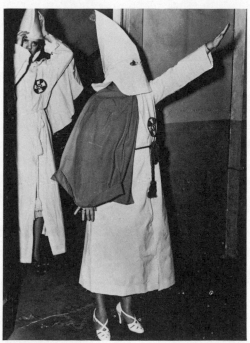

A Klanswoman gives the traditional sign of greeting as she enters a Den. Another woman adjusts her hood in this 1937 photo. *Wide World Photo*

By 1939, however, Evans was no longer the Imperial Wizard, for shortly before he had sold the Klan outright, charter and all, to Dr. James H. Colescott, a veterinarian from Terre Haute, and Samuel Green, also a "doctor." The new proprietors observed that Hitler's program was appealing to the same class of Americans that made up the potential Klan membership. Rather than compete with such mushrooming organizations as the American Rangers, the National Gentile League, and a revived Knights of the White Camellia, Colescott steered the Klan within flirting distance of the Fascist-Nazi groups. It required no severe adjustment of Klan ideals.

The flirtation came very close to marriage. At the German-American Bund's Camp Nordland in rural New Jersey, on the night of August 18, 1940, Klansmen joined the Bund members in a great meeting to stress true Americanism—or so they said. They burned a cross forty feet high, sang Nazi marching songs, and attracted a good deal of attention. The state legislature, after hearing the report of a state police investigation, ordered the closing of Camp Nordland. But the publicity had much the same effect as in the past, for membership in the Klan began to swing upward again. Time had dispelled the memory of both William Allen White's ridicule and the Stephenson scandal.

Colescott, always on the lookout for an effective issue, thought he had found one in the U.S.O. Its crime, in the Klan way of thinking, was its joint sponsorship and management by Protestants, Catholics, and Jews; such co-operation was obviously un-American. But the Japanese attacked Pearl Harbor and united the nation overnight. The Klan was hardly heard from again until the war was over.

When the war ended, the Klan no longer existed as a national organization. But, in the spring of 1944, the Collector of Internal Revenue presented the Klan with a bill for back taxes amounting to $685,305. How the government auditors arrived at this figure, or whether it approximated accuracy, matters very little; the important thing is that the Klan was officially judged to be no longer eligible for tax-exempt status. Colescott and Green could think of no way out other than to call one final Klonvokation in Atlanta, on April 23, 1944, to dissolve the Klan. The charter was surrendered, all titles were abandoned, and all members were relieved of any obligations.

The government did not collect the bill, but it probably had never hoped to; what the billing represented was the climax of a long federal campaign to break up the Klan.

No one seemed to foresee that once the Klan was broken up it would be harder than ever to control. The Klan simply went underground, thus becoming more like the original Klan. Fairly often, in the years since, it has come to the surface in state and local forms, sometimes legally constituted, at other times without benefit of charter. All that seems to be necessary is sufficient provocation, though even that may be missing. But in seasons of great stress, the scattered Klans, by whatever names they adopt, have been able to act with virtually the same concentrated force of the Klan during its twenty-nine years as a unified national group.

The Reconstruction Klan found it very effective to ride in columns through a town, slowly and in silence, at night, in full regalia. It was an awesome sight, one that uneducated Negroes in particular would not be likely to forget. Motorcades, the modern equivalent, are much more prosaic; nobody can mistake an automobile for a ghost. And since most states have followed the lead of Alabama in outlawing the mask, most of the mystery is gone from such processions. The Klan can still evoke a certain horror, however, by the fiery cross, that great inspiration of Colonel Simmons; it has been the prime symbol of the Klan in this century.

On Easter morning in 1933, a thousand Klansmen, some in robes, took part in a sunrise service outside Somerville, New Jersey; they saw nothing incongruous about burning a cross to herald the risen Christ. Not long afterward, the Klan staged a three-day convention near Peekskill, New York, with athletic contests, a spate of harangues, a mass initiation ceremony, and a twenty-foot fiery cross. But most such gatherings were only a kind of muscle-flexing. A more concrete excuse for demonstrating was President Roosevelt's appointment of Hugo Black to the Supreme Court in the fall of 1937. Accused of Klan membership, Black answered with a short radio statement on October 1, admitting he had once been a member but declaring total repudiation of all that the Klan stood for—a declaration he has consistently demonstrated in his behavior ever since.

But the Klan put its own interpretation on the appointment.

Fiery crosses were reported in many places in the North—in Marlboro and Worcester, Massachusetts; in Hyde Park, New York, near
the Roosevelt estate; in Mountain Lakes, New Jersey; and elsewhere.
Such is the symbolic power of the fiery cross that people in many
parts of the country still talk in subdued voices about the cross that
was burned one night years ago in the field across the road or on a
local hilltop. What it is commonly taken to mean is that neighbors
one sees every day include some who are Klan members, and that
Klaverns supposedly extinct are only dormant, ready to regroup for
action when the Klan senses that action is needed. It casts a
shadow on many a neighborhood to know that it harbors a poten-
tially hostile element which at any moment may disrupt the illusion
of peace.

Before a pipe cross festooned with cans of flaming oil, Klansmen hold an initiation ceremony at Stone Mountain, Georgia, in 1948.   *Wide World Photo*

A Klan for All Seasons

In the South, with its heritage of violence, Klansmen have been less content with the mere burning of crosses. Many of the "incidents" reported had no apparent motive but point to a revival of the Klan's self-image as guardian of public morality. In St. Petersburg, Florida, in March 1937, five Klansmen, including the local Kleagle, kidnaped Robert Cargell, a hotel manager, drove him out into the country, and mutilated him with a knife; no reason was given. In November of the same year about two hundred Klansmen in hoods and robes attacked the La Paloma night club in Miami, smashing furniture, driving the patrons into the street, and ordering the place closed. In suburban Atlanta, in the summer of 1939, Klansmen took two local men to a garbage dump and beat them for alleged immoral behavior; and a few months later the white operator of a Negro moving picture theater was flogged. On March 2, 1940, a couple were found beaten to death in an Atlanta lovers' lane; and only a few days later a local barber, Ike Gaston, was killed with a cleated belt known to have been made by Klansmen.

Without ever quite abandoning its role as guardian of public morality, the Klan in the South has increasingly turned its attention to maintaining white supremacy by intimidating Negroes from voting. In Starke, a rural north Florida town, hooded and robed Klansmen visited the Negro quarter on September 12, 1938, burning crosses and leaving notes warning the Negroes not to vote in the next day's election. Such warnings work better in the hinterland, where everybody knows everybody else, than in the big cities, where a man can be anonymous. A similar demonstration in Miami on May 1, 1939, when a fifty-car motorcade of Knights in full regalia traversed the Negro sections, failed dismally. In the primary voting next day Negroes turned out in record numbers. But even to this day, in two Florida counties with a considerable Negro population, not a single Negro is registered, and in other rural counties, mostly in what is called the "Pork Chop" area near the Georgia line, only a few of the Negroes courageous enough to register show up on election day. Where Klan attitudes are firmly held by virtually all the whites, there is little need for overt Klan discouragement of voting: The fear of losing one's job for so heinous an offense is deterrent enough.

[225]

The Supreme Court school desegregation decision, on May 17, 1954, triggered a new round of anti-Negro demonstrations—one that is still in progress. From the white supremacist point of view, every court order to admit Negro children to a previously all-white school, every CORE or NAACP sit-in or kneel-in, every report of a civil rights commission, and every visit by a Northern "do-gooder," is a threat to the white control that God ordained and that the Reconstruction Klan restored. Responsible state officials give aid and encouragement to the Klan by denouncing the federal and private efforts as violations of state sovereignty, as if the Civil War had not settled that matter for all time. And these officials preach the sanctity of private property, as if this principle were ever invoked except against the Negro.

Such officials owe their election, and their continuance in office, to the approval of the majority of the voters, who simply may not realize how much the Klan has done, over the years, to keep alive the tradition of Negro inferiority. Letters to the editor in the newspapers of 1964 bear an uncanny resemblance to published defenses of the Klan in the 1870's and the 1920's; the Klan influence has been steady and strong.

Since the breakup of the Klan after 1944, however, the continuity has not always been readily evident. During 1954 and early 1955, several new Klan-like groups were organized, with names so different from the Klan as to deceive a great many people: the American States' Rights Association, the National Association for the Advancement of White People, the National Association for Preservation of the White Race, the Heritage Crusade, the Southern Gentlemen, and, best known of them all, the White Citizens' Councils. (One of the most obvious signs of a strong Klan-like movement in a given town is the existence of an "Americanism Book Store.")

The White Citizens' Councils (sometimes without the word "White") have been quite successful. The first such Council was formed in Indianola, Mississippi, on July 11, 1954. By the following October there were thirty others, and soon they existed in virtually all parts of the South. The organizers have avoided entanglement with former Klan leaders, chiefly to escape the disrepute that the Klan has earned through its violence. But since the Councils' pro-

THE KU KLUX KLAN RIDES AGAIN
Your Country Is Calling You

The Klan Rides to
Save America!

Stop! Look! Listen!
Think! Pray!

Communism Must Go!   America, Wake Up!

YOUR COUNTRY	COMMUNISM
Love, Peace, Freedom, God.	Hate, Bondage, Prison and Starvation.
Home, Husband, Wife and Children.	Free Love, Children State Property.
Free Schools of Patriotic Thought.	Dictated Thought by a Few.
Free Speech and Free Press.	Fear to Express Thought by Speech or Press.
Government of the People.	Overthrow of All Government.
The Stars and Stripes Forever.	The Red Flag of Destruction.
Right to Worship God as we Please.	Overthrow of All Religion.

You have read of "The midnight ride of Paul Revere," calling the Minute Men to arms to free us from tyranny.

This is the MIDNIGHT RIDE OF THE KU KLUX KLAN, calling you to save our country and its institutions.

The Knights of the Ku Klux Klan is determined to drive out of the United States these vicious, alien radicals and to eradicate their radical thought from every rank, class and group of the American people, through a nation-wide concerted campaign. In this job, they are entitled to the hearty support of every true American citizen.

The Knights of the Ku Klux Klan invites and pleads for your help to save our country before it is too late. We do not want money but we need YOU and your support.

MODERN COMMUNISM CHALLENGES ALL DECENCY AND CIVILIZATION

This organization is determined to fight to the last ditch and the last man against any and all attacks on our government and its American institutions. If you are a Red Blooded, Native Born, American Citizen and believe with us, fill out the coupon below.

--------------------------------- Tear off on this line and mail. ---------------------------------

P. O. Box 1975,
Tampa, Florida.

I want to help save our country and am ready to ride with you.

NAME ....

OCCUPATION ....
                                                      (State where employed)

RESIDENCE ADDRESS ....

This leaflet was distributed in Florida in the 1930's when the Klan campaigned for God and country to save America from communism and "vicious, alien radicals."

gram is practically identical with that of the Klan—anti-Semitic, for example, as well as segregationist—it has not been possible tó deceive everybody. Hodding Carter, one of the South's most distinguished journalists, has called the Councils "the uptown Klan," and so they seem to many observers. They appeal more to businessmen than to the "wool hats" (once better known as the "red necks"), who, if they join, soon drift away because the Councils stage no parades and burn no crosses. The nearest Klan is the beneficiary; the new groups of prominent citizens provide an encouragement that the Klan appreciates. Klan and Council may not be on speaking terms, but they are blood brothers.

In joining other rightist groups in the struggle against the great monster, internal Communism, the Klan in the South is chiefly concerned about race. In Klan thinking, it is Communist prodding that keeps the Negro pressing for equal rights; according to the Southern myth so carefully developed in the nineteenth century, and so steadily kept alive by the modern Klan, Negroes are congenitally too indolent to act on their own accord.

But Communism is also at work, as Klansmen see it, in the steady pressure to unionize labor—which would presumably be quite content with its wages if left alone. The extent to which big business has welcomed the support of the Klan, or has stimulated that support by financial contributions, would make a very interesting study; but one thing is obvious—money has álways been available, from some source, to finance the Klan in its frequent campaigns against unions. In simple logic it would seem that the average Klansman, who today is on the lowest rung of the economic ladder, would welcome any proposal that might result in higher income for himself. But Klan propaganda reminds him that unions commonly demand the same wages for all workers in the same bracket, and that the better pay he might get as a union member would be no more than a Negro member of the same union would get for the same work. Whatever validity there may be in state "right to work" laws, in the South they reflect the old Klan argument that white men deserve more than Negroes because white men are innately superior.

Pay differential is one of the principal means of maintaining the illusion of white superiority. Another is the practice, hardly confined to the South, of giving Negroes only the most menial jobs. One white waitress in St. Petersburg, Florida, when asked why she opposed a federal minimum-wage law, which would at once raise her hourly pay, no doubt echoed an opinion widely shared by people of her social level when she replied that better pay meant less to her than being free to work "without some yid or nigger beside me."

One further part of the Klan propaganda is that "fair employment" codes, by forcing employers to hire some Negroes, will drive some whites from their jobs. It would not occur. to the Klan to say that in a really fair job competition, based not on skin color but on native intelligence, educational record, and willingness to work, some whites would have to yield places to some Negroes. If the Klan suspects this, it might explain the intensity of its fight to maintain the "tight-white" pattern, which favors the meanest, least ambitious, most illiterate white over the best Negro applicant. What the Klan does say, over and over in its copious "literature," is only what the great majority of poorly educated Southern whites—and many well-educated Southerners, too—have been conditioned to believe since earliest childhood.

Stetson Kennedy, in his book *Southern Exposure* (1946), put it this way: "While some modern Klansmen have conscientiously lynched under the delusion that they were protecting Southern womanhood or were promoting public morality and the like, they have actually served as storm troopers of the plutocracy which robs them and their neighbors (as well as the Negroes) of the best fruits of their labors." Of various examples that Kennedy cites of Klansmen serving as dupes of unscrupulous businessmen, one that stands out with elemental clarity is the beating of a union man in Anderson, South Carolina, because, as the Klansmen told him, he gave his wife too little money to manage their household, and beat his five-year-old son. But the victim had no son—he wasn't even married.

In the Klan-Walton war in Oklahoma in 1924, the Klan was solidly aligned with Chambers of Commerce opposing the governor. The major complaint was Walton's sympathy for organized labor. Even earlier, when the Klan was still in the control of Colonel Simmons, it issued a denunciation of a shipyard strike in Mobile, Alabama. Opposition to unions has never been stipulated in Klan constitutions and other public pronouncements, but it quite clearly has been a constant in the modern Klan's program. The hypothesis that the labor movement in the South has been retarded by the willingness of white workers to swallow the Klan line seems entirely valid. Such men may be incapable of suspecting how great a stake the more selfish kind of employer has in Klan success. Most rightist groups, of course, are pro-business and anti-labor; but the Klan stands out as the only rightist group that can be "bought" to convert anti-labor sentiment into physical action.

If Klansmen sometimes punished victims for supposed immorality without knowing that they were really helping keep local wages low, at other times they clearly understood that unionizing activity was the crime. The five men who stopped at the house of Frank Norman one evening in 1935 and took him for a ride knew what he was charged with: He and his wife had been active in helping the citrus workers in and near Lakeland, Florida, to organize for collective bargaining. The wife recognized one of the five men, a deputy sheriff from a neighboring county, but this didn't help; Norman was never seen alive after that evening, and his fate remains unknown.

The next year the Klan singled out for its full treatment a somewhat more important man, Joseph Shoemaker of Tampa, state director of the Workers Alliance. He had organized an independent political party, called the Modern Democrats, to promote the interests of labor. On election eve in 1935 he and several others active in the new party were arrested without warrants at a private home and were taken to a police station for routine questioning about suspected Communist ties. When the grilling ended, they walked out of the station and right into the midst of men in masks, who took them out of town, stripped and beat them, applied tar and feathers, and ordered them to leave town. Shoemaker, as the prime offender, was castrated. He died in agony in a Tampa hospital nine days later. Eleven men were subsequently arrested, some of them identified as Klan members, but after two years of court action all eleven were acquitted.

Enormities of this sort can hardly be laughed out of existence; William Allen White's technique of ridicule has severe limitations.

Klansmen sadistic enough to mutilate their victims, and apparently influential enough to get off when caught, would not hesitate to repeat their vile conduct the next time a similar provocation arises. Nor would they pause to inquire into the reason why their Cyclops, whose word they have sworn to obey without question, is sending them out after a particular individual. For such men the chance to commit physical harm is satisfaction enough; not even Klan principle is involved. Lynching has been stopped, and violence can be, too, if sufficient public sentiment can be roused against it. But this may take a long while. Employer resistance to unionism does not stop when all employees are unionized, and neither does the tendency of public officials to side with the money interests in small communities.

Yet enforcement officers cannot be blamed for performing their duties in ways approved by the majority of their constituents; and where most of the voters subscribe to white supremacy and oppose unions, the police and the magistrates can be expected to be more severe toward Negro offenders than white, and particularly harsh toward union organizers. The average policeman would laugh at the notion of his being an intellectual or a liberal. But he can almost always be counted on to obey orders. Policemen would not use tear gas or police dogs or electric cattle-prods if dominant citizen groups strongly disapproved.

A free press, not subservient to local business interests, might do much to rouse the public conscience against violence and to expose the propaganda of the Klan and its blood brothers. Few small-town newspapers, however, enjoy such independence. The freelance journalist is in a particularly good position to serve as an instrument of communication. In recent years the most famous of the independent writers opposed to the Klan has been Stetson Kennedy.

Born in Jacksonville in 1916, Kennedy attended the University of Florida and the New School for Social Research before launching himself as a writer. In *Palmetto Country* (1942), the Florida volume in the American Folkways Series, he revealed the particular interest in the Klan that has made him, in time, its number one enemy. *Southern Exposure*, cited earlier, amplified that interest. But his anti-Klan masterpiece is *Passage to Violence* (1954). This is the American title; the British title is a better indication of its contents—*I Rode with the Klan.*

This book begins like a spy thriller. When the reader discovers that what at first he took for extravagant invention is based on actual experience, it takes on a peculiar horror, for Kennedy is a marked man, one no true Klansman could ever forgive. For the rest of his life he runs a strong risk of being assassinated. So far he has been lucky, although one house he lived in, on the bank of the St. Johns River south of Jacksonville, was burned to the ground one night. He was not at home. Today he is living abroad.

What Klansmen are unlikely to forget is that Kennedy, using an assumed name, joined a Klavern in Atlanta, attended meetings regularly and took an active part in Klan "errands," all the while supplying copious detailed information to a confederate in the Georgia Bureau of Investigation. He even had the nerve to publish articles describing some of the errands he took part in, so that all the Klavern knew there was a spy among them. He had taken elaborate pains to win the complete confidence of several members, who vouched for his loyalty without question. Even so, there were many tense moments in the Klavern when the Cyclops damned him by name and described the punishment awaiting this Stetson Kennedy if he was ever identified. It was a large Klavern, providing a certain safety in numbers; the Cyclops could have had no idea which of the two hundred or so members was guilty. But it would be hard to imagine a more dangerous situation—outside of wartime espionage and spy fiction.

It was soon obvious to Kennedy that most of the Klavern members had to be furnished with assignments on a regular basis; otherwise their appetite for violence would flag and they would settle down to comfortable fraternalism. At a given meeting the Cyclops would describe the offensive behavior of some individual and gradually work the members up to a fever pitch of excitement. The selected victim was usually somebody of no importance, one with no political influence, surely, but guilty of some such heinous crime as extending credit to Negroes, or giving a Negro or a Jew a job that a "white man" could have handled, or making white customers wait while Negroes were being served, or letting a union organizer use his property for a meeting, or lodging a complaint of any sort against a Klansman. At the right moment the Cyclops would call for volunteers, and from those who stepped forward he would choose a squad —enough men to fill one or two cars—and give the specific instructions. Since holding back would have drawn attention to himself, Kennedy had to volunteer and, when chosen for the squad, to help enforce the Klan variety of justice. Whenever possible, he tipped off his friend in the state government, but when he wasn't able to, he could subsequently give exact details of what had happened. The utter senselessness of some of the assignments made it all seem like some grim practical joke; it was hard to believe that men could egg each other on to such sadism.

The elaborate and dangerous game ended when Kennedy had to testify in court against some of his fellow Klavern members, thus exposing himself as the viper who they had known was lurking in their midst. But he had played the game long enough to collect more than enough for one book. Someday an industrious scholar will piece together the complete story of the Klan-Kennedy war from the files that he deposited in the Schomberg Collection of Negro History in the New York Public Library.

After his day in court Kennedy could no longer stay in Atlanta, but the Klan was active in other places, too, and he had no difficulty in learning more about its varied procedures. On September 7, 1944, he records, the State of Florida issued a charter to the "Ku Klux Klan of Florida, Inc." as a tax-exempt charitable fraternal order. Less than five years later, during Fuller Warren's administration, the state authorized "Original Southern Klans, Inc." to establish Klaverns throughout Florida; the Grand Dragon was Bill Hendrix of Tallahassee, the state capital. In 1952 Hendrix joined with the Grand Dragons of Alabama and South Carolina in forming a new Klan, called "Southern and Northern Knights of the KKK," with headquarters in Jacksonville.

In Florida anybody who can afford the qualifying fee of five per cent of the annual salary can run for governor in the party primary elections. In 1952 Hendrix resigned temporarily from the Klan, paid the fee, and polled 11,200 votes. This poor a showing created the general impression that both he and the Klan were harmless. Kennedy thought otherwise. By tracing the license number of the limousine heading a Klan parade in Jacksonville, he deduced, whether correctly or not, that the Grand Wizard of the new Klan, who signed himself "Nathan II," was none other than the Duval County chairman of the Democratic Party. Kennedy was further convinced that it was due to this man's influence—and, by implication, the Klan's influence—that heavily Democratic Florida gave General Eisenhower an astonishing majority in the national election of 1952. State leaders of "Democrats for Eisenhower" would no doubt indignantly reject the suggestion, but it is easy to imagine Bill Hendrix chuckling to himself over the result.

The multiplication of small and even rival Klans in recent years has tended to confirm the belief that the Klan can be dismissed as impotent. One editor wittily remarked in print that there were now so many Grand Wizards, Dragons, and Keagles that it was impossible to tell them apart without a program. During 1949, in addition to the Hendrix outfit in Florida—the "Original Southern Klans, Inc." —there were at least these others:

Association of Georgia Klans, in Atlanta; Dr. Samuel Green, Imperial Wizard.

Original Southern Klans, Inc., in Columbus, Georgia; Alton Pate, Imperial Wizard.

Federated Ku Klux Klan, Inc., in Birmingham; William Hugh Morris, Grand Dragon.

Knights of the Ku Klux Klan of America, in Montgomery; Dr. Lycurgus Spinks, Imperial Emperor.

Whether the first of these replaced an earlier "Den No. 2" in Atlanta, headed by Wizard Sam Roper, or developed as its rival for control of Georgia, might be impossible to determine. The entire Klan structure has become so confused that attempting to keep it straight would be futile, for the pattern current at any one moment is sure to change fairly soon. There would be a great deal more confusion, however, if numerous Northern and Western states had not outlawed the Klan permanently, by whatever name. In New York, for example, anybody convicted of organizing a Klan faces a fine of $10,000.

A less stringent but very effective state action against the Klan has been the passage of laws requiring the Klan to unmask. Always before, the concealment of faces had been a major aid to Klansmen in carrying out their illicit errands; it made detection and punishment almost impossible. In 1949 officials in a western Alabama county reported to Governor Jim Folsom that conditions had gotten out of control, and the governor called upon the legislature to act. It did, with a firm 84 to 4 vote outlawing the wearing of masks on public property. By 1952 thirteen states had written such a law into their statute books, allowing masks only for such occasions as Mardi Gras and Halloween.

Still, the outlawing of the mask has not killed the Klan; new Klans keep cropping up wherever there are legal loopholes. Some of them have been better publicized than others, or are known because state officials took firm steps to suppress them. During 1950, for example, the Imperial Wizard of Carolina Klans, Thomas L. Hamilton, made a bold move to extend the Klan across the line from South Carolina to North Carolina. On July 22 a motorcade he had organized made a circuit of Horry County, S.C., and Columbus County, N.C. It was the opening signal for a reign of terror. Almost nightly there were floggings of both whites and Negroes for alleged immorality. Two editors of weekly newspapers, Horace Carter and Willard Cole, openly opposed the Klan—and later shared a Pulitzer Prize for their courageous reporting and editorials. Malcolm Seawell, solicitor for the Ninth Judicial District of North Carolina (and subsequently Attorney-General under Governor Luther Hodges) was no less alert. But the state line proved a great handicap: Klansmen could operate in one state and then duck back across the line.

But it was the state line that finally undid the Hamilton campaign. Klansmen abducted a white man and woman and took them across the line to flog them for not attending church. The Federal Bureau of Investigation, using the "Lindbergh Act," promptly moved into the case. The first ten men who were rounded up implicated others, until finally Hamilton himself was arrested. Twenty-three Klansmen were given prison terms, and fifty-eight others paid fines totaling about $20,000. The entire episode ran its course swiftly, thanks to the alertness of two editors and the co-operation of law-enforcement agencies. The Klansmen's victims will carry through life the marks of the floggings.

The Klan has never thrived in North Carolina since the Hamilton case, but seven years later, on November 25, 1957, the Association of South Carolina Klans was in business again. On that date it adopted a set of resolutions which run to ten mimeographed pages. Whether the action represents the reorganization of an existing Klan or the creation of a new one, the structure reveals no great change from the original drawn up by Colonel Simmons. "The Exalted Cyclops and his Twelve Terrors" are listed as the officers for any local Klan, as follows:

EXALTED CYCLOPS, president.
KLALIFF, vice-president.
KLOKARD, lecturer.
KLUDD, chaplain.
KLIGRAPP, secretary.
KLABEE, treasurer.
KLADD, conductor.
KLORAGO, inner guard.
KLEXTER, outer guard.
NIGHT-HAWK, in charge of candidates (the only title carried over from the Reconstruction Klan).
KLOKANN, a three-member board of investigators, auditors, and advisors; each member to be called a KLOKAN.

The term of office was twelve months, with the election to be held at the first Klonklave in December, and installation at the first Klonklave in January. Strong emphasis was laid on paying dues on time, under penalty of suspension, and on returning all paraphernalia and copies of the Kloran (the Klan "Bible") upon leaving the order.

Virtually all the rules and regulations follow those that governed the Simmons-Evans Klan. One interesting section of the ten-page set of resolutions spells out "Offenses and Penalties." Offenses were divided into major and minor. The major offenses included treason against the United States, violations of the Klan oath, disrespect of virtuous womanhood, conspiring against the Klan, excessive or habitual drunkenness, habitual profanity or vulgarity, and "being responsible for the polluting of Caucasian blood through miscegenation or the commission of any act unworthy of a Klansman." Minor offenses were identical with the major, only in a milder form. Considerable verbiage was spent on the procedures for trying offenders and for appealing from convictions.

The final section set the schedule of payments. Each Klavern was to remit to the State Grand Treasury $2.00 for each new member up to one hundred, and $1.00 for each member beyond that number. Local dues were not mentioned; they were apparently left to the individual Klan or Klavern. If South Carolina is representative, the Klan is no longer a machine for transferring large sums of money from initiates to Grand Wizards and Emperors; perhaps state organizers have discovered that prospects are not as easily gulled as they once were.

If it is asked how new Klans can continue to take form, despite the general hostility to the term "Klan," and when other groups with quite different names but with the same program are available, the one obvious answer is the Klan's fraternal nature. From Christmas Eve in 1865 down to the present, the Klan has always stressed its opportunity for fraternalism. Whatever principles it may announce, whatever form its activities take, and however venal its leaders may be, the Klan is and always has been a brotherhood in which men can find congeniality and a ladder of offices to climb, if they so aspire. This fraternal character gives the Klan a continuity that is not seasonal and an internal cohesiveness that groups such as the White Citizens' Councils are not organized to provide. The Klan could, if necessary, survive on its fraternalism alone, for a class of men that might be blackballed in most Masonic orders. In its heyday many Masons did join the Klan, but that was before it sank in the general public estimation.

If the Klan had remained what its founders in Pulaski first conceived it to be, a purely social club, it would today be only one more of the numerous fraternal orders that Americans like to join, and books like this would not be written. Viewed in one way, the Klansmen at all times have been the dupes, willing or otherwise, knowing or innocent, of groups and individuals with dirty work to be done. Today it would seem that the Klan is being used chiefly by the extreme right wing of reactionaries. In October 1955 a new Klan organization was chartered in Georgia, the Aryan Knights of the Ku Klux Klan, but its principal propagandist is a Texan—Horace Sherman Miller of Waco, who seems to have the means for turning out great quantities of literature. One leaflet he has distributed is called "History Repeating"; it is a reprint of an article by Thomas Dixon, Jr. (author of *The Clansman*) that first appeared in the *Metropolitan Magazine* for September 1905: "The Original Ku Klux Klan that Saved the South." At the close of the leaflet, readers are told that for $1.00 they can get two copies of the Dixon article together with "The Saddest Story Ever Told," by the Honorable Oliver Allstrom of Chicago, concerning interracial marriages. Copies ordered in larger numbers cost less; there is even a money-back guarantee.

In another hand-out, Miller quotes from remarks by William Jenner, when he was a Senator from Indiana, about the "hidden government" of the United States as a preamble to an attack on the alleged Jewish control of press, radio, television, theater, charities, foundations, and many schools and educational associations. Readers wishing to help eliminate this "Jewish menace" are invited to send donations to "The Aryan Views, Box 5062, Waco, Texas."

Another Miller masterpiece is a photocopied letter from a seaman recruit of Davenport, Iowa, to then Secretary of Defense Charles Wilson, with carbon copies to President Eisenhower, Herbert Hoover, and the editors of *Life,* insisting that arms must never be sent to Israel. "From now on," the young seaman wrote, "we will fight our true enemy—THE JEWS! I call on the American Government to arm the Arabs, and help them drive the Jews and Jewish parasites into the sea."

In other Klan material issued by Miller, readers are urged to boycott the Ford Motor Company and the makers of Philip Morris and Marlboro cigarettes, because some of the profits from these companies were being used to support the Urban League. Readers are also advised not to support United Funds, Red Feather, and Community Chests because these are not sufficiently discriminatory in dispersing funds; some money goes to agencies that Miller considers Communist fronts. Employees are specifically urged to oppose payroll deductions to support such fund drives.

Miller has one great advantage over most propagandists—a poet named June Hendricks, ready to turn out anti-Communist verse at a moment's notice. Here are two examples, pitched at exactly the right level, we may suppose, to appeal to the membership of the Aryan Knights:

THE RATTLESNAKE AND HIS BROTHER
By June K. Hendricks

You cannot spank a Rattlesnake,
    Then put him off to bed
And trust him not to bite again
    Until he is really dead.
Just like his brother, Commie
    Who does not own his name—
Called NAACP and Urban League
    And other titles tame.
But when he sinks his poison fang
    In a vital, healthy spot,
The body then is paralyzed
    And the soul begins to rot.
His serpent coils will grip us tight
    And squeeze away our hopes
Reducing us to servitude
    And isolated dopes.

Arouse you sleeping soldiers
    And rally to the call—
The Commie is among us
    Determined we must fall.
They're rooted in our politics
    From the grassroots to the top,
To destroy our Aryan people
    And they do not mean to stop.

Let us rally to our children—
    Won't you lend a helping hand,

To preserve the white child's future
  In a free and happy land.
Now, we folks can ban [*sic*] together—
  At least, we've found a way,
For The Aryan Knights are marching
  And thank God, they're here to stay.

SEGREGATION - OUR SALVATION - ARYAN SURVIVAL
By June K. Hendricks

I want my grandson to look like me—
  Be intelligent, Loyal, Happy and Free.

No tell-tale marks upon his face
  To brand him with a Mongrel Race.

Be loyal to the Nation and the South
  With active deeds and word of mouth,

Preserve the Aryan Race—the Whites
  And ready to battle for their rights.

The negro should also want his grandson
  To always be and look like one

Of his own Race, and in color and shade,
  Be like the negro the good Lord made.

He should not want a spot of white
  To deny his grandson his inborn right

To be as Black as the Lord decreed—
  Like his old Ancestor when he was Freed.

The Mulatto is the Mark of Death,
  Should cause both Races to hold their Breath.

He defies what the good Lord has in mind
  When He said—"EVERYTHING AFTER ITS KIND."

He's an open challenge to WHAT GOD HATH WROUGHT
  And brings both Races down to Naught.

Neither Race can be free again
  After they fall to the Mulatto plane.

Note: A mulatto is a person of half white, half negro blood. The word is from the Spanish mulo, from the Latin mulus, "a hybrid." The mule is so called because it is a half-breed between the horse and the donkey. To be clearly pronounced say: mew-LAT-oh.

You may help me get this mailed to a million people

HORACE SHERMAN MILLER   ARYAN KNIGHTS - KU KLUX KLAN,

Box 5062, Waco, Texas
(For reprints order by Number 265 - 20 for $1)

Miller may be a little fuzzy in his logic, but he hammers away at his major points with great consistency. Every so often in his *Aryan Views* he inserts this box with its strong black outline:

JEW COMMUNISTS

SAY

INTEGRATE

ROB—RAPE—RIOT—KILL

And he also uses a smaller box, with letters white against a black background, with this slogan: "For racial privacy today and forever join K.K.K. now. Write to Box 5062, Waco, Texas." Alongside the words is a picture of a Klansman in regalia, astride a horse and carrying a lighted torch.

The separate Klans today agree on the same general principles, but are free to follow particular lines of action. In the late summer of 1960, liberal newspapers in Florida exposed to the public view an organized movement to persuade citizens not to pay any federal income taxes, as a way to "get the chains of the beaurocrats [*sic*] off their necks." The movement was traced to the Knights of the White Camellia, which listed as its address Box 47, in Oldsmar, not far from Tampa. This turned out to be the box used by Bill Hendrix. In 1960 Hendrix made another attempt at the governorship, though with no better success than eight years before. But merely announcing oneself as a candidate is one way of attracting attention.

A four-page mimeographed leaflet with the title "Choose Sides" was widely distributed. It asserted that the federal income tax is "a Communist trick to control Americans," and it proceeded to say: "Put the damper on the tax vampires. Here's how. Take the Fifth Amendment. Answer no questions. Send in no money . . . cut off the wolves' money and watch them whine." There followed personal attacks on Drew Pearson, Eleanor Roosevelt, and Nelson Poynter, editor of the St. Petersburg *Times*. Omitted from the leaflet was the fact that Bill Hendrix himself was facing prosecution for failing to report his income.

A reporter sent to interview Hendrix was informed that the proposed boycott was entirely lawful. A graduated income tax was listed by Karl Marx as the second of his ten points in the Communist Manifesto; ergo, it was Communist-inspired. Hendrix went on to express satisfaction over the fact that four state legislatures had voted to abolish the federal income tax; thirty more states, and that would be the end of it.

"Hate literature" is distributed in every state—for example, "NIGGER! You too can be a JEW!" In Florida, much of this sort of thing has been traced to Hendrix as the perennial kingpin of

Confronting one another without their eyes meeting, a Negro picket and a Klan leaflet peddler share the same sidewalk in front of an Atlanta hotel. The confrontation occurred in 1962 during a peaceful NAACP demonstration against discrimination in Atlanta hotels, motels, and restaurants.   *Wide World Photo*

[242]

whatever Klan is momentarily in existence. One leaflet calls Leroy Collins "the color-blind governor of Florida who has traded southern principal for negro votes." The bombings of synagogues is flatly attributed to the Jews themselves, who are repeatedly identified as the leaders of world Communism. "We intend to fight fire with fire. Smear with Smear. We hope it does not take violence to win our country back from the U.S. Extreme Court." Further information is promised for anybody who sends $1.00 to Box 47 in Oldsmar.

Citizens in general have no way of realizing how steadily the Klan maintains its effort to dupe them and to influence their thinking. The generality of conservatives would no doubt flatly deny even the possibility of such influence, but it is always there. The Klan cannot be said to have invented all the propaganda it uses, but it certainly has used every available means of keeping that propaganda in the public consciousness. Hendrix has identified as Communist programs the fluoridation of drinking water, so-called home rule for large cities, all central taxes, the United Nations, court opposition to religious exercises in public schools, and mental health clinics. And he tells people how to combat the Communists: "Join your Citizens Councils . . . Committees for Free Government—States Rights Groups—KKK's or join the fastest growing of them all—the National Christian Church—Whose slogan is— For God, Country and Race. Any white Christian can join us, but we reserve the right to refuse many so-called white Christians who are afraid to fight for the true doctrines of Christ." This church is easily joined: by sending $5.00 to Box 47 in Oldsmar.

The National Christian Church sounds like the unitary Protestant church that Colonel Simmons dreamed of as a counterfoil to the Catholic, Mormon, and Jewish "religious governments." In an age when nationalism and the American way of life seem to be replacing strictly religious reasons for church-going, as Will Herberg suggests in *Protestant-Catholic-Jew,* such a church may have a chance to succeed. Its members may be no more aware that Evans first proposed it than most white supremacists are aware that the Klan has systematically kept racial tensions at white heat.

The Klan, of course, says just the opposite: that racial tensions would never exist without being fomented by outside "do-good-ers," and that they are largely a figment of the distorted imagination of outsiders. Even responsible officials deprecate the reports of tension. The Governor of Florida, in an Associated Press dispatch from London, where he was making a pitch for more British tourists to his state, was quoted on August 16, 1963, as saying that "we haven't had one single incident of violence," and that "we in Florida have no problem of integration because the laws of our state ban discrimination." A few days later, back from his trip, he was quoted as saying that he might or might not read the fact-finding report submitted to the United States Civil Rights Commission by its Florida advisory committee; the report, he intimated, was of no direct significance to him because the committee, though made up entirely of Floridians, was established and sponsored by the federal government. Local motion picture theatres, at that very time, were being picketed by Negro (and some white) college students in protest against their discriminatory policies. A few weeks earlier, city swimming pools in Tallahassee, built partly with federal funds, were closed when Negroes sought admittance; and, on advice of the city attorney, a city commission meeting was cut short when one of these Negroes tried to present her views.

The general conclusion of the Civil Rights Advisory Committee —that Florida in 1963 remained a "tight-white" state—was particularly resented by officials at all levels because it is a slurring paraphrase of the white supremacy definition of a peaceful community: one in which Negroes accept docilely the inferior place set for them by the whites. Prompt police and .court action to suppress all overt expression of Negro unrest is rationalized as maintaining the peace; the old Klan used the same argument to suppress comparable Negro efforts to gain equality after the Civil War. Relatively few members of local police and sheriff's departments are Klansmen today, as most of them were in Reconstruction days. But some are, in some Southern communities, and they do not always make a secret of the fact. The modern Klan depends somewhat more on fueling the fires of racism through propaganda, and it will no doubt continue to lead, and subtly influence others to follow, in the course of resisting civil rights legislation passed by the majority of Americans, through their representatives in Congress.

The old Klan seldom directly publicized its principles. It didn't need to, for most Southern editors of newspapers were only too ready to defend both its principles and its program of action. Modern editors, generally a more cautious breed, are inclined to leave the defense to the writers of letters to the editor. "Becoming a 'first-class citizen' is not a right," one resident of Quincy, Florida, wrote on September 9, 1963, "but a privilege earned by one's willingness to accept responsibilities of full, first-class citizenship." This writer may not have realized the irony of his words, for Gadsden County, which centers in Quincy, has one of the worst records in Florida of official resistance to Negro voter registration. For a hundred years, the writer continued, Negroes have had the opportunity to achieve first-class citizenship but have not seized it; thus they themselves are to blame for their second-class status.

Such an argument should make members of the old Klan turn in their graves, for it was their boast that they thwarted the determined effort of freedmen to achieve first-class citizenship. And defenders of white supremacy should protest, too, for in their view Negroes are innately incapable of attaining equality. No amount of Negro effort could avail, and no amount of aid by misguided outsiders could possibly alter, the inherent inferiority that is cited to justify continued discrimination.

Meanwhile the tired old argument of the sanctity of private property is being trotted out in refurbished form. In an agrarian economy, crops are the source of income and hence the basis of property; for workmen to withhold their essential labor was tantamount to destroying that property. White men, conditioned through generations to incapacity for working the money crops, needed the Negroes as much as they needed the land, the sun, the rain, and the seed. From the time of the very first Klan parade through the night streets of Pulaski it was evident that Klan mysteriousness, with or without the addition of violence, could be used to persuade the Negroes to resume their God-given labor and to refrain from destroying property through idleness.

As workmen employed by whites, the freedmen could not hope to enjoy social equality with whites any more than they could have as slaves. Black men existed to produce the property, not to enjoy its benefits, such as travel, eating at restaurants, staying at hotels, or attending theaters or sports events. The Klan, by winning for Southern whites the exclusive privilege of enjoying property, reduced to virtual zero the chance for any Negro to "accept responsibilities of full, first-class citizenship."

Southern whites have clung to another form of property, too—real estate. Far fewer Negroes than whites have ever been able to own their own land and the houses they live in. Some who were industrious enough to buy homes learned from Klan visitations the error of their ways; the majority are familiar with the Sunday morning rounds of white landlords to collect the weekly rent. In the thinking of genuine white supremacists, Negro acquisition of property is as much a threat to the traditional racial pattern as is Negro voting or mixed schools.

Klan reasoning goes something like this: Whites are superior to Negroes in every respect. To extend to Negroes all the privileges enjoyed by whites is to jeopardize that white superiority. Landed property is one of the most obvious of white privileges, whether in ownership or in sharing its use. Most whites are probably unaware of adopting this line of reasoning when they say, in great seriousness, "I think a property owner has the right, guaranteed by the Constitution, to use his property in any way he chooses, and to withhold its enjoyment from anybody he chooses, whether the individual is blue, green, or black." Since there are no blue or green people, this argument applies only to the black of skin, and it is a profound distortion of the principle of property rights that all Americans hold in high regard. Another distortion is to subscribe to "the inalienable rights of life, liberty, and the pursuit of happiness" and then to add the Klan rider: "for whites only."

A statement read by a Southern governor to the U.S. Senate Committee on Commerce, in 1964, expressed the conservative Southern white position very clearly:

The real issue you must resolve is between conflicting demands for freedom.

On the one hand the traveler demands the freedom to buy what he wishes to buy, in a hotel, a theater, or anywhere that there are things for sale.

I believe that he should have that freedom—provided, of course, he does not violate the freedom of others.

This is the crux of the matter.

And indeed it *is* the crux of the matter, for the freedom of others that is here referred to, and that is defended in hundreds of comparable Southern arguments, is the freedom of white property owners to refuse service to Negroes. The Ku Klux Klan led the fight after the Civil War to preserve this freedom to discriminate, this freedom of the dominant race to declare another race ineligible for full American citizenship. In our century the Klan has resumed the fight, broadening its base to exploit nativistic fears of Catholics, Jews, and recent immigrants. The Klan's goal is to preserve the right of a minority to declare itself superior to the rest of the population and to define true Americanism in terms of its own special traits, traditions, and interests. All Americans should be free, the Klan insists, as long as they do not violate the freedom of this minority to maintain its special privilege.

The old Klan won its fight. The modern Klan is no more abashed at the odds against it than the old, and no less determined to win. Who can say with confidence that it will not?

Chapter Thirteen

FORECAST: CONTINUED TURBULENCE

From the beginning, the American people have always had a pretty high opinion of themselves. God, it was explicitly believed by the more pious of the Founding Fathers, took a personal interest in the English settlements and intended them to flourish—as they did. Their success, and the continuing success of the nation they grew into, has confirmed the pleasing sense of being singled out of all mankind to serve as God's agents, or partners, in the glorious venture. Material prosperity has been the clinching argument: God would not have rewarded any group so handsomely if he did not approve of the way they were doing things —if they were not, in a word, his chosen people.

People look to their historians to interpret their past, and the generality of American historians have provided a solid basis for this myth of divine favor. Not every historian has been so serenely confident of the future as William Bradford, first governor of Plymouth, or John Winthrop, his counterpart in Massachusetts Bay, or so sure that the divine plan was developing properly as was Cotton Mather in 1700 and George Bancroft early in the nineteenth century. Mather read natural phenomena as messages from God, and Bancroft believed that "God is visible in history." But even though some of our historians have been more cautious, the record as it has usually been interpreted offers ample room for self-congratulation. The first migrants are viewed in retrospect as men and women courageous enough to risk the Atlantic crossing, wise enough to foresee a great future for America, and pious enough to remember that God shapes the destinies of individuals and nations. Subsequent Americans, by and large, have viewed themselves as no less virtuous, and as worthy to continue the implementing of the divine plan.

One special concern along the way has been defining the term "Americans." Not just anybody could be the genuine thing. The lazy men in Jamestown were obviously not to be bracketed with the ambitious workers. Neither were Thomas Morton and his followers, whose pagan May-pole revels at Merrymount mocked the sober-sided builders of nearby Plymouth. Since a wilderness is not tamed in a day, the virtue most in demand was willingness to share in the hard work of converting raw nature to human uses. Later, when the original urgent need for labor was past, the material success that sustained work commonly produces could be substituted for work itself as the central criterion. In a land where God offered copious rewards for all who helped themselves, as Poor Richard reminded his countrymen, poverty came to be viewed as prima-facie evidence of insufficient piety. Conversely, material substance, whether gained by one's own hard work or by the work of others, became a chief means of identifying the "real Americans."

For the first two centuries and more, the great majority of Americans were Protestants of English descent—though they preferred to call themselves Anglo-Saxons. It was only natural, then, for the definition of "real Americans" to shape up like this: "White Protestant Anglo-Saxons whose faith in God is demonstrated by their material well-being." If some Protestant Anglo-Saxons were so lacking in applied faith as to remain poor, their children could always get religion, expiate their fathers' sin by working hard, and regain their birthright. The "poor whites" in Appalachia have always been a reproach, for they seemed to prefer to stay on an economic level with groups not considered eligible for "real American" status.

The two chief groups of ineligibles were easy to identify by their racial characteristics. Toward the close of the seventeenth century, historians reporting the Indian wars reflected a profound shift in attitude: at the outset, Indians were regarded as pagans ripe for conversion, for the greater glory of God, but within half a century of contact they had become subhuman savages without souls to be saved, fit only for extermination. The notion endured. Its classic form is attributed to a famous nineteenth-century general: "The only good Indian is a dead Indian." The other and larger nonwhite group, imported from Africa as slaves, were likewise readily excludable as subhuman; their very presence in the population, relieving white men from the harder kinds of labor, helped confirm the myth of Anglo-Saxon superiority. European elements such as the Dutch and the French, meanwhile, posed no serious challenge to the concept, being few in number, confined to small areas, and readily assimilable, in time, by the Anglo-Saxon majority.

The Revolutionary War, in the logic of the "100-percenters" of the period, proved two things: that the divine plan for America included independence, and that the American variety of Anglo-Saxon was superior to the English variety or its mercenary troops from the same northern parts of Germany that produced the original Angles and Saxons. The Tories who made up a third of the colonial population hardly agreed with the patriots; and another third, indifferent to the war and its outcome, were indifferent on this point too. The patriotic third could take all the credit for independence; it added greatly to their awareness of being "real" Americans and of earning the gratitude of generations yet unborn, all of us, certainly, who prefer to be free of control by Europeans. It never bothered the patriotic "real" Americans, incidentally, that they were a minority of the population.

Flushed with victory, the patriots indulged in a veritable binge of proud nationalism. They tried to deify General Washington, in the Roman *pater patriae* tradition, but had to settle for his unanimous choice as President. They demanded of artists and authors works equaling if not excelling the best of Europe, to prove the nation culturally as well as politically independent; what they got was a windy epic by Joel Barlow, *The Vision of Columbus,* reminiscent of the *Aeneid* except in durability. Culture, apparently, could not be achieved on short order. But the question "What hath God wrought?" was easy to answer: within less than two centuries he had wrought a civilization unlike anything the world had ever known before, and better than any other, past or present. If some Europeans (and some Americans) could not see this, it only proved their myopia; all "real Americans" were sure of it, and proud that they had not let God down—for He could not have done the job alone, but depended on their Anglo-Saxon genius, American variety, to implement his will.

Even Henry Thoreau, archcritic of American materialism, thought highly of the American people. In "Civil Disobedience" he insisted that it was the people, rather than the government, that had done all that had been done; and he added that they would have done somewhat more if the government had not sometimes got in the way. In this he was echoing another historically constant American attitude: distrust of centralized power. European authoritarianism had been—for some of the migrants, if not all—one of the reasons prompting their removal to America; and the limits set to the powers of the new government, in the body of the Constitution and especially in the first ten Amendments, reflected a lively fear that personal freedom might one day be sacrificed on the altar of federal might. Since God's plan for America included maximum individual freedom, it was the duty of "real Americans" to resist the national government whenever it exceeded its delegated powers by stepping on their toes.

Given such long-established and deeply ingrained attitudes, how could "real" Americans be expected to view the sudden surge of new immigration after 1835 that brought thousands of people who were not qualified for true citizenship according to the° definition? And how could white Southerners be expected to view the post-Civil War federal effort to overthrow the definition by enforcing racial equality? The Know-Nothing movement and its successors were clearly predictable, and so was the Southern white refusal to accept the Negro as equal in any way to the white man. The "real" American would have been exceptional not to protest; this was an egregious betrayal of the contract that free men had entered into, and it justified the misgivings that had made them hesitate in 1787. The federal government, by not stemming the flood of immigrants, and by its positive action to equalize the races, was flouting the divine plan for a nation controlled by the "real" Americans who had been its builders. When historians just before and just after 1900 justified the Reconstruction Klan as a necessary evil, doing more good than harm, they were reflecting the historical notion that God intended this to be a "white man's country," and Anglo-Saxon at that.

Despite the statistical evidence that white Protestants of English descent are no longer the majority of the American population, the notion persists that these, and only these, are genuine Americans, and that all others are impostors, Americans by tolerance, perhaps, but on a distinctly lower level. People of recent migration have themselves contributed to this notion by their readiness to accept the Anglo-American as the model to emulate. Some of the newer groups quickly, and others over a longer period, have eliminated the traces of difference. The legal change of name from one obviously foreign to one safely English symbolizes a deliberate effort to accommodate; the motive is strong. Other outgroups, unable or unwilling to abandon their identification, stand apart in various parts of the country—Catholic French-Canadians in northern New England, for example, or Mexicans in the Southwest, or Nisei in California, or Negroes everywhere. Even when such groups have gained full civil rights and do not face overt discrimination, they can never be accepted as fully American by those who cling to the restrictive old definition of the "real" Americans.

These self-consciously "real" Americans are genuinely sincere people who view with alarm the steady drift away from the ideals and attitudes held by their forebears who planted the civilization and gave the nation its distinctive institutions. To such people, social change is a subtle, insidious revolution. They feel that it is their duty to both God and country to resist this revolution with the last full ounce of devotion. In their uneasiness they suspect a deliberate plot for subversion; they may be incapable of realizing that the change is largely the result of out-group pressure to gain status comparable to their own. They enjoy this status by birth; they never had to fight for it; and the struggle to gain it seems undignified and alien. The encouragement given to the strugglers by other Americans as "real" as themselves is impossible for them to understand; even the moderates, those who do nothing at all to defend *or* to change the social pattern, seem guilty of contributing to the enemy cause by simple inaction.

The original Klan was organized in defense of Americanism as the Klansmen, and white Southerners in general, conceived it. The federal program for Reconstruction was honestly viewed as a vindictive effort to destroy the definition of "real" Americans that prevailed in the region. The Klan resistance continued until the federal program was abandoned, which meant that control was restored to the white Protestant Anglo-Saxons who had historically held the control and were convinced that they always should.

The modern Klan was also formed in defense of Americanism against the mounting pressures from groups that many older Americans considered ineligible. Modern Klansmen (excluding the cynical leaders) have been sincere in supposing that the challenging groups mean to subvert all that is best in America; and they have justified their tactics as the means of preserving the great tradition and of continuing the orderly fulfillment of the divine plan for the country.

The Reconstruction Klan at the height of its power numbered about half a million members, a small fraction of all white Americans but able to succeed because most white Southerners endorsed the principles that the Klan put into practice and helped the Klansmen evade arrest and punishment. The modern Klan at its peak numbered about five million, a somewhat larger fraction of the total population but less successful because most of the nation's whites neither endorsed its principles nor threw up a protective shield for its members. The success of the Reconstruction Klan has been a constant challenge to modern Klansmen; if a minority movement could successfully resist, in the 1870's, a federal program to destroy the traditional definition of "real" Americans, a minority today, by sheer persistence, may hope to repeat the success. As long as some Americans sincerely believe that true Americanism is being subverted by government officials and by groups not eligible for full status as Americans, the Klan will survive. As in Reconstruction times, it may change its name, and even some of its tactics, but its essential character will not be changed. Continued turbulence is the only reasonable forecast.

There is a widespread notion that education can dispel the prejudice and the misdirected behavior of Klan members and their like. In Klan thinking it is *not* prejudice and misdirected behavior, but ideal Americanism and behavior in defense of divine will. Youngsters, preferably orphans, might be educable in ways the national majority consider democratic, but persuade a Klansman to abandon his commitment to white supremacy? Impossible! Any abandonment of white supremacy, to one who is committed to it, would lead to mongrelization, the worst eventuality that Klan thinking can conceive. If democratic equality is an ideal for the majority, a pure American race is no less strong an ideal for the white supremacist. And to assume that one ideal is necessarily superior to another leads nowhere, for the white supremacist is just as devoted to his ideal as the democratic equalitarian can be to his. It is also futile to belabor people for not living up to ideals set for them by others; ideals are not universally recognized, or permanent in content, or concrete actualities, though commencement speakers may assume they are.

What *is* possible is an educational program designed to show how the myth of racial difference—whites innately superior, Negroes innately inferior—was deliberately developed in the years before the Civil War to justify slavery, and that it rests chiefly on relative advantages dictated by the slave-owners. If Negroes were demonstrably inferior, it was because the owners found it to their advantage to keep them so. As for the alleged superiority of Anglo-Saxons over all other varieties of human beings, again it might be possible to demonstrate how people came to think so; and in the process the supposed purity of Anglo-Saxons as a "race" could be exploded. Such an educational program would have no effect at all on hard-core Klansmen, but it could reduce the possibility that other citizens would be seduced by their propaganda.

Another possibility is the use of force. But, though force is possible, and though it may be the only effective alternative, its use is nevertheless debatable. Whether the federal government should resort to force, even for purposes considered good by the majority, is at the heart of any civil rights discussion. If force is the decision, it will reflect an impatience with Klan-like theories and practices, and a kind of consensus never before reached by the groups the Klan has attacked. It will also reflect a growth of a kind of intolerance unfamiliar in American annals—the intolerance of intolerant behavior. As a nation we incline to the notion that intolerance will wither on the vine, and we shrug it off as of no particular significance.

Before we develop the intolerance of intolerance that would induce us to adopt force against the Klan, and Klan-like groups by any name, we would have to become more familiar with the Klan program and principles than most of us are. There is no lack of expository material published by the Klan to educate the American public, and instead of suppressing it, we might profit by multiplying copies and inviting all voters to read it. One of the best examples is not new; it was issued in 1922 by J. S. Fleming of Goodwater, Alabama: *What Is Ku Kluxism? Let Americans Answer—Aliens Only Muddy the Water*. No enemy of the Klan, and no scholar trying to present it objectively, could produce a more revealing portrait.

Fleming saw the Catholic Church as a religious government seeking deliberately to "Romanize" the United States. Every Catholic elected to public office, or employed to teach in a public school, was a conscious agent of the Church to subvert American ideals and to replace them with dangerous foreign notions. Catholic young people were encouraged to marry outside the Church, so that the wife or husband, and any children they might have, would become Catholics. Catholic opposition to Prohibition was part of the plot, a particularly vicious means of destroying the moral fiber of true Americans. And Catholic opposition to the Klan was a dead giveaway, since no true American could possibly oppose or discourage an organization pledged, as the Klan was, to uphold all that was best in America. Catholics feared the Klan, Fleming wrote, because they knew it was their greatest enemy in the struggle for control of the country. Catholics knew, Fleming added in one of his finest non-sequiturs, that "once the old Klansmen defied the world to destroy the Anglo-Saxon race through the diabolical process of miscegenation, and won."

Only degenerate white men, or subscribers to alien doctrines, could work for racial equality, Fleming continued. The original Klan deserved "the everlasting gratitude of all lovers of pure American principle throughout the nation." Klansmen were "Real White Men, with a racial pride based on the unrevoked decree of Almighty God." Color-blind Catholics could not be "real White Men" as such men defined themselves. The Catholic Church was patently guilty, Fleming insisted, of exploiting the gullibility of Negroes by raising their hopes of equality.

But the Roman Catholic Church was not the only religious government intent on overthrowing true Americanism, he warned. Two others that Fleming mentioned were the Mormon hierarchy, which was merely waiting for the right moment to align itself with the Catholic Church "to suppress our American Ideals," and the Jews. "All these aliens know they can make no progress in America, until Americanism is destroyed." It is incumbent upon the "various religious sects loyal to our pure American Ideals" to oppose these religious governments, especially when the federal government is so obviously lax concerning the danger. All this is orthodox Klan thinking.

Identifying the Mormon Church as alien tips Fleming's hand, especially when he refers to its genesis in upstate New York. By the term he means any group, whether of foreign or native origin, that diverges measurably from "American Ideals" as the Klan conceives them. In the forty years since his pamphlet was published, Klan doctrine has changed very little, although "alien" has given way to "subversive," which is closer to what Fleming was really driving at. Catholics are today no longer the prime target, and Mormons have dropped completely out of Klan suspicion. Federal laxity is currently emphasized, although the Klan charge of subversive infiltration of the federal government is only a continuation of one of its original contentions, dating as far back as 1867. Klan thinking, past and present, is "black and white." Once its basic assumptions 'are established, everything that deviates is attacked as false and dangerous, whether the deviation is total or only slight. To a Klansman, there can be no middle ground.

If the modern Klan had not followed the old Klan in its resort to violence, if its leaders in the formative period had all been men of good character, neither exploiting the membership nor guilty of individual vices, it is probable that the general public would not have repudiated the organization as thoroughly as it has. The Klan gave expression to great popular myths beloved by the public, and appealed to the concern of all for the perpetuation of the nation in the form we all desire. Henry Grady was right, in the 1870's, when he urged the Klan to refrain from overt action and to maintain itself as a moral force. But, early and late, the fear of subversion and the impulse to punish supposed enemies of Americanism have been too strong to control. The more perceptive the individual observer, the greater the gulf appears between Klan principle and overt behavior. The modern Klan's greatest mistake, by this reasoning, was to suppose it could gain its ends by adopting the illegal tactics that gave the old Klan its sweeping victory in the South.

Despite the disreputable public image of the Klan today, its program has enough appeal to idealistic "real" Americans to warrant the prediction that it will be with us for a long time to come. Not all Americans who are "real" in Klan logic endorse its program—a fact that makes the Klan sector an even smaller fraction of the population than Klan leaders may suppose it to be. When the "real" Americans who oppose the Klan are added to the groups the Klan attacks, the total is an overwhelming majority of the population. But because the Anglo-American remains a model for emulation by groups new in the land, the majority has no cohesive unity. Every American of recent vintage who achieves full acceptance and then proceeds to discriminate against individuals and entire groups still struggling for status contributes to the atmosphere favorable for Klan action. Special privilege is so attractive that all too many people, once they have gained it, find a particular enjoyment in flaunting it, and looking down on others who have yet to achieve it. The Klan capitalizes on this tendency.

Time no doubt is on the side of the "minorities" that are collectively the great majority, but the constant pressure on individuals to slough off their minority identification puts the minorities at a peculiar disadvantage. The thousands of light-skinned Negroes who "pass" each year, and who thereafter enjoy the privileges limited to whites, can easily be forgiven for abstaining from the struggle for Negro equality; they have won the fight on an individual basis and have no wish to reopen it. Their abstention, however, weakens the campaign that Negro leaders are able to mount. In roughly the same way, grandchildren of Jewish immigrants who changed their names by legal action and joined Protestant churches can be forgiven for a disinclination to stir up dying embers. They may not even know what their grandfathers did. Negroes who "pass" have even better reason for concealing the action from their children, with the result, ironic and rather bitter, that their children may be as active as any of their classmates in making life miserable for Negroes assigned by court order to newly integrated schools. The extreme of protective coloring would be former Negroes, now accepted as whites, joining the Klan. Though this seems highly improbable, what present Klansman, especially in the South with its antebellum concubinage system, can be absolutely sure that he has no Negro blood?

Nobody is born with any awareness of his genetic makeup. The "real" Americans who take pride in being Anglo-Saxon have no way of sensing the racial mixing in England before the migrants crossed the Atlantic. Harry Golden has devastated the myth of Anglo-Saxon superiority, and long before Golden's time, Daniel Defoe demolished the myth of its purity in "The True-Born Englishman." But myths develop with slight reference to facts, and survive despite all the logic and scientific evidence that can be patiently assembled. Men who pride themselves on their racial purity and fight to preserve it from contamination are immune from argument because they so deeply *wish* that purity to be true. Nor would there be any strong reason for disabusing them of the notion if they confined their belief to abstract thinking and never used it to justify overt discrimination against other human beings they honestly consider inferior.

Who would have dared predict in the year 1100 that within two centuries the Anglo-Saxons in England would absorb their demonstrably superior Norman conquerors and would proceed, in successive centuries, to produce a Chaucer, a Shakespeare, a Milton, and a Keats? It is likely that somewhere in England the myth of Anglo-Saxon inferiority, based on the abysmal ignorance and primitive level of Anglo-Saxon culture in past ages, survives among descendants of the once superior Normans. The same mental process enables modern Klansmen to ignore the cultural achievements of any element in the American population other than the Anglo-Saxon, even though an objective comparison would show other elements superior in specific ways: in the fine arts, for example, or the entertainment world. A claim to world recognition of the United States based narrowly on contributions by citizens of English descent would be as thin as it would be absurd. The education program suggested earlier might well include a catalogue of contributions made to American culture by the elements the Klan attacks as un-American. It would not convince the die-hard Klansmen, but it would limit the effectiveness of their appeal to prejudice. Myths hold on tenaciously, but they cannot be sustained forever in the face of evidence to the contrary. Prejudice burns hot and long, but it does burn out.

The Ku Klux Klan, at every stage, has been the active expression of great American myths, especially those of divine plan and a chosen people—specifically, white Protestant Anglo-Saxons. Actual Klansmen, and those who approve their principles, are generally very sincere in their wish to maintain these myths; it is an illusory countermyth to suppose they are insincere because some of their leaders have been. Klansmen may be categorized as men with an authoritarian personality, akin to Hitler's Nazis, but what they seek to do is what *all* Americans should be seeking to do—to make the United States in fact the great nation we want it to be, and to keep it great. Their method, however, has a built-in futility; they are against every group and program that they consider alien to American tradition, and this denial of alternatives proves, on close examination, to be obsolescent in terms of the direction the country is taking. One of their great weaknesses is their inability, or refusal, to recognize their own obsolescence. But as long as the American people adhere to the myths that the Klan has exploited, and as long as they refuse to recognize their decreasing relevance to modern actualities, the Klan can hope for some success. Perhaps more than "some," for it is clear that other groups have accepted the Klan logic, knowingly or not, in the current rightist attacks on supposed subversion.

In the keynote speech of the Republican National Convention in June, 1964, Governor Hatfield of Oregon repudiated the Klan logic: "There are bigots in this nation," he asserted, "who spew forth the venom of hate. They must be overcome, and this applies to the Ku Klux Klan, the John Birch Society, the Communist Party, and the hundreds of others like them." But the convention itself did not choose to endorse such a statement by making it part of its platform, and the acceptance speech of the nominee for president included a statement in startling contrast with the keynoter's thinking: "Extremism in the defense of liberty is no vice. Moderation in the pursuit of justice is no virtue."

Next day, one of the unsuccessful candidates was openly critical: "To extol extremism—whether 'in defense of liberty' or 'in pursuit of justice,' is dangerous, irresponsible and frightening; . . . the extremism of the Communists, of the Ku Klux Klan and of the John Birch Society—like that of most tyrants has always been claimed by such groups to be in defense of liberty." The Democrats, in their own convention at the end of August, wrote into their platform a strong statement on the subject: "We condemn extremism, whether from the right or left, including the extreme tactics of the Communist Party, the Ku Klux Klan, and the John Birch Society."

During the spring and summer of 1964 the South had been shocked by fiery crosses, bombed homes and motels, burned churches, even murders—the Klan had been at work. Despite these exhibits of extremism, the Republican vice-presidential candidate in a television interview on August 2 declined to reject the backing of the John Birch Society and the Ku Klux Klan. Then, after the so-called Unity Conference of Republican leaders at Hershey, Pennsylvania, on August 21, Senator Barry Goldwater reversed his running-mate's stand by agreeing to "repudiate character assassins, vigilantes, Communists and any other group such as the Ku Klux Klan that seeks to impose its views through terror of threat or violence." So Klan votes went begging after all; neither party, officially, wanted them.

Conflict, it has seriously been suggested, is the best climate for productive change. The challenge posed by the Klan to other groups making up the population should, sooner or later, produce a valuable examination of what the majority of us think Americanism really is, and what it should be. Weather without turbulence, by this reasoning, is dangerous as an invitation to apathy. But there is slight possibility of unbroken calm. The Klan can be counted on to provide the right sort of weather: continued turbulence.

Torch-bearing Klansmen encircle a flaming cross during a 1963 rally in Salisbury, North Carolina. In the flickering light of the 25-foot cross, some 2,000 persons heard Imperial Wizard Robert M. Shelton condemn the civil rights movement as communistic (*Jacket photo*).   *Wide World Photo*

BIBLIOGRAPHICAL NOTES

Chapter One, "The Birth of the Klan"

The one-story former law office of Judge Jones, half a block from the southwest corner of Pulaski's courthouse square, is now a television repair shop. The Klan plaque is just to the left of the door. About a quarter mile farther west, at the crest of a small hill, is the Martin mansion, overlooking the modest deeply shaded campus of Martin College, named for the family. The Spofford mansion, once again a private residence, is about three blocks south of the square.

Susan Lawrence Davis, author of *Authentic History: Ku Klux Klan, 1865–1877* (New York, 1924), was a daughter of the Colonel Davis who organized the second den, at Athens, Alabama; the Romines, as residents of Pulaski, would seem to be more reliable concerning local landmarks in their pamphlet, *A Story of the Original Ku Klux Klan*—which also appeared in 1924, the year when the modern Klan was at its peak in membership and influence. The Pulaski *Citizen*, which printed the Romine pamphlet, still occupies the same office facing the courthouse that it used when it was founded a few years before the Civil War.

[265]

Efforts to discover any fraternity affiliation of John Kennedy at Centre College have been unavailing.

"A Note on the Origin of the Ku Klux Klan" by Ward Allen, in the *Tennessee Historical Quarterly*, XXIII (June, 1964), 182, suggests that the word *kuklos* came from a passage in Pausanias, *Description of Greece*. The Phocians, when the circle of the moon was full, craftily smeared themselves with chalk and, clad in white armor, slaughtered the Thessalians who thought gods were attacking them. Allen cites the phrase *ton kuklon tes selenes*, "the circle of the moon." In an age when Greek was part of every college student's required curriculum, Kennedy might well have read Pausanias. Pulaski still has a classical tradition; in April 1964, the Giles County High School Latin Club produced a play in Latin.

The most authoritative book about the Reconstruction Klan is *Invisible Empire, the Story of the Ku Klux Klan 1866–1877* by Stanley F. Horn (Boston, 1939), but unfortunately it was written without benefit of modern Reconstruction historiography.

The original Klan robes from white sheets were copied by the new dens, along with cone-shaped hats built up to add height. Since the uniform was homemade, both style and color varied. In some areas red was the popular color for robes, usually with white trim. The hat or headdress could be quite grotesque. Some dens favored horns; others sported long imitation white beards. A mask might have a long tongue sticking out, and large teeth. Other dens preferred black robes. The Klan stimulated the sale of calico—white, red, black. James Melville Beard in *K.K.K. Sketches, Humorous and Didactic* (Philadelphia, 1877), pages 34–36, describes a Klan raiding party. The horses were covered with black cloth and masks with white plumes for decoration and the letters "K.K.K." on the cloth. Each rider had "a long black robe, extending from the head to the feet, and decorated with innumerable tin buttons, an inch and a half in diameter, which, under the influence of the starlight, shone like miniature moons. These robes were slit in front and rear . . . and were secured about the waist with scarfs of red silk. Over their faces they wore masks of some heavy white material, the apertures for the eyes, nose, and mouth . . . being lined with red cloth. The head-dress . . . consisted of tall black caps, helmet-shaped . . . decorated with the regulation button, and, when worn by officers of commissioned rank, supplemented by gorgeous plumes, white, red, or blue, according to rank. Each individual wore . . . a belt supporting two large army pistols, in scabbards; and on the flaps of the latter, embroidered in white characters, appeared the devices of the order—skull and crossbones, and mystical KKK. The banners which were three in number . . . were of black silk, supporting in the centre two lions rampant on either side of the regulation skull and crossbones, and on the right, left, and middle, at top, the mystic 'K.' "

Sir Walter Scott was undoubtedly popular in the South, but so were several other British novelists, including Dickens, Thackeray, G. P. R. James, and Disraeli. Scott was equally popular in the North without creating there the notion of an idealized feudal society. To credit him with being the dominant influence in shaping Old South thinking seems unwarranted, according to James Driskell, *Reading Interests in the Lower South 1842–1860* (unpublished M.A. thesis, Florida State University, 1959).

The Reconstruction Act became law on March 2, 1867. Other legislation serving as provocation of Klan resistance included the 13th Amendment in 1865, which guaranteed Negro emancipation; the Freedmen's Bureau Act, also 1865; the Civil Rights Bill, 1866; the 14th Amendment, 1868, which forbade any state to "deprive any person of life, liberty, or property, without due process of law" and confirmed the Supreme Court as final arbiter of state actions; and the 15th Amendment, 1870, which forbade abridgment of the right to vote on account of "race, color, or previous condition of servitude." It is still argued by Southern states' righters that the three Amendments—13th, 14th, and 15th—are not valid because they were adopted when the Southern states were at a political disadvantage and could not present their viewpoint. Legislation specifically designed to curb the Klan included three "Force Bills" commonly known as the "Ku Klux Acts," passed on May 31, 1870; February 28, 1871; and April 20, 1871. The last of these declared that Klan activity was tantamount to rebellion, and empowered the President to suspend the writ of habeas corpus when in his opinion conditions warranted.

Of several books about Bedford Forrest (1821–1877), the best is by Andrew Nelson Lytle, *Bedford Forrest and His Critter*

Company (New York, 1931); but it has little about Forrest's connection with the Klan.

The Prescript of the Klan (1867), together with a Revised and Amended Prescript (1868), a proposed Constitution of a Local Order, and various other official documents were included in John C. Lester and D. C. Wilson, *Ku Klux Klan, Its Origin, Growth and Disbandment,* edited by Walter L. Fleming (New York, 1905), with notes and appendices. This is an enlarged form of the book as originally brought out by Lester and Wilson in 1884. Miss Davis called it spurious, and charged that Wilson used facts given him by Lester, one of the Klan founders, who had planned to write a Klan history. Walter Lynwood Fleming's *Documentary History of Reconstruction* (2 volumes, Cleveland, 1906–7) is useful background material for the Klan, as is James P. Shenstone's *The Reconstruction; A Documentary History of the South after the War: 1865–1877* (New York, 1963).

Chapter Two, "White Supremacy"

President Leland's book is *A Voice from South Carolina* (Charleston, S.C., 1879). Senator Beveridge's remarks are taken from Claude G. Bowers, *Beveridge and the Progressive Era* (New York, 1932). The statements by Ruth Benedict (from *Race: Science and Politics,* pages 153–54), John Stuart Mill (from *Political Economy,* Vol. I, page 390), and Jacques Barzun are all taken from Barzun's *Race, A Study in Modern Superstition* (New York, 1937), page 299. A more recent volume on the same subject is Thomas F. Gossett, *Race; the History of an Idea in America* (Dallas, Texas, 1963).

The shift in "Anglo-Saxon" status from majority to minority is evidenced in the official United States census records. Kipling's phrase is from his poem "Recessional," which reminded the people of Great Britain to remain humble despite the great power they had amassed in creating the British Empire. The pertinent stanza reads:

> *If, drunk with sight of power, we loose*
> *Wild tongues that have not Thee in awe,*

> *Such boastings as the Gentiles use,*
> *Or lesser breeds without the Law—*
>
> .   .   .   .

Power brings responsibility; the superior race, in Kipling's view, must assume the "white man's burden" of guiding and governing inferior peoples.

Oscar Handlin's remark is from his *Race and Nationality in American Life* (Boston, 1957), page 38. *Theodore Weld: Crusader for Freedom*, by Benjamin P. Thomas, was published in New Brunswick, N.J., in 1950. The white Mississippian being tried for murder was Byron de la Beckwith. Pap's harangue in *Huckleberry Finn* (1884) is in Chapter VI. The lurid speech at a Klan gathering just outside St. Augustine in September, 1963, was reported in the *Newsletter* of the Florida Council on Human Relations, October, 1963.

The reference to "the national intention concerning the freedmen" should perhaps be to "the Northern intention." But as Jack B. Scroggs has pointed out in "Southern Reconstruction: A Radical View," *Journal of Southern History*, XXIV (November, 1959), 407–29, the struggle for control of the South was not simply one between Southern whites and Northern Radical Republicans. Southern Unionists bitterly accused the former rebels of virtual treason to the Union, while Southern Radicals disagreed among themselves and also with the national Republican policy-makers. The eventual failure of the congressional program for reconstructing the South was chiefly the result of waning popular support in the North, but this in turn owed much to the fatal dissensions among Southern supporters of the federal program.

The five historians and their key books are as follows:

James Ford Rhodes, *History of the United States from the Compromise of 1850* (7 volumes, New York, 1892–1906).
John W. Burgess, *Reconstruction and the Constitution* (New York, 1902).
Woodrow Wilson, *A History of the American People* (5 volumes, New York, 1902; Documentary Edition, 10 volumes, New York, 1917–18).
Walter Lynwood Fleming, *Civil War and Reconstruction in Ala-*

bama (New York, 1905) and *Documentary History of Recon-*
struction (2 volumes, Cleveland, 1906–7).
William A. Dunning, *Essays on the Civil War and Reconstruction*
and Related Topics (New York, 1898) and *Reconstruction,*
Political and Economic, 1865–1877 (New York, 1907).

Of these five, the most influential was probably Dunning, for members of his graduate seminar at Columbia turned out Reconstruction histories of virtually all the Southern states, as published Ph.D.
dissertations.

The "revisionists" have made substantial headway in the scholarly
journals if not in the textbooks used in our public schools. The
Journal of Southern History, perhaps logically, has been the fore-
most vehicle for revisionistic writing. Francis B. Simkins, "New
Viewpoints of Southern Reconstruction," V (February, 1939), 49–
61, has recently been reprinted in Simkins's book, *The Everlasting*
South, Louisiana State University Press, 1963. T. Harry Williams,
"An Analysis of Some Reconstruction Attitudes," XII (November,
1946), 469–86, shows ways in which revisionists have forced modi-
fications in the story of Reconstruction. But the strongest statement
is by Bernard Weisberger: "The Dark and Bloody Ground of Reconstruction Historiography," XXV (November, 1955), 425–47. One
pioneering revisionist statement appeared in the *American Histor-*
ical Review: Howard K. Beale, "On Rewriting Reconstruction History," XLV (July, 1940), 807–27. One of the finest selected bibliog-
raphies for Reconstruction appears in John Hope Franklin, *Recon-*
struction after the Civil War (Chicago, 1961), pages 232–42, "Suggested Readings." Franklin's own revisionist statement is "Whither
Reconstruction Historiography?" *Journal of Negro Education,* XVII
(Winter, 1948), 446–61.

A few recent school texts apply revisionist scholarship, but most
perpetuate the old stereotypes: illiterate Negro legislators duped by
carpetbaggers and scalawags intent only on becoming rich. *The*
Making of Modern America by Canfield and Wilder (1950, with
biennial revisions since) in a section "The South Suffers from Misrule" blames the region's woes on "the attempt to force Negro rule
upon the South." *Wests' Story of Our Country* revised by Gardner
(1961) calls carpetbaggers venal and adds, "There were also dis-

honest Southerners, called *scalawags*" (p. 336). *Goals of Democracy* by McCutchen, Fersh, and Clark (1962) asserts that under carpet-bag leadership Southern state governments became "profligately corrupt" (p. 133). *Our United States* by Eibling, King, and Harlow (1962) calls these governments "shamefully inefficient" after the carpetbaggers "hurried down from the North to enrich themselves in Southern politics" (p. 389). *Exploring American History* by Schwartz and O'Connor (1963) refers to carpetbaggers and scala-wags as "two groups of greedy white men" (p. 287). *Our Country's History* by Muzzey and Link (1964), despite a conscious effort to incorporate modern research, by implication attributes the "fla-grantly corrupt" Southern state governments to carpetbaggers and Negroes who "were not competent to govern wisely" (p. 326). Muzzey, in the long series of school histories that made him perhaps the most successful of textbook authors, disdained implication in describing what he considered an orgy of extravagance, fraud, and incompetence that made a travesty of government. One won-ders how many thousands of adult Americans owe to Muzzey's books their stand on civil rights.

Claude G. Bowers, *The Tragic Era* (1929), became a best-seller; it used all the traditional views of the older historians, and popu-larized those views for a new generation.

A colleague of the author has suggested that Woodrow Wilson, staunch Presbyterian that he was and thereby a firm believer in predestination, would have been likely to assume divinely intended Negro inferiority. Kathleen Long Wolgemuth, in "Woodrow Wil-son's Appointment Policy and the Negro," *Journal of Southern History*, XXIV (November, 1958), 457–71, shows that in spite of his pre-election promise to deal fairly with Negroes, Wilson appointed virtually no Negroes to federal positions, retained only a few from Taft's administration, and permitted an increase in segregation within several federal departments.

The development of Jim Crow legislation is admirably treated in C. Vann Woodward, *The Strange Career of Jim Crow* (New York, 1955). The Northern record of discrimination is alluded to in Woodward's "The Antislavery Myth," in *The American Scholar*, XXXI (Spring, 1962); he points out that there have been antislavery myths in the North complementing proslavery myths in the South. A good study of Northern myth and practice is Leon F. Litwack, *North of Slavery: the Negro in the Free States, 1790–1860* (Chicago, 1961). Neither the Northern free Negro nor the Southern slave, according to Litwack, was, by 1860, as passive, meek, and subservient as the conventional stereotype.

Gustavus Myers treats the Klan, both old and new, in his *History of Bigotry in the United States* (New York, 1943).

Chapter Three, "The Klan Impeaches a Governor"

The prime source for details of atrocities committed by the Klan prior to 1871 is the 13-volume report, commonly called "The Ku Klux Conspiracy," but officially titled *The Testimony Taken by the Joint Select Committee to Inquire into the Condition of Affairs in the Late Insurrectionary States* (Report no. 22, parts 1–13, of the Reports of Committees of the House of Representatives for the 2nd Session of the 42nd Congress, 1871–1872), published in 1872. The same report, as submitted to the Senate, is Senate Report No. 41. The thirteen parts or volumes are as follows:

> I. Report of Committee and Views of the Minority
> II. North Carolina
> III, IV, V. South Carolina
> VI, VII. Georgia
> VIII, IX, X. Alabama
> XI, XII. Mississippi
> XIII. Florida

As might be expected, the minority views given in Volume I strongly attack the majority findings, *e.g.* (page 289): "The atrocious measures by which millions of white people have been put at the mercy of the semi-barbarous negroes of the South, and the vilest of the white people, both from the North and South, who have been constituted the leaders of this black horde, are now sought to be justified and defended by defaming the people upon whom this unspeakable outrage had been committed." Elsewhere the minority opinion discounts the reports of the Klan, and asserts that an armed conspiracy never existed in more than one-tenth of the area of the South. In strong opposition to the assertions of many defenders of the Klan that Klansmen were the cream of Southern white manhood, the minority report insists (page 292) that "the men and the bands by which such outrages are perpetrated are almost universally regarded by the intelligent people of the several States as the worst enemies of the South." But it further insisted that the federal action was the stimulus to all such outrages, and charged that "the Ku-Klux bill, and the proceedings thereunder are the grossest outrage, the foulest calumny, ever perpetrated or circulated upon or against a helpless people by their rulers—who ought, for that reason if for no other, to be their friends instead of being their relentless enemies and calumniators." Later in the report, the minority branded the Radical rule in South Carolina the most oppressive that ever disgraced humanity, and said (page 515) that "bad government will produce bad men among the best people on earth; and that has clearly been the cause of Ku-Kluxism in South Carolina." Similar circumstances, the report continued, produced the Carbonari in Italy, the Free Companions in France, the Moss Troopers in England under the Normans, and even Robin Hood.

Holden's impeachment was not the first attempted in the Reconstruction South; Governor Reed of Florida was impeached three times—in 1868, 1870, and 1871—but never successfully.

North Carolina background is supplied in Hugh Lefler and Albert Newsome, *North Carolina: The History of a Southern State* (Chapel Hill, 1955). More specific details are furnished by Cortez A. M. Ewing, "Two Reconstruction Impeachments," *North Carolina Historical Review*, XV (July, 1938), 204–30; Otto H. Olsen, "The Ku Klux Klan: A Study of Reconstruction Politics and Propaganda," *ibid.*, XXXIX (July, 1962), 340–62; J. R. Davis, "Reconstruction in Cleveland County [N.C.]," *Trinity College Historical Society Papers*, Series X (Durham, N.C., 1914); and W. K. Boyd, "William W. Holden," *ibid.*, Series III (1899), 39–78, 90–130.

The first six chapters of Hamilton's *Reconstruction in North Carolina* were originally printed privately as a doctoral dissertation at Columbia University in 1906; this was one of the long series of volumes produced under the direction of Professor William A. Dunning, covering individual Southern states and helping confirm the older interpretation of Reconstruction history.

Bedford Forrest was not alone in charging that Union League insolence prompted the formation of the Klan as a defensive organization; the charge is basic to all defenses of the Klan. No full treatment of the Union League has been published. Its ritual is described in Simkins and Woody, *South Carolina during Reconstruction* (Chapel Hill, 1932).

The troubles in Alamance and Caswell Counties have been variously described in state histories, in "The Ku Klux Conspiracy," and in Horn, *Invisible Empire,* pages 190–213. Chapter 10 in the present volume, "The Battle of the Books," shows how strong an appeal the "Kirk-Holden War" has had for authors of Klan novels.

The Negro militia has been well examined by Otis A. Singletary, *Negro Militia and Reconstruction* (Austin, Texas, 1957). One point commonly (and, for pro-Klan writers, perhaps willfully) overlooked is that Negroes were almost never the sole members of state militias, or even the majority of those militias during Reconstruction.

Patsy Barton's affidavit was given to Albion W. Tourgée when Tourgée was serving as a federal judge in Greensboro, N.C.; it was one of the large number of documents he later drew upon in writing his anti-Klan novel, *A Fool's Errand,* which is discussed in Chapter 10. A photocopy of Lea's deposition is owned by the author; permission to quote excerpts has been given by the State of North Carolina Department of Archives and History. The term "carried" in the passage "beckoned to Stevens and carried him downstairs" is regional for "led" or "took." Perhaps the most remarkable thing about this deposition is that it is one of the very few ever given by former Klansmen, yet it cleared up one of the most widely known of all Klan incidents.

Chapter Four, "South Carolina: The Lawless Temper"

The term "lawless temper" is taken from a letter written on November 22, 1871, by the Attorney-General of the United States, Amos Tappan Akerman. Excerpts from this and a second Akerman letter, both in the Akerman letterbooks in the University of Virginia Library, are included in this chapter by permission.

Reconstruction in South Carolina, as in other Southern states, has been quite differently reported at different times by writers of different predilections. The "classical" Southern interpretation is well exemplified by James S. Pike, *The Prostrate State* (New York, 1874; reissued New York, 1935, with an introduction by Henry Steele Commager). A fairly recent restatement of the Pike thesis is Henry T. Thompson, *Ousting the Carpetbagger from South Carolina* (Columbia, S.C., 1926). Robert Durden, *James Shepherd Pike: Republicanism and the American Negro* (Durham, N.C., 1957), shows how Pike's book has served as a major prop for the "classical" history of South Carolina; James Ford Rhodes, for instance, cited Pike seventeen times in a single chapter in Volume VII (covering 1872–1877) of his *History of the United States*. B. F. Simkins and R. H. Woody, *South Carolina during Reconstruction* (Chapel Hill, N.C., 1932), is a pioneer in the modern "revisionist" interpretation. The evolution in historical viewpoint is reviewed in Neill W. Macaulay, Jr., "South Carolina Reconstruction Historiography," *South Carolina Historical Magazine*, LXV (January, 1964), 20–32. Herbert Shapiro, "The Ku Klux Klan during Reconstruction: The South Carolina Episode," *Journal of Negro History*, XLIV (January, 1964), 34–55, re-examines the political turmoil in the state and suggests that the Klan strengthened the morale of Southern conservatives.

The testimony of former governor James L. Orr at the Congressional hearings of the Ku Klux Klan in 1871 is recorded in "The Ku Klux Conspiracy." John L. Leland's book, *A View from South Carolina* (Columbia, S.C., 1879), offers an interesting contrast with Orr's testimony. The suspension of habeas corpus in South Carolina in 1872 was probably the most significant application of this punitive measure which was authorized by the "Ku Klux Acts" of 1871. At the Klan trials in Columbia, the presentment of the grand jury, signed by "Benj. F. Jackson, foreman," expressed great shock at what had been learned, especially the fact that Klan members included "the leading men of those counties . . . large numbers of the most prominent citizens," and it added that "many of these men who were openly and publicly speaking against the Klan, and pretending to deplore the work of this murderous conspiracy, were influential members of the order, and directing its operation even in detail."

The Joe Crews syllogism could just as well have read, "Joe Crews is a Radical. All Radicals are vile, vicious men. Joe Crews, therefore, is a vile, vicious man." So sweeping was Conservative Southern denunication of Radicals that the denunciation of any particular Radical invites, at least in retrospect, generous discounting. President Leland, for example, may never have suspected how many Radicals were accused of inciting freedmen to arson by mentioning the low cost of matches; simple repetition of this accusation makes it sound, in time, like the very stuff of legend. This is not said with the intention of whitewashing all Radicals operating in the South, or to suggest that not one of them was vile or vicious; a few of them no doubt were, just as a few Klansmen may have been, too.

This chapter refers to counties in South Carolina. Prior to 1868, the only divisions of the state were judicial districts. Of the numerous reforms produced by the constitutional convention held in Charleston in January, 1868, one of the most important was the conversion of the judicial districts into counties and the stipulation that all the county officials be elected by popular vote.

The standard work on the Freedmen's Bureau is George R. Bentley, *A History of the Freedmen's Bureau* (Philadelphia, 1955). McNeilly's *Religion and Slavery: A Vindication of the Southern Churches* was published in 1911, eleven years after it was read as a paper.

Alfred T. Williams, in *Hampton and His Red Shirts* (Charleston, S.C., 1935), reports that the Klan was relatively quiescent by the time of the crucial election of 1876. But during that campaign one effective device used by Democratic candidates was first to announce that they had been accused of former Klan membership and then to challenge the accusers to step forward with proof. General knowledge of Klan activity, or of opposition to the Klan, Williams indicates, did affect the voting in 1876; but a split in the Radical ranks had a greater bearing on the outcome. This split, according to Williams, deprived the Union League "of the absolute power it had possessed since the Ku Klux Klan, the one effective force, had been destroyed by demoralization and treason within its ranks and the relentless—frequently tyrannical and illegal—attacks of the United States authorities." The habit of calling action of duly constituted federal authorities illegal seems to be quite firmly fixed in the thinking of some Southerners.

Chapter Five, "The Way of the Scalawag"

The minority report in Volume I of "The Ku Klux Conspiracy" offers (page 297) an interesting definition of a "scalawag" by General James H. Clanton of Alabama: "southern men we call scalawags. The name originated in a fellow being kicked by a sheep so that he died. He said he didn't mind being killed, but he hated the idea of being kicked to death by the meanest wether in the whole flock—the scaly sheep. We mean by a scalawag a meaner man than a carpet-bagger."

Allen W. Trelease, "Who Were the Scalawags?" *Journal of Southern History*, XXIX (November, 1963), 445–68, shows that the caricature of the scalawag as a traitor to race and region gained currency with passage of time. David H. Donald, "The Scalawag in Mississippi Reconstruction," *ibid.*, X (November, 1944), 447–60, sympathetically presents the Unionist Whig predicament and especially the insuperable problems faced by Alcorn as governor.

Reconstruction in Mississippi has been treated with an emphasis on the state's Negroes in volumes twenty years apart: Jesse Thomas Wallace, *A History of the Negroes of Mississippi from 1865 to 1890* (Clinton, Miss., 1927, written as a Columbia dissertation), and Vernon Lane Wharton, *The Negro in Mississippi 1865 to 1890* (Chapel Hill, 1947, the twenty-eighth volume in the James Sprunt Publications of the University of North Carolina). The Wallace volume has a kind of left-handed distinction of having been produced at the institution where the Dunning influence so long dictated a classical interpretation of Reconstruction. The Wharton volume has been described as the ideal kind of Reconstruction history; that it was produced at a Southern institution, under the direction of a Southern professor of history, should astonish nobody who is aware of the solid historical research in the South today.

James M. Wells, *The Chisolm Massacre: A Picture of "Home Rule" in Mississippi*, was published in Washington in 1877 by the Chisolm Monument Association; there was a second edition in 1878. The full title of James D. Lynch's answer is *Kemper County Vindicated, and a Peep at Radical Rule in Mississippi* (New York, 1879).

Lynch also wrote *Redpath; or the Ku-Klux Tribunal. A Poem* (Columbus, Miss., 1877).

Judge Chisolm's faith in the federal authority to protect him seems, at least in retrospect, somewhat naive; the United States Army had too few troops even to provide adequate protection for such agents as employees of the Freedmen's Bureau. Florida's Governor Stearns (see Chapter 8) made several appeals for troops but without success. Native Radicals under Klan attack had no chance at all.

It is unfortunate that "Dixie," a fine song which originated in ante-bellum Negro minstrel shows, and contains no concrete referent to white-Negro relationships, should have acquired its enduring emotional connotation. White students at Southern universities, who spring to their feet when its lively strains begin, are generally as ignorant of the song's history as they are of its adverse connotation to Negro classmates. Sporting the Confederate flag on convertibles and fraternity house flagpoles has comparable symbolic significance that may be unrecognized. To a racial moderate, the Negro sensitivity must seem exaggerated, for most of the whites who respond to "Dixie" and flaunt the Stars and Bars are not deliberately seeking to remind Negroes of the racial discrepancies. Klansmen using these symbols, whether at the Chisolm serenade or at rallies today, may be presumed to be less innocent.

Chapter Six, "The Klan and the Northern Teacher"

The files of the American Missionary Association, housed in a special room on the top floor of the Fisk University Library in Nashville, comprise a unique collection of material related to the Northerners teaching in the South during Reconstruction. I am grateful to Fisk University for permission to use and quote from this material. The bulk of the material is in the form of letters, mostly from individuals in the North who contributed to the support of the schools which the A.M.A. organized for the freedmen. Most of the donations were small—seldom as large as ten dollars; and most of the contributors lived in small towns scattered all across the Northern tier of states. The teachers came from more prosperous families, as a rule, than those sending their mites; many of the letters reflect very limited education. It may be doubted whether so many small, humble donors have ever, collectively, produced such magnificent results—the Negro schools and colleges that have survived, poor in endowment but rich in dedication to principle, providing the chief means by which the freedmen and their descendants have overcome the overwhelming barrier of ignorance.

Since not all the money needed to sustain a teacher in the South could ever go to salary, it is doubtful whether any Northern teacher in the South ever received as much as $400 a year; and it is probable that most of them were partially subsidized by their families. Much of the factual information used in this chapter is from Henry L. Swint, *The Northern Teacher in the South, 1862–1870* (Nashville, 1941) and Ralph E. Morrow, *Northern Methodism and Reconstruction* (East Lansing, Mich., 1956). Some of the details about Southern disdain for the teachers come from testimony given by teachers at the Congressional hearings in 1871; this testimony closely corroborates Albion Tourgée's comments in *A Fool's Errand*. Southern men were reportedly less hostile than their wives toward the Northern teachers, perhaps from ingrained male chivalry, but also, no doubt, because as soldiers they had learned in contact with Union soldiers that not all Northerners were ogres or the low, mean creatures of Southern propaganda. In any war, the stay-at-homes are likely to be more belligerent than the men in service. One reason for the Klan's year-by-year degeneration is that it attracted younger men, who had never been in uniform and had been nurtured in hate by their homebody mothers and neighbors.

Most of the Klan messages and warnings were presented in evidence at the Congressional hearings in 1871. The Klan letter to Schneider is printed in James Wilford Garner, *Reconstruction in Mississippi* (New York, 1901). The two Corliss letters are in the A.M.A. files at Fisk.

Not all Northern teachers were treated badly, and not all of them were critical of white Southerners. A. A. Safford, writing on May 4, 1871, from Talladega, Alabama, to E. M. Cravath in New York, had this to say: "There is no mistake about it—there certainly is no place in this state where 'nigger teachers' are treated with such respect as here. I think too many of the teachers south have acted upon the principle that the *colored* man is worth *ten white* men. I think one as good as the other provided each behaves himself, giving my preference to him that behaves best, be he white or black."

J. T. Trowbridge was only one of numerous Northerners who visited the South immediately after the Civil War and reported their impressions to the people back home. Edward Eggleston, for example, made a quick trip to Virginia, collecting details enough for a popular lecture; there was no limit to Northern curiosity about the South in defeat. Trowbridge wrote two books, both published in Hartford: *The South: a Tour of Its Battlefields and Ruined Cities* (1866), and the work quoted in this chapter, *A Picture of the Desolated States; and the Work of Restoration* (1868). His comments about "bleaching" relate to one of the greatest ironies in history—the Klan insistence on preservation of racial integrity in a region with a long history of miscegenation. To a certain extent it is the central theme of Faulkner's novels, and other observers have agreed that the resulting sense of guilt, usually subconscious, plays a major role in the continuing strain of Southern violence and discrimination.

Chapter Seven, "Georgia Scenes"

Most of the details in this chapter are from "The Ku Klux Conspiracy," but some are taken from W. E. Burghardt DuBois, *Black Reconstruction. An Essay toward a History of the Part which Black Folk Played in the Attempt to Reconstruct Democracy in America, 1860–1880* (Philadelphia, 1935). When a white scholar writes history, no reviewer refers to his "old race consciousness" as an influence upon his interpretation. When a Negro scholar writes history —especially a Negro scholar who helped found the NAACP—reviewers, perhaps unconsciously, peruse the work with a sharp eye for distortion, omission, bitterness, and partisanship. *Black Reconstruction*, with the exception of its final chapter, "The Propaganda of History," which might better have been an appendix or epilogue, is measurably less bitter, distorted, and partisan than some of the volumes produced early in this century that confirm the classical Southern view and that still exert a great influence on the teaching of history in our public schools. The sampling of contemporary reviews of this book in the *Book Review Digest* would make edifying reading for people unfamiliar with the evolution of Reconstruction historiography.

Of the Negroes taking part in the Georgia constitution convention in December 1867, the most prominent was Henry McNeal Turner. He was also the Negro leader most cordially disliked by the whites. Yet he led an effort to gain a full pardon for Jefferson Davis, and he actively supported provisions to protect banks and to prevent the sale of property for delinquent taxes. Other capable Negroes at this convention were Aaron Bradley, Tunis Campbell, and J. B. Costin. When Negroes elected to the state legislature were finally seated, Turner again proved his intelligent leadership —though he was radical on one point, urging an amendment to extend the vote to a group that had always been excluded in the past: women.

Henry W. Grady was famous later, while editor of the Atlanta *Constitution*, 1879–89, for oratory advocating economic and social progress. His most famous oration was "The New South," delivered in New York City in 1886 and subsequently printed in his *The New South and Other Addresses* (1904).

Clara Barton's testimony is included in *Report of the Joint Commission on Reconstruction at the First Session of the Thirty-Ninth Congress* (1866).

The absence of remorse in John C. Reed's *The Brothers' War* (1905).parallels the "unreconstructed" attitude explicit in Captain Lea's deposition concerning the 1870 murder of John Stephens in North Carolina, as reported in Chapter 3. The attitude has been immortalized in the ballad "O I'm a Good Old Rebel."

Chapter Eight, "Friction in Florida"

Swint, in *The Northern Teacher in the South*, gives excerpts from letters in which teachers expressed their shock at conditions they found.

Prince Murat's estimate of Tallahassee in 1827 is reflected in Emerson's *Journals*, edited by Edward Waldo Emerson and Waldo Emerson Forbes (Boston, 1909), Vol. II, page 161. The entry is from Emerson's "Pocket Note-Book": "Tallahassee, a grotesque place, selected three years since as a suitable spot for the Capital

of the Territory, and since that day rapidly settled by public officers, land speculators and desperadoes. Much club law and little
else. What are called the ladies of the place are, in number,
eight."

Reid's description of Tallahassee appeared in Whitelaw Reid,
After the War: A Southern Tour May 1, 1865 to May 1, 1866 (Cincinnati, 1866).

Conditions and events in Florida during Reconstruction have
been most effectively re-created in Joe E. Richardson, *The Negro
in the Reconstruction of Florida* (unpublished Ph.D. dissertation,
the Florida State University, 1963). Among the older, less reliable
volumes on the state and the period are John Wallace, *Carpetbag
Rule in Florida: the Inside Workings of the Reconstruction of Civil
Government in Florida after the Close of the Civil War* (Jacksonville, 1888) and William Watson Davis, *The Civil War and Reconstruction in Florida* (New York, 1913). Davis quotes frequently
from Wallace's book, and is the source of the interesting detail that
ex-Governor William D. Bloxham helped Wallace write the book.
"Ex-Governor Bloxham told me that he aided Wallace in the com-
pilation of his work" (page 265, footnote 3). Ruby Leach Carson,
in "William Dunnington Bloxham," *Florida Historical Quarterly,*
XXVII (January, 1949), 218, relates that Bloxham established a
school for Negroes on his plantation near Tallahassee and hired
an educated Negro, John Wallace, as its teacher. The Wallace
book was republished in facsimile edition by the University of
Florida Press 1964, with an introduction by Allan Nevins.

The careers of Congressman Walls and Secretary of State Gibbs
are traced by Richardson in his Chapter XIV, "Negro Politicians."
The contemporary newspaper references to Gibbs: Tallahassee *Sentinel,* February 20, 1868; Jacksonville *Weekly Floridian,* March 4,
1873. Richardson has also written an article, "Jonathan C. Gibbs:
Florida's Only Negro Cabinet Member," *Florida Historical Quarterly,* LXII (April, 1964), 363–68.

Simkins's article is "Why the Ku Klux," in *The Alcalde,* IV (June
19, 1916). The Gainesville and Monticello headlines were quoted
in the Tallahassee *Sentinel* on November 26, 1870. Correspondence
yielding evidence of Klan involvement in the "Jackson County

War" included letters from C. M. Hamilton to A. H. Jackson, December 31, 1867, and W. J. Purman to Jackson, June 30, 1868, in the Freedmen's Bureau Records for Florida. The "Ku Klux Conspiracy" volume on Florida contains the testimony of Dennis, Dickinson, Gibbs, Purman, and Johnson, together with other information about the outrages in Jackson County.

The Klan's part in the disputed election of 1876 is no easier to ascertain in specific detail than any other facet of that very confused event. Paul L. Haworth, *The Hayes-Tilden Disputed Election* (Cleveland, 1906), gives the general picture; a localized account is Jerrel H. Shofner, "Fraud and Intimidation in the Florida Election of 1876," *Florida Historical Quarterly*, LXII (April, 1964), 321–30.

Chapter Nine, "The Freedmen's Bureau"

Southern novelists, as reported in Chapter 10, "The Battle of the Books," commonly cast the Freedmen's Bureau agent in the role of villain. The minority report in the summary volume of "The Ku Klux Conspiracy" might well have served as inspiration for the novelists, for it refers to "the vilest of the white people, both from the North and South, who have constituted the leaders of this black horde. . . ."

The one scholarly study of the Bureau, George R. Bentley, *A History of the Freedmen's Bureau* (Philadelphia, 1955), while not written to refute this notion nevertheless does so effectively. General Howard emerges as one of the most honest, fair-minded agency administrators the federal government has ever employed; and most of the agents, like most of the Northern teachers, were motivated by a sincere desire to help the freedmen and, though less directly, the South itself in its struggle to recover from the war. A revealing portrait of Howard is provided by John and LaWanda Cox, "General O. O. Howard and the 'Misrepresented Bureau,'" *Journal of Southern History*, XIX (November, 1953), 427–56. Howard's own contemporary view of the Bureau, and his objectivity, may readily be seen in "Report of Major General O. O. Howard, Commissioner of Bureau of Refugees, Freedmen, and Deserted Lands," in *Report of the Secretary of War* for 1868 (House Doc. No. 1, 40th Congress,

3rd Session). The promise of "forty acres and a mule" that the Bureau was seldom able to honor is discussed in LaWanda Cox, "The Promise of Land for the Freedmen," *Mississippi Valley Historical Review*, XLV (December, 1958), 413–40.

The contention that the Southern whites during Reconstruction were at the mercy of semi-barbarous Negroes and the vilest of whites is a major point in the classical interpretation of Southern history. Recent scholarship, far from giving comfort to people who wish to continue believing the classical interpretation, has been steadily undermining it—by showing that the *few* Negroes who rose to prominent place in Southern governments were generally men of character and ability, and that most of the "carpetbaggers" were men of integrity, education, and liberality. But this is not an exclusively modern phenomenon; as early as 1901, James W. Garner in his *Reconstruction in Mississippi* objectively appraised the Freedmen's Bureau and dispersed such myths as its encouragement of Negro indolence and idleness.

Readers familiar with congressional reports on controversial subjects should know that the majority and minority conclusions, based on the same factual testimony, usually reflect the current "party lines"; in the conclusions of "The Ku Klux Conspiracy," the majority view was in line with contemporary Republican opinion, and the minority view, just as naturally, was in line with the prevailing Democratic position. The objective modern reader quite properly ignores both conclusions and forms his own judgments about the facts presented.

By this procedure of independent judgment, we would be unlikely to accept such a term in the minority conclusion as the "vilest of the white people" for men demonstrably anything but vile. John William DeForest, for example, served for fifteen months, in 1866–67, as a Freedmen's Bureau official in and near Greenville, South Carolina; he was thus a genuine carpetbagger. But today his memory is respected for a number of novels, especially *Miss Ravenel's Conversion from Secession to Loyalty* (1867, reissued 1939), hailed as a pioneer in American realism. The book owes much to his actual war experience as captain in the Twelfth Connecticut Volunteers. In 1948 his Freedmen's Bureau reminiscences were published by the Yale University Press with the title *A Union*

Officer in the Reconstruction, edited by James H. Croushore and David Morris Potter. Most of the chapters had originally appeared in magazines during 1868—*Harper's Monthly, The Atlantic,* and *Putnam's Magazine.* The final chapters describe four distinct types of Southern whites as DeForest found them: to use his own terms, "the low-down people," meaning poor whites; "semi-chivalrous Southrons," mostly small farmers and mostly in hill districts: "chivalrous Southrons," and "more chivalrous Southrons." As a sample of DeForest's good-humored style, as well as of his attitude and observation, consider the opening of his chapter on "chivalrous Southrons":

> They certainly are, these "Southrons," a different people from us Northerners; they are, perhaps, as unlike us as the Spartans to the Athenians, or the Poles to the Germans; they are more simple than we, more provincial, more antique, more picturesque; they have fewer of the virtues of modern society, and more of the primitive, the natural virtues; they care less for wealth, art, learning, and the other delicacies of an urban civilization; they care more for individual character and reputation of honor.
>
> Cowed as we are by the Mrs. Grundy of democracy; moulded into tame similarity by a general education, remarkably uniform in degree and nature, we shall do well to study this peculiar people, which will soon lose its peculiarities; we shall do better to engraft upon ourselves its nobler qualities.

J. T. Trowbridge, in *A Picture of the Desolated States* (1868), may have been thinking of the group DeForest called "the low-down people" when he wrote (pages 664–65):

> The prime cause of Southern want is the laziness of the whites. The Southern climate is notoriously enervating, and is made the excuse for not working by the "privileged classes." At every crossroads doggery, every shop, and every store in every town and village, is to be found a crowd of long-haired, stalwart fellows engaged in whittling sticks, chewing tobacco, and cursing the negro—three things which they do so well and industriously. follow up. Without a dollar, save what they make or defraud their laborers out of, they spend their time, week in and week out, in idleness, regretting "old times," instead of turning to work and industriously striving to retrieve their fallen fortunes. They have land in abundance. . . .

Trowbridge had little to say about the Freedmen's Bureau, and what he did say could not have failed to offend most Southern readers. Slave-owners who had formed profitable liaisons with Negro women by selling the resulting offspring, so Trowbridge reported, now had to support both the women and the children—forced to do so by the Freedmen's Bureau. The Bureau also interfered in another way: it enforced thousands of wills leaving property to former slaves, wills that had hitherto usually been suppressed by white heirs in line with the old saying that "Black men have no rights that white men are bound to respect." In Richmond, Trowbridge learned that white people outnumbered Negroes ten to one in drawing Bureau rations; he heard one white woman say (page 163), "You ought to do something for us, for you've took away our niggers." He saw no indolent Negroes in Richmond, and remarked (page 178) that "the frequenters of bar-rooms, and loungers at taverns, were white of skin. To get drunk, especially, appeared to be a prerogative of the chivalry." Winding up this obviously partisan catalogue of Southern traits is a quotation that Trowbridge (page 287) attributes to General Fisk, that Negroes "are more industrious than the whites. You see young men standing on street corners with cigars in their mouths and hands in their pockets, swearing the negroes won't work. . . ."

It was a time, apparently, when men of different regions considered it proper and desirable to trade insults, leaving us to judge for ourselves which pots were calling which kettles black. Northern observers had the initial advantage of a ready market for their books and articles; but this advantage was lost to the Southerners when, about 1900, historians lifted epithets from the minority conclusion of "The Ku Klux Conspiracy" to give the Freedmen's Bureau an enduring bad name.

Chapter Ten, "The Battle of the Books"

The most recent and best-documented Tourgée biography, Theodore L. Gross's *Albion W. Tourgée* (New York, 1963, in the Twayne United States Authors Series), is somewhat compromised by the author's acceptance of the classical interpretation of Reconstruction history.

A Fool's Errand by One of the Fools was published anonymously in New York in 1879. The full title of the 1880 reissue is *A Fool's Errand, By One of the Fools; the Famous Romance of American History. New, Enlarged, and Illustrated Edition. To which is added, by the same author, Part II, The Invisible Empire: a concise review of the epoch in which the tale is based* (New York, 1880). *Uncle Tom's Cabin* was serialized in *The National Era*, 1851–52, and was issued as a book in 1852. *A Key to Uncle Tom's Cabin* was published in 1853. The first dramatization (produced without Mrs. Stowe's consent) was in 1852.

Tourgée called himself "one of the fools" because it was his ultimate opinion that only foolish men would have gone south as he did after the war with the hope of really helping the South. His use of the term "wise men," for men who were more cautious and stayed North, suggests that Tourgée recalled the saying, "Fools rush in where wise men fear to tread." At the same time, there is a veiled indictment of these "wise men." History, which eventually reaches a balanced judgment on all dubious matters, may well decide that Tourgée was not so foolish as he supposed in 1879. Otto H. Olsen, "Albion W. Tourgée," *North Carolina Historical Review*, XL (Autumn, 1963), 434–54, surveys evolving opinions of Tourgée from abusive denunciation to admiration and praise. It is Olsen's opinion that Tourgée's hand was felt in the Supreme Court school decision of 1954.

The pro-Klan novels considered in this chapter are as follows: N. J. Floyd, *Thorns in the Flesh. A Voice of Vindication from the South in Answer to "A Fool's Errand" and Other Slanders* (Philadelphia, 1884); Thomas J. Jerome, *Ku Klux Klan No. 40* (Raleigh, N.C., 1895); Thomas Nelson Page, *Red Rock* (New York, 1898); Joel Chandler Harris, *Gabriel Tolliver: A Story of Reconstruction* (New York, 1902); Thomas Dixon, *The Clansman: an Historical Romance of the Ku Klux Klan* (New York, 1906).

Jonathan Daniels, *Prince of Carpetbaggers* (Philadelphia, 1958), is a sympathetic biography of an actual carpetbagger. In a preface Daniels suggests that the carpetbagger became the scapegoat, both North and South, for all that went awry during Reconstruction.

The Lost Clan of Cocletz in *Thorns in the Flesh* recalls the suggestion, reported in Chapter I, of a hypothetical visitor from Georgia when the Klan founders in Pulaski were casting about for a name.

Theodore Huff's Shot Analysis of D. W. Griffith's *Birth of a Nation* was prepared for the Museum of Modern Art (New York) Film Library in 1961.

Chapter Eleven, "The Klan Revived"

Of the numerous books and pamphlets about the Klan issued in the early 1920's, the titles are not always indicative of the contents or of the viewpoints of the authors. Here, divided pro and con, and in their chronological order, are the works used in the writing of this chapter:

WORKS DEFENDING THE KLAN:

Winfield Jones, *Story of the Ku Klux Klan* (Washington, 1921).
J. S. Fleming, *What Is Ku Kluxism?* (Goodwater, Alabama, 1923).
Leroy A. Curry, *The Ku Klux Klan under the Searchlight* (Kansas City, 1924).
Blaine Mast, *K.K.K. Friend or Foe: Which?* (no place given, 1924).
Winfield Jones, *Knights of the Ku Klux Klan* (New York, 1941).

WORKS ATTACKING THE KLAN:

W. C. Witcher, *The Unveiling of the Ku Klux Klan* (Fort Worth, Texas, 1922).
Ku Klux Klan Secrets Exposed, published by Ezra A. Cook (Chicago, 1922?).
Howard Tucker, *History of Gov. Walton's War* (Oklahoma City, 1923).
W. C. Witcher, *The Reign of Terror in Oklahoma* (Fort Worth, 1923).
Aldrich Blake, *The Ku Klux Kraze: A Trip through the Klavern* (Oklahoma City, 1924).
John J. Gordon, *Unmasked* (Brooklyn, 1924).
Marion Monteval, *The Klan Inside Out* (Chicago, 1924). This book is copyrighted by F. N. Littlejohn, perhaps a pseudonym for Monteval, although a later author on the Klan thinks it may be a pseudonym for Edgar I. Fuller.
John Moffat Mecklin, *The Ku Klux Klan: A Study of the American Mind* (New York, 1924).
Edgar I. Fuller, *The Visible of the Invisible Empire*. "The Mael-

strom," revised and edited by George L. LaDura (Denver, 1925).

Emerson Hunsberger Loucks, *The Ku Klux Klan in Pennsylvania, a Study in Nativism* (Harrisburg, 1936).

The original Klan may on occasion have used a fiery cross, but it is doubtful whether it was ever the fixture that it has been for the modern Klan. Winfield Jones, in *Knights of the Ku Klux Klan*, discounts the notion that the Pulaski founders had the Scottish clans in mind. When those clans planned gatherings, messengers were sent out bearing a blazing torch, but, Jones said, it is a mistake to think that the Klan's fiery cross originated with this summoning device used in Scotland. The opening section of the Kloran details the opening ceremonies, as Colonel Simmons devised them; therein appears this passage:

> As he leaves the s.a. [sacred altar], the Night-Hawk (in his absence, the Kladd) will advance to the s.a. with the F.C. [fiery cross] and place it at and against the center of the s.a. on side facing the E.C.'s station, light it, and take position no. 4 facing the s.a.
>
> The Klokard . . . addresses the E.C. [Exalted Cyclops] as follows:
>
> Klokard: "Your Excellency, the s.a. of the klan is prepared, the f.c. illumines the klavern."
>
> E.C.: "Faithful Klokard, why the f.c.?"
>
> Klokard: "Sir, it is the emblem of that sincere, unselfish devotedness of all klansmen to the sacred purpose and principles we have espoused."
>
> E.C.: "My Terrors and Klansmen, what means the f.c.?"
>
> All: "We serve and sacrifice for the right."

The Klan uniform was no longer made at home by wives and daughters, as during Reconstruction, but was actually rented for five dollars from headquarters, and had to be returned when the member left the Klan. It was a white robe with a patch on the left shoulder—a white cross on a red background. The headdress was a white mask and peaked hood with a red tassel. The officers had more elaborate costumes of silk with braid and embroidery.

The ten test questions are contained in a 21-page manuscript copy of the Kloran, a complete initiation ritual, owned by the Department of Special Collections of the University of Kansas Library, which has given permission for quotation here. The Library of Congress has copies of *The Constitution and Laws of the Knights of the Ku Klux Klan*, as amended by various Imperial Klonvokations, as well as a *Klansman's Manual* (1924), a Kloran (1916), *Minutes of the Imperial Kloncilium* (1923), *Catalogue of Official Robes and Banners* (1925), and other pamphlet material issued by the Klan.

The A.P.A. is described in J. Desmond Humphrey, *The A.P.A. Movement: A Sketch* (Washington, 1912). A comprehensive report on nativism is Roy Allen Billington, *The Protestant Crusade, 1800–1860: A Study of the Origins of American Nativism* (New York, 1938).

C. Vann Woodward, *Tom Watson, Agrarian Rebel* (New York, 1938), page 450, says there is no evidence that Watson helped launch the modern Klan. "Yet if any mortal man may be credited (as no one man may rightly be) with releasing the forces of human malice and ignorance and prejudice, which the Klan merely mobilized, that man was Thomas E. Watson." At Watson's funeral in 1922 the largest floral offering at the grave was from the Klan.

Fuller's *The Visible of the Invisible Empire* contains copies of the Hiram Evans memoranda and orders, the telegram from Clarke about the Rev. Wilmer and the answers, the telegram from Stephenson to Evans, and the material about the New York Masons.

"The Klan's Fight for Americanism" by Hiram Evans, identified as Imperial Wizard and Emperor, Knights of the Ku Klux Klan, appeared in the *North American Review*, CCXXIII (March-April-May, 1926), 33–63. The quoted material is from pages 49–51. The next issue had papers giving the opposing view, written by a Catholic, a Jew, and a Princeton professor. Evans is credited with several books, including *The Public School Problem in America by Dr. H. W. Evans . . . Outlining Fully the Policies and the Program of the Knights of the Ku Klux Klan toward the Public School System* (no place given, 1924); *The Rising Storm; An Analysis of the Growing Conflict over the Political Dilemma of Roman Catholics in America* (Atlanta, 1930); and—though I have not tracked it down—*The Menace of Modern Immigration* (1923).

William Allen White's skirmish with the Klan is amply recorded in books by and about White: *Forty Years on Main Street*, compiled by Rüssell H. Fitzgibbon from the columns of the Emporia *Gazette* (New York, 1937); Everett Rich, *William Allen White, the Man from Emporia* (New York, 1941); Frank C. Clough, *William Allen White of Emporia* (New York, 1941); David Hinshaw, *A Man from Kansas, the Story of William Allen White* (New York, 1945); *The Autobiography of William Allen White* (New York, 1946); *Selected Letters of William Allen White 1899–1943*, edited by Walter Johnson (New York, 1947); and Walter Johnson, *William Allen White's America* (New York, 1947).

A good study of the Klan's political involvement in the 1920's is Arnold S. Rice, *The Ku Klux Klan in American Politics* (Washington, 1962). In 1922–26 the Klan was especially influential in Texas, Indiana, Colorado, Oregon, and Maine, but its membership was nation-wide.

Two recent studies of Klan activity in the 1920's are David Chalmers, "The Ku Klux Klan in the Sunshine State: the 1920's," *Florida Historical Quarterly*, LXII (January, 1964), 209–15; and Charles C. Alexander, "Secrecy Bids for Power: The Ku Klux Klan in Texas Politics in the 1920's," *Mid-America*, LXVI (January, 1964), 3–28.

Chapter Twelve, "A Klan for All Seasons"

The story of the Stephenson scandal has often been told, but never with more gusto than in Robert Coughlan's "Klonklave in Kokomo," the 1923 entry in *The Aspirin Age: 1919–1941*, edited by Isabel Leighton (New York, 1949).

Colonel Simmons, dedicated lodge man that he was, showed a gusto of his own in creating the vocabulary of the modern Klan. The local den he renamed a Klavern. Of the original titles of den officers he kept only two: Cyclops, which he expanded to Exalted Cyclops, and Night-Hawk. To the old state and regional titles, such as Grand Dragon and Grand Titan, he added Grand Goblin and Grand Kleagle (for a recruiter). The national legislative body he called the Klonvokation; the judicial committee he named the Kloncilium. The initiation fee, so vital to the Klan as he and his successors conceived it, became the Klecktoken.

In addition to devising new titles, Colonel Simmons lovingly invented a secret language. The first letters of words in a sentence

[291]

became a word that could be pronounced, e.g., "Ayak?" meaning "Are you a Klansman?" to which the proper response was "Akia"— "A Klansman I am." "Itsub" meant "In the sacred unfailing bond," and "Kigy" meant "Klansman, I greet you." The supreme production was a motto, *Non silba sed anthar.* The first and third words were familiar Latin, but Simmons had to explain that *silba* meant "self" in Latin while *anthar* was Saxon for "others." *Not for self but for others.*

The Library of Congress owns a copy of the ten-page "Rules & Regulations Applicable to the Association of South Carolina Klans," copyrighted by Robert E. Hodges in 1957. Samples of the material put out by Horace Sherman Miller of Waco, Texas, are in the Alderman Library of the University of Virginia. Copies of material issued by Bill Hendrix of Oldsmar, Florida, have been furnished the author, in photocopies, by an appointed official of the State of Florida. Use of the rattlesnake by June Hendricks, in her poem "The Rattlesnake and His Brother," may remind readers of the harangue at a St. Augustine Klan rally quoted in Chapter 2.

The author is not one of those who can say with any confidence that the Klan will not win again. A bulging file of editorials and letters to the editor in Florida newspapers indicates wide support for what the Klan stands for, some of it from highly respectable individuals. It may be sheer coincidence that these people, including some who proudly acknowledge their membership in extreme rightist groups, share the Klan thinking on such subjects as opposition to fluoridation of water supplies and mental health programs, impeachment of Earl Warren, blanket condemnation of university faculties as dangerously tolerant of Communist subversion, and repeal of the income tax amendment. They may not realize that such planks were in the Klan platform long before rightists began to espouse them. Many of the "best people" during Reconstruction either belonged to the Klan or supported its activities, making its success possible. It can happen again.

Chapter Thirteen, "Forecast: Continued Turbulence"

"History is a pageant, not a philosophy," according to Augustine Birrell. Others call it an art. German-trained historians tried to make it a science, shortly after the Civil War. Awareness of the evolving concepts of historiography, and of the shifting variety of particular approaches and emphases, may shake the lay reader's faith in all historians—but a little shaking, of the sort attempted in this volume, may be of benefit.

History has never been interpreted solely in terms of myths—meaning the great popular beliefs that we hold to so tenaciously, in inverse proportion to their susceptibility to proof or disproof. So fiercely do people defend their myths that even an effort to examine them critically may be resented. According to Michael Argyle in *Religious Behavior* (Glencoe, Ill., 1959), 96 per cent of all Americans believe in God (though only 35 per cent can name the four gospels). To speak out about "divine favor" and the "chosen people" notion is therefore risky. If an author then proceeds to question such myths as that of "real Americans," and hints that many whites in the population—21 per cent by one estimate—have some Negro blood, he runs a grave danger of alienating the very readers he would most like to reach.

But the risks must be taken. As a nation we must somehow be shocked into recognizing the mythic basis of much of our behavior. Many of us would like to forget the past and face modern issues with modern facts and modern logic; but our myths hold us back. As long as we tolerate school textbooks that hail the restoration of Southern white control as a triumph over carpetbag-scalawag-Negro misrule, we impose a handicap that the Klan gladly exploits. How can there be real hope of reducing resistance to equalization of civil rights when most of our history textbooks parrot the almost universal nineteenth-century conviction of the Negro's innate inferiority? And how can any minority hope for achievement of full acceptance as long as the myth prevails that one minority, and one only, comprises the "real Americans"?

The Klan's inclusion of the Mormon Church among the groups Fleming attacked as "these aliens" may be a carry-over from the general nineteenth-century hostility toward Mormons because of their practice of plural marriage. It is ironic in view of the Mormon rule, which the church is now reconsidering, against admitting Negroes to full membership. This rule is a source of embarrassment to modern Mormons, who insist they are above prejudice; apparently the church founders were prejudiced enough to write the anti-Negro bias into the Mormon theology, where it will stay until removed by a new revelation.

Hodding Carter, in the preface to his fine book *The Angry Scar* (New York, 1959, in Mainstream of America Series), remarks that "it has been almost as unfortunate for our nation that the North has remembered so little of Reconstruction as that the South has remembered so much." And his final words (page 409) parallel the prediction of this chapter though without naming the Klan:

> How long will the memory of the Reconstruction period affect the South and the nation?
> There can be no certain answer. The South is reacting in predictable fashion to old and new racial pressures. The doctrine of nullification has been advanced as fervently as it was ever propounded by John C. Calhoun. Today the Southern moderate is as suspect as were his Reconstruction prototypes. Today a more determined Negro is again faced by a nearly unified white South no less determined than in 1868 to circumvent the intent of the federal government. Today the singing of "Dixie," the waving of a Confederate flag, and the stump orator's passionate appeal to the past are as sure fire as in the 1870's.
> And the end is not in sight.*

If the authors of two books published in 1963 are both right, they also underscore the prediction in this chapter. John P. Roche, in *The Quest for the Dream: The Development of Civil Rights and Human Relations in Modern America,* asserts in his preface that "civil liberty has a meaning in contemporary American life which never existed in the past," and he adds that never before has there been such a concern for the basic principles of decency and civility. Ben Haas, in a book called simply *KKK,* describes the Klan as "fattening on the hatreds generated by the current battle for integration, growing and strengthening itself and becoming a formidable force-in-being once more." If both are right, if the Klan is girding for renewed action at the very time when a concern for civil liberty is growing, our forecast should perhaps be not "continued," but "greatly increased turbulence."

---

* From *The Angry Scar,* by Hodding Carter. Copyright © 1959 by Hodding Carter. Reprinted by permission of Doubleday & Company, Inc.

INDEX

Index

[299]

William Peirce Randel, Professor of English and Director of American Studies at the Florida State University, lives in the South (Tallahassee, Florida), but maintains his roots in the North (most particularly at a farm in York County, Maine). New York-born, Randel earned his doctorate at Columbia University. He has taught at the University of Minnesota, the Missouri School of Mines, the University of Helsinki, the University of Athens, and in Italy and the West Indies.